EMBODYING IRISH ABORTION REFORM

Gender and Sociology

Series Editors: **Sue Scott**, Newcastle University and **Stevi Jackson**, University of York

Presenting high-quality research from established scholars and early-career researchers, the *Gender and Sociology* series is aimed at an international audience of academics and students who are interested in gender across the social science disciplines, particularly in sociology.

Scan the code below to discover new and forthcoming titles in the series, or visit:

bristoluniversitypress.co.uk/gender-and-sociology

EMBODYING IRISH ABORTION REFORM

Bodies, Emotions, and Feminist Activism

Aideen O'Shaughnessy

First published in Great Britain in 2024 by

Bristol University Press
University of Bristol
1–9 Old Park Hill
Bristol
BS2 8BB
UK
t: +44 (0)117 374 6645
e: bup-info@bristol.ac.uk

Details of international sales and distribution partners are available at bristoluniversitypress.co.uk

© Bristol University Press 2024

British Library Cataloguing in Publication Data
A catalogue record for this book is available from the British Library

ISBN 978-1-5292-3643-9 hardcover
ISBN 978-1-5292-3645-3 ePub
ISBN 978-1-5292-3646-0 ePdf

The right of Aideen O'Shaughnessy to be identified as author of this work has been asserted by her in accordance with the Copyright, Designs and Patents Act 1988.

All rights reserved: no part of this publication may be reproduced, stored in a retrieval system, or transmitted in any form or by any means, electronic, mechanical, photocopying, recording, or otherwise without the prior permission of Bristol University Press.

Every reasonable effort has been made to obtain permission to reproduce copyrighted material. If, however, anyone knows of an oversight, please contact the publisher.

The statements and opinions contained within this publication are solely those of the author and not of the University of Bristol or Bristol University Press. The University of Bristol and Bristol University Press disclaim responsibility for any injury to persons or property resulting from any material published in this publication.

Bristol University Press works to counter discrimination on grounds of gender, race, disability, age and sexuality.

Cover design: designer: blu inc
Front cover image: iStock/colnihko
Bristol University Press uses environmentally responsible print partners.
Printed and bound in Great Britain by CPI Group (UK) Ltd, Croydon, CR0 4YY

This book is dedicated to the many activists who generously shared their time and stories with me.

Contents

Series Editors' Preface		viii
About the Author		x
Acknowledgements		xi
1	Introduction	1
2	Living under the 8th: The Gendered Burden of 'Abortion Work'	25
3	Tracing the 'Embodied Infrastructure' of the Movement to Repeal the 8th Amendment	43
4	On the Physicality of Protest: The Politics of Revelation	63
5	Embodying Respectability: The Politics of Concealment	86
6	Changed Bodies? Life after Repeal	109
7	Conclusion	133
Notes		146
References		149
Index		166

Series Editors' Preface

Sue Scott and Stevi Jackson

This book is a very welcome addition to the series. It brings a highly original perspective to the history of abortion rights, and the movement for them in Ireland, and also makes an intellectual contribution with relevance far beyond the immediate context of the research. It is an extremely timely contribution when abortion rights are being contested and disputed in a number of countries. The book is much more than a case study of abortion politics in Ireland; it develops a strong conceptualization of 'abortion work' and the 'embodied consequences of social movements' which can be applied to the interpretation of protest in other contexts where abortion rights, sexual freedoms, and bodily autonomy are threatened.

Progress with regard to women's[1] right to control their reproductive bodies was never stable in the 20th century and any gains have been subject to repeated challenge. The apotheosis of this state of affairs can be seen in Supreme Court in the United States overturning, in June 2022, *Roe* v *Wade* (a 1973 ruling which stated that the right to abortion was protected by the Constitution), thus destroying a milestone of second-wave feminism. Despite critiques of the progress model of modernity, and contestation by far right and religious movements, reproductive rights did seem to have been moving in a positive direction. This has certainly been the case in Ireland with the repeal of the 8th amendment in May 2018. What is most shocking about the Irish context, however, is not that change took so long to achieve, or the 'meeting itself coming back' situation of the change happening after the repeal of *Roe* v *Wade*, but that the 8th amendment, which recognized 'the equal right to life of pregnant women and the unborn', was inserted into the Irish Constitution as late as 1983. Also shocking – and we are not easily shocked – is the example that the author gives of a poster campaign in the run-up to the 2018 referendum on the 8th amendment:

> This image was of a black-and-white line-drawing of a pregnant woman's body. On the left-hand side of the image was a line which went from the top of the woman's head, all down her left side, to her feet. Pointed to this line was an arrow, connected to a speech bubble.

Inside the speech bubble was text which read 'Your body'. On the right-hand side of the image was another line which ran from the top of the woman's abdomen to just above her hips. A separate arrow pointed to this portion of her body. This arrow was connected to a second speech bubble which had text inside it reading 'Not your body'.

The author refers to the concept of 'affective dissonance' which Claire Hemmings (2012) describes as the experience of being confronted with the disjuncture between how one views and understands one's own self/body, and the ways in which one's self/body is conceptualized and represented. Hemmings goes on to argue that this dissonance is crucial to the emergence of feminist solidarity and feminist politics. This idea takes us to the heart of the book, to the analysis of the personal testimonies of 43 Irish abortion activists campaigning for the 'repeal of the 8th'. This rich data, in the form of interviews, enables an understanding of how bodily experiences 'are shaped by systems of reproductive coercion' and how these experiences, in turn, go on to produce embodied activism in an attempt to resist and transform these coercive political structures. O'Shaughnessy understands the struggle for abortion rights as an aspect of reproductive justice more widely, and, by taking an intersectional approach makes a strong analytic connection with gendered, racialized, and colonial relations of power, and the ways in which these are also embodied and experienced.

We very much hope that the book will be read, internationally and across disciplines by all those – academics and activists – with an interest in abortion, feminism, social movements, and political change, in Ireland and beyond. An in-depth understanding of embodied political activism is essential if we are to develop the most successful strategies for what is likely to be a continuing struggle for reproductive justice.

About the Author

Aideen O'Shaughnessy is Lecturer in Sociology at the University of Lincoln, UK. She holds a PhD in Sociology from the University of Cambridge, an MA in Gender Studies (Research) from Utrecht University, and a BA (Hons) in Sociology and French from Trinity College Dublin. Her research interests include embodiment, emotions, affect, reproduction, and feminist protest movements.

Acknowledgements

I have been privileged to have been mentored and guided throughout the undertaking of this research by Professor Sarah Franklin (University of Cambridge) and Dr Lucy Van De Wiel (Kings College London). Thank you to Professor Franklin, Dr Van De Wiel, and to all my colleagues in the ReproSoc (Reproductive Sociology) research group at the University of Cambridge, where I carried out this project as part of my doctoral studies in Sociology from 2018 to 2022. This research was made possible by funding from the Economic Social Research Council DTP (Training Grant reference number: ES/P000738/1). I would also like to take this opportunity to express my gratitude to the Cambridge Commonwealth, European and International Trust. I gratefully acknowledge the funding I received as part of my Cambridge Trust European Scholarship, without which it would not have been possible to complete my PhD research. I would also like to acknowledge the financial support provided to me in the form of several grants which I received from Newnham College (University of Cambridge) and the Annette Lawson Charitable Trust which allowed me to write up my doctoral thesis.

I am particularly grateful to Professor Barbara Sutton (State University New York) whose work has been a constant source of inspiration for me and who was invaluable in supporting me in the pursuance of this book. I would also like to thank Professor Sutton and Dr Francesca Moore (University of Cambridge) for their feedback and comments on my doctoral thesis which were fundamental in the preparation of this book manuscript. I would also like to take this opportunity to thank Dr Sonja Mackenzie (Santa Clara University), Dr Sydney Calkin (Queen Mary University London), and Dr Mairead Enright (University of Birmingham) for their encouragement and advice during the process of writing this monograph. Thank you, as well, to Dr Ali Meghi for judiciously answering all my book-writing related questions. In addition, I would like to express my sincere thanks to my colleagues in the School of Social and Political Sciences at the University of Lincoln for their guidance and support over the past two years.

On a personal note, I would like to say a heartfelt thank you to my friends and colleagues, Dr Stella Pryce, Amanda-Rose O'Halloran-Bermingham,

Dr Paul O'Halloran–Bermingham, Dr Rachel Roth, Anna Carnegie, and Dr Lorraine Grimes, for always so willingly and generously discussing ideas with me at various stages. Thank you, as well, to my family for their support. Finally, an inexpressible debt of gratitude goes to Dr R. Sánchez Rivera for their unwavering faith and belief in me and in my work.

1

Introduction

Conception stories: religion, women's bodies, and the foundation of the state

As a child, I often slept at my granny's house. Several times a week, my mother would scoop me up, full of sleep, from my own bed, bundling me into the car. Through the stiff winter frost, she drove, eventually reinserting me under the sheets with her own mother before heading off to work at the hospital where my grandmother herself had also been employed as a young woman. My maternal grandmother was born in 1932, ten years after the founding of the Irish Free State, which ended the Irish War of Independence between the Irish Republican Army, the National Army, and British Crown forces in 1922. Following 800 years of British rule, the Anglo-Irish Treaty would create a separate state in 26 of the 32 counties of Ireland, with the caveat that the country remains a dominion of the British Empire. In 1937, when my grandmother was five years old, a new Constitution would be ratified, creating the office of the President of Ireland, which would ultimately replace the colonial office of the Governor-General of Ireland, when the country transitioned to a Republic in 1948 (Tithe an Oireachtais – Houses of the Oireachtas 2020).

Co-authored by then Archbishop of Dublin, John McQuaid, and President Eamon De Valera, the 1937 Constitution of Ireland 'enshrined the patriarchal nuclear family as the cornerstone' of the new Irish Free State (Martin 2002, 67). As anthropologist Angela Martin (2002) explains, at this time, Irish men were engaged in a project to 'establish a nationalist masculine identity in counterposition to Irish colonial feminisation under British rule' (67). The Irish Free State had two key preoccupations: re-emasculating men (and conjointly, subordinating women) and repopulating the country after centuries of colonial decimation. Efforts to control women's sexuality were thus compounded by nationalist motivations and religious ideology, as well as by economic developments, stretching back to the mid-19th century. The Great Famine of 1845–1852 (also a product of British colonial policy

1

in Ireland) wiped out the cottier class, shoring up the power of the landed farming community who, with the backing of the Catholic Church, imposed a strict code of sexual behaviour on women intending to be matched with rural landowning males (Ferriter 2009). Sexual morality came under increasing surveillance with the nationalist cultural revival of the late 19th and early 20th century, which saw efforts to promote the unique virtues of Irish women (Ferriter 2009).

Article 41.2 of the 1937 Constitution formally established that the place of Irish women in the new state would be confined to the sphere of the home (Scannell 2007). As Irish legal scholar Yvonne Scannell (2007) argues, the legislature attempted to keep women in the home by 'foul rather than fair means' (73). Contraception was made illegal under the Criminal Law Amendment Act 1935. In 1956, the government of the Irish Republic passed the Civil Service Regulation Act. This legislation obliged women previously employed in civil service or (semi-)state sectors to resign from their positions upon marriage (Scannell 2007). Having only completed her nursing training in 1954, my grandmother worked for four years before she was forced to resign her post after marrying my grandfather in April 1958. The 'marriage bar', as it was colloquially known, was gradually abandoned in various employment sectors before being conclusively abolished under the Employment Equality Act in 1977, the same year that my mother began her nursing training.[1]

When I was a child, both of my parents worked long hours. My father, the eldest of a family of eight children, was forced to leave school at age nine to take up employment as a local farmhand. He would eventually establish his own business as an agricultural contractor, where he continues to work alongside my younger brother. My mother completed her nursing training and continued to work when my elder sister and brother were born in 1986 and 1989, respectively. Consequently, my maternal grandmother took on a great deal of the caring responsibilities in my family, regularly looking after myself and my three siblings. As a result, I woke up in my grandmother's bedroom quite frequently. In her room, there were two beds – a double and a single – enough to accommodate her, myself, and my brothers and sister. The vanity against the wall held her perfumes and powders, and a cross on which she hung her various rosaries. My grandfather, an amputee with a prosthetic leg, slept in a specially configured bed in another room.

One morning in late 2000, I woke up in my grandmother's bed; blood pooled on the mattress beside me. The sheets were thrown back, crumpled on the floor, the door of the bedroom flung open. I heard voices on the landing, the hot press being opened. Gently, I pulled myself out from underneath the heavy wool blankets and jumped onto the floor. Swiftly, I moved to the opposite wall of the bedroom, to where the hallway and bathroom came into sight. There, I saw my grandmother, pulling bed sheets around her calf, twisting and tightening them methodically. The sheets did their job, turning crimson and then pink. Quickly, the voices stopped. My mother returned, in her nurse's uniform. She explained that varicose veins were a professional hazard for nurses, who spent many hours every day on their feet. Later, I examined the bandages and the purple bruises on my granny's legs, as she danced around the kitchen, cigarette in hand.

A devoted Catholic, my grandmother went to mass every day and took communion. She lived in an era when, after giving birth, women were sectioned off to a particular portion of the chapel, where they would be housed until the priest declared them to be 'clean' again – a process known as 'churching'.[2] The days I stayed with my grandmother, mass was a requirement. We always sat in the pews on the left-hand side of the chapel (formerly, the 'women's side'). I would pass the time examining the intricate plaster mouldings of the Stations of the Cross which decorated the walls on either side of the altar. After mass, I would join my grandmother to light candles for family members who had passed – including one for my elder brother who died in 1996, aged seven. At the back of the chapel, above the candleholders, was a statue of the Virgin Mary. She stood, head bowed and arms outstretched, draped in her blue and white robes. Tears streamed down her face and a rosary hung from her right hand. There she remained, all throughout my childhood; a silent, pitiful figure.

For centuries, Catholicism has acted as the 'religious signifier of Irishness', constituting an integral element of the process of postcolonial 'disidentification' with Protestant Britain (Fletcher 2005, 378). In the early years of the Irish Free State, Catholic doctrine offered the 'ideological justification' for the conservative gender roles espoused by the new nation-state (Fletcher 2005, 378). The Irish nationalist revival of the late 19th century was informed specifically by the religious tenets of Devotional Marianism. The figure of the Virgin Mary, the suffering mother who sacrificed her only son, was perceived as mimetic of the Irish nation, for whom generations of sons (and less adorned daughters) had forfeited their lives for Irish freedom (Martin 2002). The bodies of Irish women would thus be disciplined to 'correspond to an ideal of femininity' embodied by the Virgin Mary (Martin 2002, 81). This 'labour of representation', Martin states, involved 'very real material consequences for the body, self, and nation' (Martin 2002, 67).

Accompanying my granny on her daily travails, I became increasingly interested in what I perceived as these curious contradictions between the idealized feminine embodiment that the figure of the Virgin Mary represented – stationary, passive, dolorous – and the reality of gendered bodily life that my grandmother exemplified for me. I began to wonder how these hegemonic conceptualizations of maternal embodiment – which centred around the figure of the Virgin Mary – acted as a disciplinary or regulatory force in my grandmother's life and in the life of other women around her. I would discover the answers to some of these questions while conducting my doctoral research in the winter of 2019. During a visit to my parents' home in the southeast of Ireland, my mother shared a recent discovery about the reproductive politics of our own family. Piecing together marriage certificates and birth records, she discovered that when my grandmother married my grandfather in April 1958, she was already six months pregnant.

In the discussions which followed, we debated what would have happened had my grandparents not married. It was speculated that my grandfather had intentions to emigrate to the United States, to take up employment alongside thousands of his compatriots in the burgeoning construction sector there. Instead, he married my grandmother, with whom he would go on to have four other children. I wondered what would have happened if my grandfather had followed through on his emigration plans. What fate would have befallen my grandmother, as an unmarried mother in Ireland in 1958?

Historian Maria Luddy (2011) describes how with the foundation of the Irish Free State in 1922, the 'unmarried mother' became a 'symbol of unacceptable sexual activity and a problem that had the potential to blight the reputation not only of the family but of the nation' (110). Although the 'idealisation of motherhood' was a prominent feature of political rhetoric inside the Irish Free State, the 'unmarried mother' was constructed as a 'social and political problem' and was 'categorised as part of the "undeserving poor"' (Luddy 2011, 112–113). From the late 20th century onwards, unmarried mothers would be systematically detained inside Mother and Baby Homes, 'county homes', or Magdalene Asylums; carceral institutions designed to 'rehabilitate' these 'fallen women' and manage the risk of contagion of 'sexual deviants' (Luddy 2007, 84; O'Sullivan and O'Donnell 2012). A moral hierarchy was applied to 'unmarried mothers' inside of these institutions; with 'first offenders' categorized as 'redeemable', while those with multiple pregnancies outside of marriage were pathologized as 'mentally deficient' (Luddy 2011, 115).

Feminist theorist Clara Fischer argues that this 'vast system of institutionalisation' in Ireland was buttressed by a 'gendered politics of shame' (Fischer 2017, 754). Fischer (2019) foregrounds the 'co-constitutive relationship between the gendered politics of shame' and 'women's occupation of space' (41). Institutions like the Magdalene Laundries, Fischer (2019) explains, operated to hide the country's 'assumed national blemishes' (41). The postcolonial, nation-building project, Fischer (2019) argues, 'relied on shame', in its efforts to constitute the Irish nation as 'a particular, gendered place' (33). In other words, by systematically removing 'transgressive' women – the objects of shame – from the landscape, the nation-state sought to preserve a version of 'national identity which was premised on the gendered purity and moral superiority' of Irish women (Fischer 2019,

38). From the founding of the Irish Free State until 1996, approximately 10,000 women were incarcerated in these institutions, forced to carry out unpaid labour (as part of these institutions' commercial businesses) and subjected to sustained psychological, emotional, and physical abuse (Justice for Magdalenes Research 2021).

Mary Gilmartin and Sinead Kennedy (2019) position the institutionalization of unmarried women as one element of a politics of *reproductive mobility* which aimed to regulate and control women's reproductive capacities in Ireland. Institutionalization, they argue, constituted a form of 'reproductive immobility' where women were forcibly 'removed from their family homes or incarcerated in institutions for the duration of their pregnancy or, in some instances, for significantly longer' (Gilmartin and Kennedy 2019, 125). Historical records from the 1940s onwards illustrate that many of the children of these incarcerated mothers were 'exported' to the United States, 'through an informal (and possibly illegal) overseas adoption scheme' (Gilmartin and Kennedy 2019, 125). The second form of reproductive mobility identified by Gilmartin and Kennedy (2019) utilized to discipline female fertility in Ireland was the forced emigration of pregnant Irish women. As historian Lorraine Grimes (2016) explains, the legalization of adoption in Britain in 1926 meant that Irish women could travel to Britain, give birth, and place their babies up for adoption before subsequently returning home.

It is not unreasonable to assume then that, if my grandmother had not married my grandfather in 1958, she may have found herself being forced to emigrate or incarcerated in an institutional workhouse for unmarried mothers. If my granny had desired to procure an abortion, her options were equally limited. Abortion itself was illegal in Ireland under the 1861 Offences Against the Persons Act – a colonial law, which criminalized the 'unlawful procurement of miscarriage' (Irish Statute Book 1861). 'Backstreet' abortions were common in Ireland in the early 20th century, however, and increased when 'travel to England was restricted, for example, during the Second World War' (Connolly 2002, 160). Gilmartin and Kennedy (2019) explain that the introduction of the 1967 Abortion Act in Britain made 'a third form of reproductive mobility' possible for Irish women (126).[3] Between 1968 and 1989, an estimated 50,000 women travelled from Ireland to Britain to access abortions (Gilmartin and Kennedy 2019, 126). While 'travelling' may have allowed Irish abortion-seekers to exercise some agency within highly constraining circumstances, the act of travelling is generally perceived as 'a punitive and stigmatizing form of "banishment"' (Sethna and Davis 2019, 10).

Since she died when I was only eight years old, I never had the opportunity to discuss with my grandmother what options she had considered when she became pregnant with my uncle in 1957. I never had the chance to ask her how she felt about the institutionalization and forced emigration of her peers, who may have found themselves in similar circumstances to her own. Equally, I do not know how my grandmother voted in 1983, when a referendum was held on whether to insert the 'pro-life' 8th amendment into the Constitution. While conducting research for this book, I found an image of a Society for the Protection of the Unborn (SPUC) rally in 1982 (Barry 1988). The group of activists depicted carry a banner which reads 'Natural Family Planning. Pro-Life. "Billings"'.[4] After forwarding the image to my mother, she confirmed that indeed, the women depicted hailed from her hometown in the southeast of Ireland. She identifies them as Mrs Hennessy and Mrs Foley, the latter of whom, my mother contributes, had a "big family" of "nine or ten children".[5]

The SPUC formed part of the Pro-Life Amendment Campaign, which had begun lobbying the Irish government in the early 1980s to insert a 'pro-life clause' into the Irish Constitution (Connolly 2002, 160). Concerned by various 'secularizing trends' – including the foundation of the first Women's Right to Choose group (in the late 1970s), the partial legalization of contraception in 1979, as well as the opening of the first Irish Pregnancy Counselling Centre in 1980 – the Pro-Life Amendment Campaign launched a 'highly-organised countermovement' which borrowed tactics and strategies from the Human Life Amendment Campaign in the United States (Connolly 2002, 162; McAvoy 2013, 51).[6] I imagined that my grandmother would have received several 'pro-amendment' (anti-abortion) pamphlets from Catholic organizations such as the Knights of Columbanus and Opus Dei, which systematically canvassed Sunday mass-goers in 1982 and 1983 (Connolly 2002). Sociologist Linda Connolly (2002) describes how involvement in the 'pro-choice' Anti-Amendment Campaign involved 'high personal cost and alienation' for those involved (172).

On 7 September 1983, the Irish electorate went to the polls, opting by a margin of two to one to insert the 8th amendment into the Constitution (Connolly 2002). According to the 8th amendment (or Article 40.3.3 of the Constitution), the Irish state would henceforth 'acknowledge the right to life of the unborn and, with due regard to the equal right to life of the mother, guarantee in its laws to respect, and, as far as practicable, by its laws, to defend and vindicate that right' (Irish Statute Book nd).

The 8th amendment effectively worked to 'copper fasten' the right to life of the unborn, which arguably, was already protected under the 1861 Offences Against the Persons Act (which outlawed abortion in all instances) (Connolly 2002, 163). As policy analyst Ursula Barry writes, 'the consequences' of the 8th amendment for Irish women 'have been severe' (Barry 1988, 59). With the insertion of the 8th amendment, Barry explains, Irish women were 'recategorized to be equal to that which is *not yet born*' (Barry 1988, 59, my emphasis). Barry (1988) forewarned the 'legal ramifications' of the

8th amendment, which now reconstituted pregnancy as a 'conflict between the life of a pregnant woman and her foetus' (59).

As legal scholars Fiona de Londras and Mairead Enright (2018) explain, the 8th amendment would treat the foetus as a 'constitutional person', entitled to its own 'legal representation' (1). After the 8th amendment was inserted, there were several occurrences wherein groups intent on prohibiting access to abortion initiated court proceedings against individual pregnant people, acting 'on behalf of the foetus' (de Londras and Enright 2018, 2). In accordance with the 8th amendment, any attempts to 'provide or access' abortion in Ireland would be criminalized (de Londras and Enright 2018, 2). This produced far-reaching effects for the provision of healthcare to pregnant people, related or unrelated to their maternity. Under the Health Service Executive National Consent Policy, an 'otherwise healthy pregnant person' could be 'subjected to unwanted medical treatment under the 8th amendment' (de Londras and Enright 2018, 9). Likewise, in cases where a pregnant person became ill and required, for example, access to cancer treatments, this treatment would have to be stopped wherein it produced potentially harmful effects for the development of foetal life.[7]

Before I ever picked up a book, it was my grandmother who taught me that the body is a bridge between the personal and political. Observing her arduous, joyful, and complicated intimate bodily life, my grandmother showed me how the gendered body is at once a site of labour, control, and suffering, at the same time as it is a source of agency, strength, and, sometimes, even pleasure. Taking forward these lessons that my grandmother bequeathed me, this book outlines an alternative 'embodied' approach to the study of Irish abortion politics. In short, while the implications of Ireland's constitutional abortion ban in law and medicine have been extensively surveyed, no research has thus far examined how the structural and social transformations brought about by the 8th amendment were experienced in the bodies of Irish women. This book addresses this gap and poses the question of how the embodied subjectivities of women and others who may become pregnant were moulded through the implementation and subsequent repeal of Ireland's constitutional abortion ban.

The first aim of this book then is to understand the embodied experience of living under Ireland's 8th amendment. By foregrounding the everyday experiences of women and others who may become pregnant living under the constitutional abortion ban, my goal here is to illuminate how Ireland's anti-abortion laws and regulations have been felt and inscribed at the level of the gendered body. In this vein, this book reinscribes the gendered body as a site of power and offers an alternative framework for understanding the embodiment and temporality of 'reproductive governance', which I understand according to Morgan and Roberts's (2012) definition as 'mechanisms through which different historical configurations of actors – such as state, religious, and international financial institutions, NGOs, and social movements – use legislative controls, economic inducements, moral injunctions, direct coercion, and ethical incitements to produce, monitor, and control reproductive behaviours and population practices' (243). In this book, I conceptualize the 8th amendment as a uniquely potent mechanism of reproductive governance and as typifying a broader, historically embedded, system of reproductive governance in this context.

Understanding that the gendered body is always already a site of both power and resistance, I have chosen to take the embodied experience of abortion activists as the point of departure for this analysis. My goal here is to focalize the agency of those living under the 8th amendment and to emphasize the ways in which these individuals have variously experienced, negotiated, and resisted the forces of reproductive oppression impressed upon them. Emphasizing the capacity of the embodied subject to both act and be acted upon by various social structures and cultural forces, I operationalize the concept of embodied experience as the ongoing process by which the subject is made and is making the world around them. Foregrounding the location of the body at the intersection of the personal and political, this book explores not only how the conditions of activists' bodily existence are shaped and formed by systems of reproductive governance, but how activists, through their embodied experiences, transform political structures in their own right.

The second aim of this book then is to examine the role and experience of the gendered body in the social movement for abortion rights in Ireland. Examining the connection between dynamic patterns of emotional and embodied experiences, the changing social consciousness of Irish women, and processes of collective mobilization, as well as the role of the body in wider movement activity within the Repeal the 8th campaign, this research attempts to put forward a novel perspective on the significance of the gendered, reproductive body in processes of social and political transformation in Ireland. As such, this book builds upon existing feminist research on the role of the body and emotions in politics (Parkins 2000; Sutton 2007). It investigates how women's bodies have both changed and been changed by the shifting political and cultural landscape in Ireland, specifically in relation to the historical transformation of Ireland's reproductive laws.

This book is inspired by a wealth of feminist studies, on the philosophy of the body, medical anthropology, Black feminist theory, the sociology of emotions, and new social movement studies (Hill Collins 2009 [1990]; Franklin 1991; Sutton 2007; Ahmed 2014a; Dolezal 2015). Much of this scholarship has in common clear social, political, and epistemological aims; to revalue the lived experiences of women and marginalized groups, and to prioritize 'bottom–up' methods of knowledge production which recognize the 'situatedness' of all embodied perspectives (Hill Collins 2009 [1990];

Haraway 1988). This book contributes to what Argentinian sociologist Barbara Sutton calls 'a politics of visibility', putting forward an alternative portrayal of the intimate bodily and emotional lives of women and gestating people living under and fighting against Ireland's 8th amendment. To paraphrase feminist anthropologist Emily Martin (2002), this book aims to tell a 'different story' about women's bodies and Ireland's historic constitutional abortion ban.

Studying the movement for abortion rights in Ireland: an alternative approach?

In a 2018 editorial for *Feminist Legal Studies*, Irish scholar Ruth Fletcher wrote that 'figuring out Repealed the 8th will take many tellings' (233). Indeed, in the years since the referendum, a wealth of scholarship has been dedicated to understanding how the Repeal the 8th movement achieved its success and why indeed conditions were apparently ripe for abortion reform at this historical moment. Historians, sociologists, legal researchers, and social movement scholars have studied the role of political opportunity structures, legal transformations, transnational solidarity, and the relevance of changing social and cultural norms in both the domestic and international landscapes (Reidy 2019; Connolly 2020; de Londras 2020; Fitzsimons 2021; McKimmons and Caffrey 2021). Before describing the parameters of my 'embodied approach' to the study of the Irish abortion movement, I want to outline what I understand as some of the key historical events and transitions in the timeline of the Repeal the 8th campaign.

As social movement scholar Linda Connolly describes, the foundation of numerous women's rights groups in the 1960s and 1970s marked the end of a long period of 'abeyance' in women's political organizing in Ireland (2002, 111). A core demand of groups including the Women's Liberation Movement and Irish Women United (founded in 1970 and 1977, respectively) was access to contraception which would be legalized under the *McGee* ruling in 1979 (Connolly 2002).[8] Following the foundation of the first Irish Pregnancy Counselling Centre in 1980, feminist activists convened a conference in Trinity College Dublin in early 1981 on the theme of 'Abortion, Contraception, and Sterilisation' (Connolly 2002). At this same moment, the Irish 'pro-life' campaign set about lobbying for a constitutional referendum on the 'right to life of the unborn' (Connolly 2002). Women's rights organizations responded by setting up a coalition of activist groups under the banner of the 'Anti-Amendment Campaign'. Importantly, these groups did not campaign explicitly for the right to abortion, but rather against the insertion of a constitutional abortion ban in 1983.

McKimmons and Caffrey (2021) note that abortion activists in Ireland felt 'disillusioned' after the 'pro-life' constitutional amendment was passed by popular vote in 1983, leading into another period of relative stagnation for the movement. Despite this, the 1990s and early 2000s saw a slew of referenda on abortion in Ireland. Debate was catalysed primarily by Ireland's signing of the Maastricht Treaty and its concurrent economic integration to the European Union (EU) single market.[9] Abortion became a 'national boundary issue', as Angela Martin (2002) explains, intimately linked with efforts to (re)define Ireland's moral and political identity inside of the EU (66). Public attitudes towards abortion would begin to change in the early 1990s with the now infamous 'X case'. 'Miss X', a 14-year-old girl, who had become pregnant through rape, was prevented by court injunction from travelling to England to access abortion services. After declaring that she was suicidal, Miss X was eventually granted permission to travel but ultimately experienced a miscarriage on her way to England. As Martin (2002) claims, debate around the possible liberalization of Ireland's abortion laws in line with EU standards 'played out across the terrain of Miss X's body' (76).

Following debate surrounding the X case, a referendum was held in 1992 to insert a further clause into the Constitution to protect the 'right' to travel abroad to access abortion services. With the passing of the 1992 referendum, abortion campaigners Carnegie and Roth (2019) explain, the country's 'exportation of reproductive healthcare was enshrined in law' (111). Demonstrating minimal liberalization, the right to access information in relation to abortion services abroad was also inserted into the Constitution by the same vote (de Londras and Enright 2018). In a 2002 referendum, anti-abortion activists attempted to have suicide explicitly excluded as possible grounds for obtaining an abortion under Irish law: this proposal was ultimately rejected by the voting public. The Protection of Human Life in Pregnancy Bill 2002 also sought to increase the penalties associated with aiding the provision of abortion but was rejected by Irish voters by a slim margin of 50.4 per cent.[10]

The Irish campaign for abortion rights has historically been an all-island, as well as a transnational movement. Although the six counties of Northern Ireland form a part of the United Kingdom, the Abortion Act 1967 was never extended to this jurisdiction. Until October 2019, both accessing and providing abortions constituted a criminal offence in Northern Ireland under the Offences Against the Persons Act 1861 (Bloomer and Fegan 2014). Statistics from 2012 illustrate that approximately 20 women per day were travelling from Northern Ireland to mainland Britain to access abortion services, encountering expenses of anywhere between £200 and £2,000 (Bloomer and Fegan 2014, 111).[11] Groups such as the Irish Women's Abortion Support Group (IWASG) and Speaking of Imelda operated to assist abortion-seekers from Northern Ireland and the Republic navigating their journey to undergo procedures in Great Britain (Rossiter 2009) Members of the IWASG met Irish abortion-seekers at airports, accompanied them

INTRODUCTION

to clinics, and opened their homes, offering hot meals and couches to sleep on (Rossiter 2009).

Indeed, transnational feminist solidarity has historically played an important role in the Irish abortion movement. The IWASG, whose activities also included 'running an information line, organising appointments for women at abortion clinics, negotiating with the clinics about price', was also supported since its inception by various health and welfare organizations in Britain, as well as by international abortion activist groups, like the Spanish Women's Abortion Support Group which offered similar services to Spanish abortion-seekers travelling to access services in Britain and beyond (Calkin et al 2020, 8). The work of other abortion 'accompaniment' organizations, such as Need Abortion Ireland, which provides support to people self-managing abortions at home, have become increasingly important across the last decade with the uptake in the importation of illegal abortion pills.[12] Need Abortion Ireland borrows its strategies and tactics from the work of similar organizations in Latin America, specifically in Guatemala, Honduras, and El Salvador (Walsh 2020).

In 2001, the Dutch non-governmental organization (NGO) Women on Waves sailed its 'abortion ship' to Ireland, helping to strengthen the global visibility and reach of the Irish pro-choice movement (Clifford 2002). Setting out on the maiden voyage of the *Aurora*, Dutch doctor and abortion activist Rebecca Gomperts intended for the vessel to act as a 'floating abortion clinic' (Clifford 2002, 385). Gomperts was invited to Ireland by Irish abortion activists but was ultimately unable to administer abortions to Irish patients after being denied the relevant medical licence (Rosen 2016). More than 25 Irish activists did board the ship, however, in a fervent display of international solidarity. International activist groups like Abortion Support Network (ASN) – set up in London in 2009 – continue to play a fundamental role in assisting Irish abortion-seekers to access services abroad, even post-repeal of the 8th amendment (Duffy 2020). ASN caters to abortion-seekers from Ireland, Northern Ireland, Malta, Gibraltar, Hungary, France, and Poland (as well as some other EU countries).

The movement for abortion rights in Ireland intensified substantially following the death of Savita Halappanavar in 2012. Ms Halappanavar, a dentist who had migrated to Ireland from India, self-referred to Galway University Hospital on 21 October 2012. Ms Halappanavar was 17 weeks pregnant at the time and was complaining of lower back pain. Ms Halappanavar was sent home but returned later the same day complaining of 'unbearable pain' (McCarthy 2016, 10–11). She was subsequently diagnosed with an 'inevitable/impending miscarriage' but because a foetal heartbeat was still detected, medical practitioners declined to intervene to pre-emptively evacuate the pregnancy from her womb (McCarthy 2016, 10–11). Ms Halappanavar went on to develop sepsis and died on 28 October 2012, aged 31 years. Ensuing reports into her death identified 'gross inadequacies' in the 'basic elements' of her care, as well as confusion surrounding the legality of providing abortions in the case where the woman's life is at risk (McCarthy 2016, 11).

Such confusion surrounding the legality of abortions in the case of risk to the woman's life stemmed from the 1992 X case ruling, according to which abortion was deemed to be technically lawful in Ireland, wherein there was 'real and substantial risk to the life of the mother' (Carnegie and Roth 2019, 112). Despite the X case ruling, the Irish Supreme Court never enacted legislation to regulate legal abortion access. Ms Halappanavar's death occurred two years after the deaths of two other migrant women in Irish maternity services. Ms Bimbo Onanuga, a Nigerian woman, died of cardiac arrest in the Rotunda Hospital after being induced for treatment of late intrauterine foetal death in 2010 (Lentin 2013, 131). In the same year, Ms Dhara Kivlehan, from India, developed pre-eclampsia and died from HELLP syndrome in Sligo General Hospital following a Caesarean section (AIMS Ireland 2017). It is worth noting that although they accounted for only 23.7 per cent of births in the period accruing from 2009 to 2021, 31 per cent of maternal deaths which occurred during this time were among women born outside of the country (O'Hare et al 2023).

The Abortion Rights Campaign (ARC) – a grassroots activist group campaigning for free, safe, legal abortion on the island of Ireland, founded in July 2012 – gained considerable support in the aftermath of Ms Halappanavar's death. McKimmons and Caffrey (2021) point to Ms Halappanavar's death and the establishment of the ARC as a key moment in the 'bureaucratization' of the abortion movement, wherein the campaign began to take on a more streamlined structure and approach. ARC established itself as a non-hierarchical organization which drew upon a wide range of tactics including policy and advocacy work, social media campaigning, and direct actions. Acknowledging that stigma–busting, as well as constitutional change, would be core to the organization's mission, the ARC made the conscious decision to put the word abortion 'front and centre' in its name (Carnegie and Roth 2019, 111). ARC organized its first annual 'March for Choice' on 28 September 2012, to coincide with International Safe Abortion Day.[13] The numbers in attendance at the annual March for Choice would grow exponentially from an estimated 2,500 participants in 2012, to an astounding 40,000 in 2017 (Carnegie and Roth 2019).

By late 2012, the Irish government's inaction around the abortion issue had become untenable (Carnegie and Roth 2019). Ireland was being put under increasing pressure from international human rights bodies, including the European Court of Human Rights, which ruled against Ireland in the 'ABC judgement', finding that the state's failure to enact effective abortion laws and procedures amounted to a violation of Ireland's obligations under Article

8 of the European Convention on Human Rights, the right to respect for private life (Goold 2014). In 2013, the Protection of Life During Pregnancy Act (PLDPA) was introduced, outlining for the first time a 'framework regulating abortion into Irish law' (Murray 2016, 667). This legislation maintained a 'two-tier' approach to abortion provision in Ireland however, permitting abortion only in the cases where 'the life of the woman is at risk' (Murray 2016, 667). The PLDPA was introduced, legal scholar Claire Murray explains, 'to comply with Ireland's obligations under the European Court of Human Rights' (Murray 2016, 668). It is practical application in terms of widening access to healthcare for Irish abortion-seekers proved meagre, however.[14]

Between 2012 and 2017, the abortion rights movement in Ireland gained increasing momentum. The ARC hosted values clarification training and civic engagement workshops across the country and began to produce and sell a range of feminist and 'pro-choice' merchandise including buttons, t-shirts, and tote bags, increasing the visibility of the movement in the public sphere (Carnegie and Roth 2019). In 2013, the Coalition to Repeal the Eighth Amendment was formed, bringing together a diverse range of organizations, some of whom did not share an explicitly 'pro-choice' stance, but did support the repeal of the 8th amendment of the constitution in its current form (Griffin et al 2019). Over the course of a five-year period, the Coalition to Repeal the Eighth Amendment grew from having 12 constituent members to over 100. Constituent groups included the National Women's Council of Ireland, AkiDwA (a network of migrant women in Ireland), Termination for Medical Reasons, and the Association for Improvements in Maternity Services – Ireland.

Scholar and activist Camilla Fitzsimons (2021) described the burgeoning 'repeal sentiment' in Ireland from 2016 onwards as reflective of a global 'awakening of consciousness' taking place among young women, citing the #MeToo campaign and the Ni Una Menos movement against femicide as emblematic of this international mass movement (xv). It is fair to say, I think, that Irish campaigners drew inspiration as well from the 'Marea Verde' or the 'Green Wave' for abortion rights across Latin America. The triangular green kerchief, which became so emblematic of the Latin American abortion movement, was first used at the 2003 National Women's Meeting in Rosario, and took on new life during the 2018 protests when the Argentinian Senate rejected a bill to legalize abortion in the first 14 weeks (Vacarezza 2021a). Irish and Polish abortion activists, too, fostered solidarity through actions like the Black Monday/CzarnyProtest, with Irish activists demonstrating outside the Polish Consulate in Dublin on 3 October 2016.[15]

Legal scholar Mairead Enright called the Repeal the 8th campaign a 'floating signifier' (2018, 9). Indeed, as momentum gathered behind the campaign in the years preceding the 2018 referendum, it became increasingly clear that the Repeal movement had become a kind of 'hold all' for a collective reckoning with Ireland's history of sexual and reproductive oppression. A particular sequence of events on home grounds between 2015 and 2018 cemented the status of the Repeal campaign as part of a broader feminist and reproductive justice initiative. In 2015, in response to a report by historian Catherine Corless into the Bon Secours Mother and Baby Home in Tuam, County Galway, the Irish government launched an investigation into practices at Catholic Church run Mother and Baby Homes between 1922 and 1988. The 'Homes' investigated by the Mother and Baby Homes Commission of Investigation housed 56,000 unmarried mothers and about 57,000 children during the period under review (Commission of Investigation into Mother and Baby Homes 2021).

The Commission's report (2021) cites 'appalling physical conditions' in these institutions and describes that the women held there were subjected to 'physical' and 'emotional abuse' (2–3). With regards to the treatment of children in these institutions, it is estimated that upwards of 6,000 children may have died in these homes, while others were 'sold' as part of an illegal overseas adoption scheme (Grimes 2016). Many of these children suffered from malnutrition and some of them were also subjected to unsanctioned vaccination trials (Fitzsimons 2021). An excavation project carried out at the Bon Secours Home between November 2016 and February 2017 uncovered an unmarked, mass grave of approximately 800 children and babies. The discovery of the mass grave in Tuam sparked anger, outrage, and sorrow among reproductive rights campaigners who highlighted the hypocrisy of the Catholic Church and its 'pro-life' stance. How could an organization responsible for the abuse and death of thousands of Irish women and children now legitimately position itself as a defender of mothers and of 'the unborn'?

In early 2018, two other events occurred which added further fuel to the fires of Irish feminist activism. In March 2018, two Irish rugby players were found not guilty of raping a woman at a party in Belfast in 2016. When the verdict was publicized, feminists north and south of the border took to the streets with placards reading 'I Believe Her' in a show of support for the woman at the centre of the case. Details of the case, including a leaked transcript of a text conversation between a group of rugby players wherein the men discussed the events of the party where the alleged incident took place, brought into focus the deep-seeded misogyny which continues to permeate Irish society. Feminists were appalled at the misogynistic line of questioning in the court, with the woman at the centre of the case being asked to describe the type of underwear she was wearing on the night in question (Safronova 2018).

A month after the conclusion of the 'Rugby Rape Trial', news broke in the Irish media that CervicalCheck – the national cervical screening programme – had sent 'false negative' pap smear results to over 200 women who went on to receive cancer diagnoses. The CervicalCheck scandal only became public knowledge through the efforts of women's health campaigner and whistleblower Vicky Phelan. Phelan was diagnosed with cervical cancer in 2014 but was not informed until three years later that an earlier smear test from 2011, which showed a negative result, was incorrect. Phelan began litigation against the US laboratory subcontracted by CervicalCheck and refused to sign a confidentiality clause to reach an earlier settlement. A subsequent government report into CervicalCheck found 'serious gaps in the governance and expertise of the programme' and recommended 'more robust quality assurance procedures' (Scally 2018). An estimated 30 women have now died as a result of the CervicalCheck scandal, including Ms Phelan who passed away in November 2022.

Under increasing pressure from domestic activist groups and international human rights organizations, the Irish government eventually called a referendum to be held on 25 May 2018, on the issue of the 8th amendment. In the run-up to the referendum, abortion activist groups as well as various NGOs and political parties came together under the banner of Together for Yes, the civil society organization which would advocate for a 'Yes' vote. After an arduous and divisive campaign, the pro-choice movement in Ireland secured victory when the electorate chose to repeal the 8th amendment by a landslide margin of 66 per cent (Griffin et al 2019, 197). Following the referendum, the Health (Regulation of Termination of Pregnancy) Act was signed into law in December 2018 with abortion provision commencing from 1 January 2019. In practice, however, the Health Act allows for access to abortion in only a very limited set of circumstances; with abortion-seekers over 12 weeks of pregnancy, as well as those whose pregnancies have been diagnosed with severe foetal anomalies being forced still to travel abroad to access care (de Londras 2020).

Acknowledging the relevance of various 'organizational' factors in the trajectory of the Repeal the 8th movement, this book prescribes a more 'embodied' approach to the study of the Irish abortion movement. Pregnancy and abortion are embodied experiences, and abortion laws have a direct and tangible effect on the everyday, bodily, and emotional lives of women and gestating people (Kimport and Littlejohn 2021). With this book, I want to refocus the fact that women's bodies are in no way tangential to abortion politics and in fact are both 'the main cause', as well as the 'instrument' of reproductive rights protests (Sasson-Levy and Rapoport 2003, 388–398). In this vein, it is impossible, I argue, to fully understand the social, political, and cultural consequences of the Repeal the 8th movement without considering the embodied experiences of living through and participating in these historical events.

How I understand bodies and emotions and how I conducted this research

A key focus for academics and activists in the years prior to the 2018 referendum was documenting the lived experiences of women and pregnant people who had attempted to access abortion care, inside of and beyond Irish borders. Such work sought to highlight the legal, financial, and logistical hoops that Irish abortion-seekers were being forced to jump through, as well as the emotional and physical harm being inflicted on women and others who may become pregnant as a result of the 8th amendment. By focusing on the lived experience of abortion-seekers, these accounts transformed our understanding of the power of the 8th amendment beyond what was possible using only legalistic or medical arguments and evidenced the real, embodied effects for abortion-seekers of having to navigate access to abortion care. This book takes that work a step further, exploring the everyday bodily experience of being subjected to and of fighting against Ireland's strict anti-abortion laws and regulations.

As many critical feminist studies of the body and reproduction have explored, the historically contingent and culturally divergent ways in which we conceptualize and represent the (gendered) reproductive body have social and political, as well as symbolic, effects (Duden 1993; Martin 2001). Taking first-person accounts of everyday bodily life as the point of departure for analysis, this book contributes to a feminist 'politics of visibility', by depicting the bodies of women and others who may become pregnant 'in ways that are different from dominant social portrayals' (Sutton 2010, 194). Specifically, this book brings into focus how foetocentric, biomedical models of reproduction – which tend to dominate political debate and discourse on abortion – not only limit our understandings of the operation of reproductive governance, but themselves also reproduce a pattern of symbolic violence targeted at women and others who may become pregnant, by obscuring the fact that pregnancy is an embodied and 'social process' (Franklin 1991, 203).

My approach to the study of embodiment in inspired primarily by feminist phenomenology, and poststructuralism, as well as by queer and affect theory. Feminist phenomenology is a 'bottom-up' model of knowledge production, indebted to feminist science and technology studies, and to Black feminist (standpoint) theory; which were among the first areas of social science scholarship to highlight the 'situatedness' of all knowledge production, as well as the gendered and racialized specificity of embodied perspectives (Haraway 1988; Hill Collins 2009 [1990]; Pitts-Taylor 2014). Feminist phenomenology considers 'consciousness and the body together as aspects of an integrated and projective unity' (Dolezal 2015, 8). It seeks to confront histories of discriminatory scholarship which have devalued the lived, embodied experiences of women, and other marginalized groups (Weiss

2021). In line with a critical feminist phenomenological approach, while taking the embodied experiences of Irish activists as the point of analytical departure, I also consider how structural forces like racism, classism, and ableism shape their everyday bodily life.

In other words, my understanding of the body, while drawing primarily upon feminist phenomenological approaches, also integrates the work of poststructuralist theorists like Judith Butler (1988) and Michel Foucault (1978), in so far as I endeavour to pay close attention to the ways in which power relations frame and inform the embodied experiences of research participants.[16] In this sense, the feminist phenomenological framework I deploy here is also a 'queer' one, which borrows from the ground-breaking work of scholars like Sara Ahmed (2006) to analyse the ways in which bodies are affected and become 'oriented' in 'responsiveness to the world around them' (7). As Ahmed writes, 'spaces are not exterior to bodies' but are 'like a second skin that unfolds in the body' (2006, 9). In this way, and following Ahmed's line of inquiry, the model of queer, feminist phenomenology I adopt here explores the ways in which the body is 'affected' by and can also itself affect the social structures and spaces within which it operates.

The important work of feminist sociologist Barbara Sutton (2007; 2010) on women's embodiment and political resistance in Argentina has been deeply formative to the theoretical development of this research. Like Sutton, I conceptualize the bodies of Irish activists as 'sites of power inscription and contestation' (2010, 2). Returning to her country of origin during the citizens' uprising after the economic collapse of 2001, Sutton conceptualizes women's bodies as 'embattled sites' which are simultaneously 'actively engaged in the construction of a new society' (2010, 8). She poses the question of what can be learned about Argentinean society during this period by taking the 'bodily worlds' of women as the starting point of analysis. Citing Dorothy Smith, who advocated for sociologists of gender to study the 'everyday experiences' of women, Sutton describes these 'bodily worlds' as 'women's varied, overlapping and context-related bodily experience – including both every day and extraordinary events – marked by the gamut of human emotions' (Smith 1987 in Sutton 2010, 6; Sutton 2010, 2).

Sutton is careful to emphasize that while each woman's narrative around her bodily experience might be treated as an 'individual event', participants' narratives can be taken together as 'part of a social pattern' (Sutton 2010, 6). Exploring what she describes as 'five fields of power', that is, the effects of neoliberal globalization, beauty and femininity norms, reproductive politics, violence against women, and women's bodies in political protest, Sutton explores how women experience these social changes 'in the flesh' (2010, 8). By exploring the testimony of both activist and nonactivist women, Sutton demonstrates how 'powerful ideologies and institutions' in Argentina work to 'regulate and control women's bodies', while at the same time, illustrating how women 'cope, negotiate, and resist these forces' as embodied beings (2010, 2). Sutton (2010) situates her analysis of women's bodily worlds as part of an attempt to encourage 'a closer approximation of social suffering' (11).

Contributing to a rich corpus of feminist literature on embodiment and political agency, Sutton explains how the female body in Argentina becomes both 'vehicle and agent' of resistance (2007, 129). She elaborates five ways in which the body is important to political protest. First, activism happens through the body which marches in the street, carrying banners and waving flags. Second, describing the function of protest objects like scarves, clothes, and signs, Sutton explains that the protest body can be deployed as a political argument or text. Third, Sutton expands on the material needs and vulnerabilities of activist bodies which eat, sleep, and care for each other. Fourth, she explores the importance of 'massed bodies', where the existence of large crowds 'makes it harder for the State to downplay the existence of social problems' (Sutton 2007, 141; Sutton 2010, 174). Finally, Sutton (2010, 174) maintains the significance of 'embodied emotions and passions' which can sustain or undermine social movements.

This question of the role of emotions, feelings, or 'bodily intensities' in the Irish abortion rights movement constitutes an integral element of this book's mission (Gould 2009). My conceptualization of emotions borrows from the work of Sara Ahmed (2014a, 4, 9) in so far as I am less concerned with the definition of what emotions *are* and am more concerned with understanding what emotions *do* as 'social and cultural practices'. In other words, I am particularly interested in the connection between emotions and power and conceptualize emotions as one circuit through which 'power is felt' in the body (Pedwell 2021b in Pedwell and Whitehead 2012, 120). Indeed, Ahmed explains, emotions are intentional, and always already involve a 'claim about a subject or collective' which is clearly dependent on relations of power (2014a, 4). In other words, emotions provide a method to endow others with meaning or 'value'. Emotions do not reside in the subject but are passed around, displaced, or withheld as part of an affective economy.

Rather than bifurcating the emotional and the structural, then, I draw inspiration from feminist scholarship, and particularly from Black feminist theorists who have taught us that systems and structures of oppression operate on an affective level (Lorde 1981). As Sara Ahmed so eloquently describes it, feelings are the route through which structures 'get under our skin' (2010, 216). In this sense, emotional experiences can be conceptualized as fundamental sites for the production of knowledge about how power operates in society, in a broader sense. While classical social movement scholarship viewed social movement actors as 'rational' agents working in the best interest of their economic and political conditions, and consequently, conceptualized emotion as antithetical to 'rational' political activity, feminist scholars have convincingly argued that this oppositional dichotomization of the emotional and the political is indeed itself a political strategy defined to 'keep women and the feminine out of politics and political spheres' (Åhäll 2018, 37).

As Deborah Gould argues in her ethnography of AIDS activism in the United States in the 1980s and 1990s, feelings and emotions are 'fundamental to political life', not because they are antithetical to the exercise of 'rational' political agency, but in the sense that 'the political' has an inherently 'affective dimension' (Gould 2009, 3). Tracing the history of ACTUp or the 'AIDS Coalition to Unleash Power' – an international, grassroots, activist group working to end the AIDS epidemic – Gould's book offers an innovative exploration of the 'affective stimuli' and 'blockages' to political activism (2009, 3). Gould poses the question of how emotions like anger, rage, indignation, and hope might generate or foreclose specific political horizons.

Explaining how AIDS activists successfully channelled their grief and rage into confrontational action, and describing the psychological cost of their activism, Gould's book clearly delineates the importance of emotion work or emotional labour in social justice organizing. This focus on the role of embodied, emotional labour and 'feelings work' in social movement activity is one which I take forward into this book. I also borrow here from Arlie Hochschild and her symbolic interactionist approach which conceptualizes 'emotion work' as 'the act of trying to change in degree or quality an emotion or feeling' (1979, 561). Analysing the experiences of Irish abortion activists living under and mobilizing against the 8th amendment, I pay close attention to the ways in which activists strategically perform emotions through body language and facial expressions, as well as the ways in which activists grapple with and struggle to manage the 'inner shape' of their own feelings, in an everyday sense (Hochschild 2012 [1983], 36).

This book is based on the analysis of personal testimonies gathered via in-depth qualitative, semi-structured interviews conducted with 43 Irish abortion activists across two periods of fieldwork from late 2019 to early 2021. My status as an 'insider-outsider' – living in the UK but having been born and raised in Ireland and involved in various forms of abortion activism (including campaigning as part of my local Together for Yes group in the 2018 referendum and as a member of the ARC) – meant that I was able to recruit participants relatively easily through a snowball sampling method. The initial fieldwork period ran from November 2019 until March 2020. I met interviewees in hotel lobbies, cafes, restaurants, and activist spaces all over the country. After pausing fieldwork due to the COVID-19 pandemic and lockdown in March 2020, I recommenced and completed fieldwork in January and February 2021, using online and telephone interviews only. In total, 43 interviews took place; 23 interviews were conducted face-to-face and 20 interviews were carried out online or using the telephone.

The activists who participated in this research were variously affiliated to abortion rights, anti-racist, reproductive justice, disability rights, and trade union groups, among others. Participants ranged in age from early 20s to late 60s and came from all four provinces of Ireland, including a small number who lived in Northern Ireland or on the borderlands between Northern Ireland and the Republic (while these individuals spoke about their lived experience and activism in both jurisdictions, their testimonies pertained primarily to their involvement in the campaign to repeal the 8th amendment). Six participants were first generation migrants, coming from British, North American, East Asian, Anglo-Caribbean, and Western and Southern European backgrounds, respectively. The majority of research participants (approximately 86 per cent) were both White and from a 'national' background (meaning they were born in Ireland and automatically granted Irish citizenship).[17] While sexual orientation was not explicitly elicited, 15 activists identified themselves as LGBTQIA+. Sociodemographic information was also not explicitly elicited. However, several participants identified themselves as coming from an urban working-class background.

As will become evident in the proceeding chapters, I have written this book in such a way as to try to make central the voices and experiences of activists who participated in this research. This decision has both epistemological and political underpinnings. First, inspired by Black feminist standpoint theory, I want to emphasize the status of activists themselves as epistemological agents (Hill Collins 1996). The theory that those who are subordinated by interlocking oppressive structures have a unique perspective and understanding of how such systems of domination operate was seminal to the foundation of this research; as was the notion that the specific, concrete experiences of an oppressed group stimulate a unique type of consciousness concerning that material reality (Hill Collins 2009 [1990]). The idea that we can challenge dominant oppressive ideologies through the articulation of alternative imaginings of gendered and racialized embodiment, based on the lived, intersubjective experiences of subordinated groups, are core to the objectives this book strives to achieve.

Second, by centralizing the words, experiences, and feelings of these activists, I hope to contribute to a feminist 'testimonial politics' which views 'speaking out' about gender injustice as integral to the process of subject formation for marginalized groups (Ahmed and Stacey 2001, 2). I am conscious that a key feature of the patriarchal church–state apparatus in Ireland historically has been an attempt to silence the voices of women and others who may become pregnant, specifically wherein they have attempted to disclose or bring public attention to their experiences of reproductive injustice. As Sara Ahmed and Jackie Stacey describe, feminist struggles for justice are inherently 'bound up' with speaking out, testifying, or bearing witness to violence and oppression (2001, 1). The use of testimony remains an integral part of feminist politics, Ahmed and Stacey argue, as it is about 'women becoming subjects of their lives, and speaking rather than remaining silent about trauma, injustice, or violence (2001, 4).

Through analysing the embodied experiences of women and gestating people living under and mobilizing against Ireland's constitutional abortion ban, this book brings attention to the perhaps more subtle yet equally pervasive ways in which reproductive injustice operates in this context. In parts, this book takes an auto-ethnographical approach, integrating reflections of my own experiences growing up in Ireland from the early 1990s onwards, as a queer, White woman, in a rural community and reflections on my experiences campaigning as part of the Repeal the 8th movement in 2018. In taking an auto-ethnographical approach and reflecting on my own bodily and affective experience of reproductive politics in Ireland, I hope to make clear my positionality, as an academic–activist and as a member of the community under study, and to illustrate the power and richness of taking one's own body as a point of departure for the sociological analysis of gendered life.

Outline of the book

This book consists of seven chapters, taking a chronological approach to explore the experiences of activists growing up under the 8th amendment, as well their embodied and emotional experiences as part of the movement for abortion rights in Ireland. Chapter 2 explores activists' experiences of growing up in Ireland under the 8th amendment and their memories of first learning about or encountering abortion as a social and political issue. Chapters 3 through 5 analyse activists' embodied experiences of politicization and mobilization within the pro-choice movement, as well as their more recent memories and experiences within the Repeal the 8th campaign. Chapters 6 and 7 examine how the intimate, bodily, reproductive lives of activists have been transformed since the constitutional abortion ban was overturned in May 2018 and discusses the conceptual contributions of this book to broader scholarship on abortion politics, reproductive (in)justice, and contemporary feminist social movements.

In Chapter 2, 'Living under the 8th: The Gendered Burden of "Abortion Work"', I explore how the 'reproductive habitus' of women and gestating people in Ireland has historically been moulded through the 8th amendment; analysing how their everyday bodily practices and unconscious thought patterns have been shaped and reproduced through systems of reproductive governance (Smith-Oka 2012, 2276). Illustrating how Irish abortion politics have historically been deeply enmeshed with the country's postcolonial identity, activists from different age groups recount the development of an early affective attachment which associates abortion with England and 'foreign-ness' or 'going abroad'. Exemplifying the spatial organization of reproductive politics in Ireland, activists describe being always already *oriented*, both mentally and physically, towards England – the traditional destination of Irish abortion travellers.

Recounting their everyday experience of life under the 8th amendment, activists describe a general feeling of 'fear' and 'vulnerability' and explain the bodily effects of being forced to constantly 'anticipate' the possibility of needing to access clandestine abortion care. This chapter coins the term 'abortion work' to describe the cognitive, emotional, and physical bodily labour or the specific 'gendered burden' which is unequally imposed on women and gestating people as they are forced to plan and prepare for how they might go about accessing abortion care in a context where abortion is both illegal and practically inaccessible. Through the doing of 'abortion work', which I conceptualize as a distinct form of reproductive labour which has thus far been missing from feminist theorizations of abortion politics, the 'pre-pregnant' body comes to be experienced both as site of acute, gendered vulnerability, and as the location of a subversive, counter-hegemonic resistance, at the same time.

Chapter 3, 'Tracing the "Embodied Infrastructure" of the Movement to Repeal the 8th Amendment', develops a framework for what I term the 'embodied infrastructure' of the Repeal the 8th campaign. Drawing upon Sewell's (1996) 'theory of the event', I illustrate how a 2012 billboard campaign by the anti-abortion group Youth Defence sparked an alteration in normative 'feeling states', propelling Irish abortion activists towards a more confrontational form of direct action (Gould 2009, 26). The wave of anger unleashed by the 'Abortion Tears Her Life Apart' billboard campaign can be directly connected, I argue, to the founding of the ARC in July 2012 (Carnegie and Roth 2019, 109). Also in this chapter, I propose a closer approximation of the embodied encounters of Irish abortion activists with 'pro-life' protest imagery – specifically, graphic foetal imagery. I theorize that activists experience anti-abortion protest imagery on a bodily level as a form of intimidation and harassment. In this vein, 'pro-life' protest objects work to catalyse counteractivity as abortion activists feel compelled to resist their moral and physical domination of the social landscape.

Additionally, in Chapter 3, I interrogate the politics of feminist anger and white, postcolonial shame, as adhesive affective forces in the consolidation of the Irish abortion rights movement. I explain how the death of Savita Halappanavar, four months after the publication of the Youth Defence billboard campaign, fostered a deep sense of outrage and despair as activists confronted the extent of the government's betrayal of pregnant people and reconceptualized the 8th amendment itself as a 'life-threatening risk' (Connolly 2019, 51). Expressions of collective shame and anguish in relation to Ms Halappanavar's death exemplified a specifically Irish form of postracialism, I argue, which constructed Ms Halappanavar – a middle-class, married, professional woman – as a 'good' migrant whose death served to illustrate the failure of the Irish state to live up to its desired identity as a charitable, modern, multicultural nation-state (Lentin 2015; O'Shaughnessy 2021).

Chapter 4, 'On the Physicality of Protest: The Politics of Revelation', discusses the importance of 'coming out' for abortion, emphasizing how the double movement of activists publicly disclosing their abortion experiences after 2013, at the same time as campaigners took to the street, *en masse*, constituted integral elements of a 'politics of revelation' which worked to counter the stigma and shame which has historically been attached to the bodies of abortion-seekers. This chapter also explores the practice of dress as a form of situated bodily resistance. Activists describe the transformative, consciousness-raising effect of the black-and-white Repeal jumper, launched in 2016. Conceptualizing the wearing of the Repeal jumper as a form of what I term 'gestural dress', I explore how through the act of donning the black-and-white sweatshirt, Irish activists used their bodies to convey political meaning, to create additional spaces for embodied protest, and to communicate a sense of care and solidarity to abortion-seekers.

In Chapter 5, 'Embodying Respectability: The Politics of Concealment', I apply an intersectional perspective to analyse the transition from the campaign to repeal the 8th to Together for Yes (the civil society campaign which advocated for a 'Yes' vote in the 2018 referendum on abortion rights). Both during and after the referendum campaign, the politics and strategies of Together for Yes came under intense scrutiny for what has been deemed by several activists and scholars as the conservativism, Whiteness, and Eurocentrism of the organization and its message (Weerawardhana 2018; Chakravarty et al 2020). Analysing the conflicting feelings of Irish activists around the campaign's buzzwords of 'care, compassion and change' and its discursive focus on 'suffering' and 'tragedy' in relation to abortion, I argue that Together for Yes worked to effectively mobilize Catholic and postcolonial gender norms linking the suffering Motherland, the Virgin Mary, and the notion of an inherently 'sacrificial' ideal of Irish femininity (O'Shaughnessy 2021, 12).

Assimilating to this 'respectability politics' strategy, activists were required not only to dress and speak in particular ways, but to mediate their feelings and emotional expressions accordingly. Activists describe how the Together for Yes campaign encouraged them to approach their work in a positive and 'non-reactive' tone. Putting aside momentarily this debate surrounding the subversive or concessionary nature of the Together for Yes strategy, I propose that this reticence to appear as 'angry' or 'confrontational' may have been motivated by a desire to distinguish itself from the activism of women of colour reproductive justice groups who, as several activists described to me, were castigated as being 'unable' to represent the campaign. In this sense, I posit that the 'unspoken registers of race thinking' and, specifically, the affective bonds of Whiteness played an important role in securing mainstream political backing for the Repeal movement (Nayak 2007, 746).

In Chapter 6, 'Changed Bodies? Life After Repeal', I explore the 'embodied consequences' of the 2018 referendum which saw Ireland's constitutional abortion ban finally overturned. Revealing the bodily risks, investments, and demands of their commitment to the pro-choice movement, activists reveal the physical toll on their bodies of participating in the referendum campaign. Activists recount their experiences of exhaustion and 'burnout' after the referendum campaign, with some describing how they had "lost weight", became "gaunt" and felt like "physical wrecks". These accounts illustrate, I argue, the need to continue to analyse our 'protest bodies' in relation to one another, even after the Repeal the 8th campaign, such that we might appreciate how reproductive violence and social suffering continues to be embodied under the Health (Termination of Pregnancy) Act 2018 in distinctly different ways (Quinn 2018). I pose the question here of how 'abortion work' is continuing, in the aftermath of the Repeal of the 8th amendment and how such work is unequally disseminated across racial and class lines.

I conclude in Chapter 7 with an analysis of the conceptual contributions and limitations of this book. I argue that this book reveals how the constitutional abortion ban historically moulded the relationship of Irish women to their (reproductive) bodies, whether or not they ever attempted to access a clandestine abortion. It explains how women and gestating people in Ireland came to live their bodies out-of-space-and-time as 'future aborting bodies' and unveils how the quotidian embodied practices, bodily labours, spatial orientations, and affective experiences of women and gestating people were shaped by and through the need to 'prepare' for crisis pregnancies. This struggle to repeal the constitutional abortion ban in Ireland was not only a struggle to secure reproductive rights, but to alleviate an ongoing and violent condition of gendered, racialized, embodied vulnerability and labour, forcibly imposed on women and gestating people. I consider how, with access to abortion being rolled back in a number of countries worldwide, increased analytical attention is needed to understand how abortion-seekers differentially experience and negotiate these restrictions in their everyday lives.

2

Living under the 8th: The Gendered Burden of 'Abortion Work'

Finding your way (to England): spatial orientations as reproductive directions

I begin with the story of Eabha, a single mother-of-two in her early 40s. I met Eabha the week before Christmas 2019. We arranged to meet at a bar in the centre of the city where she lived. I remember seeing her come over the hill at the top of the street. She waved enthusiastically as though greeting an old friend. She was warm and welcoming and asked me about my trip. We commiserated about the weather, and I remarked that I wasn't used to the Irish wind anymore. The bar where we were supposed to meet and conduct our interview was closed for the holidays. Eabha suggested a hotel, about a mile away, as a decent alternative. As we walked, she told me all about the city, which she clearly loved, pointing out interesting landmarks along the way. At the hotel, we sat down and ordered coffee. After the waitress laid the coffee pots on the table, I asked Eabha how she got involved in abortion activism.

> 'So, I suppose I made a name for myself and because of that, students came to me who may have needed information. And there would have been some staff who would have sent students to me if they needed information. "Go to Eabha" was a thing, I suppose … crisis pregnancies and so on. So, that would have been the start of it for me.'

Eabha worked as a lecturer in a higher educational institution, a place she described as having "a very conservative ethos". She became involved in debate and activism around abortion when she noticed other staff members removing posters from the female students' bathrooms with information about pregnancy counselling services. Although, according to her own

25

admission, it "wouldn't really qualify as activism", Eabha described how she found herself staging "a little protest" in her workplace to demand that senior management reinstate the posters for 'Positive Options' – a British-based pregnancy advisory service – in the female students' bathrooms. She "went back again", she says, after noticing "internet blocks" on the college computers, prohibiting students from accessing abortion referral websites.

> 'On and off over the years, students would have been coming to me for a variety of reasons and I would have supported them in whatever way I could. ... I know the one thing I often think about was one student who had to travel on her own. She couldn't take time off work, she couldn't tell anybody, she had to get a ferry. So, she travelled for, I can't remember, was it 18 hours to get there? Had the procedure done and then had to turn around and come back overnight on a ferry. On her own, on the ferry, bleeding. And nobody knew except me. So, I was messaging her and then she had to come straight back and into work, bleeding and in distress. Couldn't tell anybody. ... It was one story but it's one of so many stories.'

As she explains here, Eabha's early activism centred around facilitating the mobility of aborting bodies – in both the online and offline space. Her "little protests" (as she described them) led to the removal of the "blocks" which had previously prohibited students from accessing abortion referral websites on the college campus. Eabha also supported students who had 'to travel' to access abortions in Britain. In Ireland, the verbiage of 'travelling' is so synonymous with abortion that it is often deployed without any explicit reference to pregnancy or abortion-seeking, as Eabha demonstrates here. Since the introduction of the Abortion Act 1967 which legalized abortion in Great Britain on specific grounds, droves of Irish abortion-seekers have made the same journey to access legal abortion there (Gilmartin and Kennedy 2019). The terminology of 'travelling' entered more colloquial usage in 1992 when, after the now infamous 'X case', Irish women were awarded the '*right to travel*' to access abortion services outside of the jurisdiction (Sethna and Davis 2019, my emphasis).

Scholarship on abortion travel in Ireland has focused heavily on what feminist theorist Clara Fischer describes as the 'co-constitutive relationship' between gender politics and 'women's occupation of space' (Fischer 2019, 41). After gaining independence from the British Empire, 'nation-building' in Ireland was premised largely on the idea of 'the superiority of the Catholic Celts and their reproducing women' (Fletcher 2005, 376). Ireland constructed itself as a bastion for the veneration of motherhood and as a protector of 'unborn' life; in opposition to England, which, it was argued, used abortion as a colonial weapon against Irish women (Fischer 2019).

As Angela Martin explains, women in Ireland were held responsible for the 'labour of representation' of the nation, wherein the 'mimetic links between women and the nation' were constructed around the figure of the Virgin Mary (Martin 2002, 67, 69).

Although the 'idealisation of motherhood' was a prominent feature of the Irish Free State (established in the aftermath of the War of Independence), pregnancy outside of marriage was heavily stigmatized and 'unmarried mothers' were ostracized in Irish society (Luddy 2011, 112–113). Unmarried mothers faced systematic confinement in a range of institutions including the Magdalene Asylums and in 'county homes' (O'Sullivan and O'Donnell 2012, 11). As O'Sullivan and O'Donnell (2012) explain, being originally built in the 1840s as workhouses for the poor, these 'county homes' were 'designed to be grim and foreboding places in order to deter all but the most desperate from seeking refuge there' (11). The disciplining of female fertility was further maintained through the forced emigration of pregnant unmarried women. The legalization of adoption in Britain in 1926 meant that Irish women could 'preserve their secret' by travelling there and giving birth, before placing their babies in the adoption system (Grimes 2016).

Following the 1937 *Rex* v *Bourne* case – which saw gynaecologist Alex Bourne acquitted after he performed a life-saving abortion on a 14-year-old girl who had become pregnant as a result of rape – the door to legal abortion provision under specific conditions was gradually being opened in Great Britain, for women from within and outside of British borders (Luibhéid 2006). After the passing of the 1967 Act, 'abortion migration' became more heavily 'institutionalised', as Luibhéid (2006, 63) explains. In the period from 1968 to 1989, an estimated 50,000 women made the journey from Ireland to England or Wales to access legal abortion care (Gilmartin and Kennedy 2019, 126). Within this framework, abortion travel can be conceptualized as part of a system of exiling transgressive women – those considered incapable of upholding the religious and moral standards required of them as symbols of the nation – through what Clara Fischer (2019) calls a process of 'gendered displacement' (33).

Geographer Sydney Calkin (2019) describes the Irish tendency to 'offshore' abortions as 'part of a larger geopolitical narrative to perform state power through the control of reproduction' (2). The 'political fiction' of an 'abortion-free Ireland', Calkin (2019) argues, 'signals more than a conservative attitude to abortion' and 'enforces a broader claim to the geopolitical position of Ireland as a bastion of moral conservativism' (8–9). Calkin's (2019) work reinforces how the spatial organization of gendered bodies is critical to reproductive politics in Ireland and conjointly to the Irish nation-building project. Through her analysis of abortion travel, Calkin (2019) illuminates the connection between 'the intimate and the geopolitical', demonstrating how geopolitical power structures are experienced in/by the body of the aborting subject (7). As of the late 1990s, estimates indicated that upwards of 6,000 people per year were travelling from Ireland to Great Britain or elsewhere to access abortion services (Connolly 2002, 160).

As Canadian and Scottish historians Christabelle Sethna and Gayle Davis (2019) argue, while the Irish case is peculiar for the quantity and consistency of abortion travellers it produces, abortion migration is not unique to Ireland. As far back as the 1960s, women were travelling from Eastern Europe to Russia, to access abortion services which were not yet legally available in their respective states (Sethna and Davis 2019). In addition, prior to the legalization of abortion under the *Roe* v *Wade* ruling in 1973, droves of mainly White, middle-class women travelled from the United States to Puerto Rico to access abortion services which were widely accessible there as part of racist, population control policies designed to decrease the fertility of Puerto Rican women (Sánchez-Rivera 2022). Interestingly, in the Irish case, the numbers of abortion-seekers travelling to Britain and elsewhere declined substantially in the period between 2001 and 2018, a fact which can be correlated with the rise in volume of people obtaining abortion pills online during this timeframe (Calkin 2020).

Listening to Eabha speak, I noted how she seemed particularly affected by the story of the student who was forced to take an 18-hour journey by ferry and train to an abortion clinic in England. Eabha appeared particularly upset at the fact that this student was "on her own" and "bleeding" on the ferry home. Political geographer Cordelia Freeman (2020) argues that bleeding serves as an 'incriminating marker' that increases the 'potential of being caught' in contexts where abortion is illegal (5). Freeman (2020) contends that while abortion scholarship emphasizes the fact that women travel, 'scant attention' is given to 'the journeys themselves and how these journeys are undertaken' (1). Through bringing our attention to the embodied reality of travelling and to the visceral, bloody experience of the student in question, Eabha's story confronts us with the inevitable 'leakiness' of the aborting-body struggling against the societal indictment to 'contain' itself (Shildrick 1997).

Freeman (2020) defines 'abortion mobilities' as 'the movement or fixity of people and things that shape abortion access' (1). She deploys the framework of 'viapolitics' to re-centre the 'vehicles, roads, and routes' of abortion travel, describing vehicles as 'sites of power and contestation' in abortion politics (Freeman 2020, 2–3). As Eabha alludes to, the ferry or boat has historically served an important emblem in Irish abortion politics. As Earner-Byrne writes, 'the "boat to England" is almost a cliché used to describe the flight to England of thousands of pregnant, unmarried Irishwomen who have fled Ireland in search of a solution to their predicament· illegitimate pregnancy' (Earner-Byrne 2003, 52). Contemporary artistic interventions have attempted to refocus the 'sensory experience and emotional burden' of abortion travel, to underscore the agency of those who have had to make this journey (19).

One of the peculiarities of pro-choice activism in Ireland then is that early iterations of the reproductive rights movement focused on securing access to abortion travel and to information or referral services (which would facilitate their accessing services outside the state), instead of systematically confronting the government to repeal the 8th amendment and legislate for the provision of abortion on Irish shores (Connolly 2002). From the early 1980s onwards, numerous pregnancy advisory and referral organizations were set up, including the Irish Pregnancy Counselling Centre (which would later become Open Line Counselling), the Women's Right to Choose Campaign, the Well Woman Centre, as well as the Irish Women's Abortion Solidarity Group (Connolly 2002). Not content with having secured constitutional protection for the 'right to life' of 'the unborn' in the 1983 referendum, anti-abortion groups in Ireland set their sights on dismantling the information networks which existed to support women and pregnant people in travelling to Britain and elsewhere, to access legal abortion care.

In 1986, under the Supreme Court's *Hamilton* ruling, the Society for the Protection of the Unborn Campaign was granted an injunction against various pregnancy counselling services, which, it claimed, operated in contravention of the 8th amendment by offering information to Irish women on accessing abortion services abroad (Connolly 2002). On the back of the Hamilton ruling and the subsequent 1987 High Court order which closed numerous family planning clinics, the commercial magazine *Cosmopolitan* received complaints from the Office of Censorship of Publications 'requesting the omission of advertisements giving abortion advice' (Porter 1996, 283). Despite the results of the *Hamilton* ruling, information networks continued to operate underground throughout the 1980s and into the early 1990s. 'Travelling' has thus been endemic to reproductive life in Ireland over the past half a century, with pregnancy advisory services playing a hugely important role in helping Irish abortion-seekers to navigate this journey, as Eimear, another activist I interviewed, explained:

> 'I had an abortion myself. I had gone to the Open Line Counselling, which was just a room in Mountjoy Square, all very grim. I think the Well Woman Clinic gave me the number, so I went in and spoke to a counsellor. But it was very difficult, the information. You were going to England really, you know, with a map and the name of the clinic and so on. It was a difficult journey anyway, but the circumstances made it even more difficult. So, I obviously then was very aware of the campaign because this had been prior to 1983 that I had an abortion.'

Eimear was in her early 60s and had two adult children. We first met almost a year previously, at a meeting for the Coalition to Repeal the Eighth Amendment in Dublin where we shared a pot of tea and bonded over our shared interest in the experiences of rural women both in accessing and advocating for abortion in Ireland. We ran into each other again at another event later that year, and I asked her if she would be interesting in taking part in my research. I finally interviewed her late on a rainy Friday afternoon in mid-January 2020. She told me about her mother, who she described as "a feminist" even though, as Eimear explained to me, "she would have had no theory of feminism herself". She talks about her excitement at the "new generation" of abortion activists in Ireland, after what she described as a relative silence around the issue in the late 1990s and early 2000s. She explained to me how, after travelling to England herself for an abortion in the early 1980s, she began volunteering for one of the telephone hotlines which provided Irish abortion-seekers with information on accessing services abroad:

> 'The community of women that were in the group, we reinforced each other, because it was illegal what we were doing. There was that sense that nobody else was doing it. We had little stickers that we put up and little booklets that we gave out to community groups. But it was that sense that, if we're not doing it, there's nobody doing it. I mean, you can't go to the paper. Back then, there was no mobile phones. Where would you go in the phone book? Back then you had to go into the GPO [General Post Office] to get the English phonebook. There was no other phonebook. The desk in the GPO. But it wasn't going to say: "A for Abortion". Where would you even go for information? Maybe you might have a doctor who would put you onto us or put you onto doctors in England.'

The GPO sits on the middle of O'Connell Street on the north side of Dublin city centre. It holds huge historical significance for Irish people as it was this building which served as the headquarters for the leaders of the 1916 Easter Rising – an armed insurrection of Irish Republicans against British rule in Ireland. The Easter Rising is regarded as the first armed conflict of the revolution, which ended in 1922 with the establishment of the Irish Free State. Today, tour guides can be seen feeling out the bullet holes which remain on the six iconic columns of the GPO's façade. I thought about the idea of a young Eimear, or other women like her, walking through those columns and into the building's still rather ornately decorated main room. How big would the English phonebook have been in those days, I wondered?

When questioned about the first time they remember being aware of abortion or abortion politics, many the activists I interviewed referred to travelling, to England, or to an early association they had made between abortion and "going abroad". Roisin, a project coordinator in her early 30s, had become involved in abortion activism as a student in 2016 when a friend invited her to a demonstration outside the Dáil (Irish Parliament) to support a bill being brought forward by Teachtaí Dála (TDs) Mick Wallace and Clare Daly proposing the legalization of abortion in the case of pregnancies with fatal foetal anomalies. She arrived at our interview head-to-toe in abortion rights garb – a Repeal jumper, 'Repealed' necklace, and a 'Free, Safe, Legal' tote bag. When I asked Roisin to reflect on her earliest memories of abortion politics in Ireland, she referred to an early association she had made between abortion and 'travelling':

> 'I didn't think anything about abortion. It was bizarre. Like, I knew you went to England. I thought it was wrong, but I also knew that if I needed to go to England, I'd think about the story that I would need to have and all of that. But I don't think I really thought about it in terms of the wider context of how restrictive it was, how degrading it was. As I said, until I was 21, I didn't think that Ireland was anything unusual. I would have thought that England was more progressive or more liberal. But it really fascinates me that I did not question those ideologies, that they were just … they weren't even invasive in the sense of being shoved down my throat, they were just there, and I just didn't question them. It was just like the norm. People went to England if they needed to go to England and it was just a common euphemism that nobody thought about. I guess the idea of changing it was never on the cards for me. I knew so little about politics; I probably didn't understand how policy change worked or if it was even possible.'

I was intrigued by the many apparent contradictions in Roisin's statement. On the one hand, she explained to me how, as a child, she "didn't think anything about" abortion. In the same breath however, she recalls that she "knew you went to England" and that she herself had thought about "the story" she "would need to have" if ever she ended up 'travelling'. In similarly contradictory terms, she recounts how while she thought abortion "was wrong", she knew that 'travelling' was "the norm" and that "people went to England if they needed to go to England". Interestingly, Roisin explains how she "didn't think that Ireland was anything unusual" in its outlawing of abortion, rather that abortion-providing England was simply "more progressive" or "more liberal". Without having had any of these ideas "shoved down (her) throat", Roisin had created the idea of abortion as somehow antithetical to Irishness; as a practice which belonged in more 'liberal' countries, such as England.

Writing in the aftermath of the referendum in 2018, feminist legal scholar Mairead Enright (2018) wrote that pregnant people in Ireland would now be spared 'the trauma of that journey to England', which she says 'has shaped our sense of Irish womanhood for generations' (8–9). Indeed, the idea that this journey to England has been historically formative to the experience of gendered socialization in Ireland appears to have reached the status of common sense and, yet, little has been done to explain the mechanisms of this process in sociological terms. Smith-Oka's (2012) concept of 'reproductive habitus' (2275) is potentially useful here. Defined as 'modes of living the reproductive body, bodily practices, and the creation of new subjects through interactions between people and structures', the reproductive habitus 'exists in the hazy, gray realm between consciousness and unconsciousness' (Smith-Oka 2012, 2276).

Thinking about the idea of the reproductive habitus as ways of living or (unconscious) practices associated with the relationship between structural inequalities and the reproductive body, perhaps it can then be argued that 'travelling' is constitutive of the 'reproductive habitus' of women and gestating people in Ireland. While activists like Roisin might not remember exactly how or when they learned about 'going to England', these internalized thought-patterns are symptomatic of how structural power relations infiltrate the mind and memory of the embodied reproductive subject to replicate patterns of social and, specifically, reproductive inequality – particularly, to exclude those who fail to uphold 'repronormativity' (that is, 'legitimate', state-sanctioned forms of reproduction) (Weissman 2017).

In other words, Ireland's abortion laws have produced within the gestating body an 'orientation' towards 'travelling' which is both mental and physical. Sara Ahmed (2006) explains how the way the body is positioned in social space, as well as the proximity of the body to certain objects, is contingent on and connected to systems of gendered and racial inequality. To be 'oriented', Ahmed (2006) describes, is to be 'turned towards certain objects, those that help us find our way' (1). For women and people who may become pregnant, the experience of reproductive embodiment in Ireland means to be always turned towards England, always turned towards planes and boats. Even for those who never have and potentially never will have to make that journey to access abortion services abroad, this mental and physical 'orientation' towards travelling is fundamental to the process of gendered socialization and to the everyday embodied experience of many women and gestating subjects.

Mediating on the concept of 'directions', Ahmed (2006) argues that the ways we are directed, the directions we 'face as well as move', are 'organized rather than casual' (15). Ahmed's (2006) framework provides us with tools to think about how the injunction to travel, or merely to 'orient' oneself towards travelling, might constitute a *disciplinary* force, which operates exclusively upon the feminized, reproductive body. That is to say, while travelling has historically functioned as a lifeline for Irish abortion-seekers, providing a way for those with the financial means and mobility privilege to access care, the 'orientation' towards England is simultaneously a 'direction' that Irish abortion-seekers are 'asked to follow' (Ahmed 2006, 17). This is particularly true for migrant and 'non-national' abortion-seekers whose childbearing has been constructed as 'subverting the nation' (Lentin 2004, 307). It is worth noting that between 2000 and 2001, ten pregnant asylum seekers were provided with documents to travel to Britain for state-funded abortions (Lentin 2003, 313).[1]

This begs the question then of how the feminized, reproductive subject can ever truly 'belong' within the project of the Irish 'nation'? If 'travelling' is both a 'line of discipline' we are asked to follow, and simultaneously conceived as an anti-nationalist movement against the 'pro-natalist' postcolonial, racial state, as well as a mimetic failure whereby Irish women neglect to uphold the feminine and maternal ideals embodied by the Virgin Mary, what *space* can there ever truly be then for the gestating or aborting subject inside of the Irish national imaginary?

"Preparing your story" and "looking up options": fear, vulnerability, and abortion contingency plans

Listening to Roisin recount her earliest associations with abortion, I was particularly struck by her assertion that if she "needed to go to England" that she would "think about the story [she] would need to have and all of that". It quickly became apparent that by 'story', Roisin meant a 'cover story', something she could tell her parents or family to explain her absence if she was forced to travel to England to access an abortion there. Roisin's testimony illustrates how for Irish abortion-seekers, 'travelling' entailed not only navigating the complicated planning and logistics associated with finding a clinic, securing an appointment, and booking travel and accommodation at the destination (as implied in the "and all of that" portion of Roisin's statement) but also, more often than not, required a great deal of mental and emotional labour to explain or 'justify' one's absence from work and home. As activist Eileen Flynn (2018) states, many women including Traveller women 'don't really have that choice to travel' as they can't explain or 'sleep away from … home or … husband for one night' (91).

During my meeting with Eithne, an activist in her mid-20s, she explained how the reality of having to anticipate and plan for potentially needing to access a clandestine abortion, as well as having to navigate the logistical challenges that this would entail, brought with it a great degree of stress and anxiety. Eithne, who moved to Ireland from East Asia when she was a child, explained to me how her experience as a migrant and her experience growing up in a single-parent household informed her desire to become involved in grassroots reproductive justice activist networks who, as she described to me, didn't just organize around "single issues". Eithne told me that while she couldn't remember when she became explicitly aware of the existence of the 8th amendment, she remembered knowing from an early stage that abortion was "just not legal here". She further explained how, when she became sexually active herself, she realized how "scary" Ireland's abortion laws were. Although, as she recounted to me, herself and her partner were using multiple forms of contraception at the time, she regularly felt "panicked" about the possibility that she might become pregnant and need to somehow navigate access to safe abortion care. She explained:

> 'I remember in the first year of college, I started going on the pill because I was having sex more regularly. That's when I realized how scary it was and how I did not want to be pregnant. I really do think it's something no one will understand unless you've been there. I was on the pill, and we were using condoms and still, every time, I would get so panicked. It was so irrational, but I was looking at all these options, and at the time there were no options. There still aren't many.'

Eithne explained how, "every time" (presumably, every month), she spent time "looking at all these options", presumably trying to put together a plan for how or where she might access abortion care. She describes feeling "sad" that her boyfriend at the time seemed unconcerned with the issue and placated her that they would simply "find a way" if the situation arose. Eithne's testimony reveals not only the intense levels of cognitive work, as well as the emotional burden associated with having to live under and navigate around Ireland's abortion ban, but how this uniquely affective and laboursome experience is generally imposed on women rather than men. Listening to Eithne, I began to wonder whether this type of work – that is, the work involved in coming up with 'cover stories' or making abortion 'travel plans' – could be conceptualized as part of the 'mental load', that is, as an element of the 'cognitive, mnemonic, or invisible work/labour' associated with planning or managing unpaid reproductive labour with which women are generally disproportionately tasked (Reich-Stiebert et al 2023).

Sadbh was a teenager in the late 1990s, a period she describes as a "fraught time" for abortion rights in Ireland. Coming from what she described as a "middle-class, professional" rural family, Sadbh told me how her parents were "probably more old-fashioned that most", with respect to relationships and sexuality. When I asked her to explain what she meant by this, she went on to elucidate how "the class aspect was very important" in terms of how she "understood the dynamic" in her own family. Sadbh told me how "the ideal situation" for women, as she learned it, was "to be vaguely virginal" until marriage. Indeed, as Diarmuid Ferriter (2009) explains, the farming class in Ireland has historically upheld strict Catholic teachings on sexuality, in the interests of controlling women's reproduction, and thereby shoring up land and assets. When I asked her about her first encounter with abortion politics, Sadbh explains that while the topic was never engaged with directly in her home growing up, she had a "very strong sense" of how her family would respond in the event of an unplanned pregnancy and that they would "want the issue resolved":

'When I was old enough to understand pregnancy and my own risk of becoming the same, it wasn't intellectual then, it was more emotional. It was, I'd need to be able to access this if I needed it, it's not an intellectual thing. I think the strongest feeling – because I always had this morbid fear of pregnancy anyway, thought it was the most awful concept, still do [chuckles] I was so afraid of the very idea, I think I thought very strongly that it would have to just be ended, I would have to make it stop. And whatever had to be done, to do that, you know. ... I do remember reading stories about people having hot baths or throwing themselves down the stairs and I do remember thinking that I would do that if I had to.'

We were sitting across the table from one another in a small, forgotten cafe when Sadbh made this statement. I remember being struck with the straightforwardness of her confession. She had just told me, without flickering an eyelid, that if she had an unplanned pregnancy, she intended to throw herself down the stairs to induce a miscarriage. I thought about the stairs in my parents' house where I was staying. I meditated on the jagged wooden steps and the cold, unforgiving, tiled floor below. Describing how her earlier "intellectual" understanding of abortion become complicated once she became "physically aware of pregnancy as a possibility", Sadbh explains how the prohibition of abortion through the law was suddenly felt the level of her affected body. Like Eithne, Sadbh describes how she was suddenly "so afraid", illustrating the intense emotional weight that came with recognizing one's vulnerability to criminalization, illness, injury, and perhaps even death, under Ireland's abortion laws.

Indeed, as social movement scholar Linda Connolly (2020) explains, the 8th amendment did not simply prohibit access to abortion for healthy, mobile women, forcing them to travel abroad to discontinue pregnancies, but posed a 'life-threatening risk and danger to pregnant, immobile, and incarcerated women in Irish maternity hospitals' (51). Listening to Sadbh recount what can only be described as her abortion contingency plans – specifically, her proposal that if she experienced an unplanned pregnancy, she would throw herself down the stairs or immerse herself in a very hot bath to induce a miscarriage – I thought about how this intense collective fear imposed by Ireland's reproductive laws had changed Sadbh's relationship to her body. I couldn't quite decide whether the body she was describing to me was intensely vulnerable, or the site of expression of a radical agency which, in refusing coerced pregnancy, powerfully rejected the state's pro–natalist regime.

Both Sadbh and Eithne appear to describe a similar experience, then, a particular state of "fear" or "panic", the product of recognizing oneself as potentially pregnant in an environment where, through constitutional mandate, pregnancy instantiated a very specific form of gendered vulnerability. Taking its origin in the Latin word '*vulnus*' (wound), vulnerability describes 'the capacity to be wounded and suffer' (Koivunen et al 2018, 4). Vulnerability can be synonymous for 'marginalisation or subordination, especially when it is invoked in connection to those who suffer or experience discrimination due to how they are categorised' (Koivunen et al 2018, 7). Vulnerability, unlike 'discrimination', however, has a distinctly more 'embodied' and 'corporeal' nature (Koivunen et al 2018, 9). It invokes the idea of 'openness' or 'injury' (Koivunen et al 2018, 9). I remember Sadbh's readiness to 'throw' her body down the stairs and think about the idea of vulnerability as both 'an existential condition' and 'socially induced' (Butler 2016, 22, 25).

Sara Ahmed (2014a) describes how the 'openness of the body to the world involves a sense of danger, which is anticipated as a future pain or injury ... the body shrinks back from the world in the desire to avoid the object of fear' (69). Ahmed continues, explaining how 'fear works to contain some bodies', restricting the body's movement 'insofar as it seems to prepare the body for flight' (69). Reflecting on the testimony of these activists, it becomes evident how these affective states of fear and vulnerability were constitutive of the quotidian embodied experience of women and people subjected to Ireland's constitutional abortion ban. Elaborating further on the correlation between space and affect, Ahmed contends that there is a 'relationship to space and mobility at stake in the differential organisation of fear' (68). Ahmed continues, explaining how 'fear works to contain some bodies', restricting the body's movement 'insofar as it seems to prepare the body for flight' (69).

In the case of Ireland, it can be argued that fear did indeed prepare the body for flight(s) ... as well as for boats, and for stairs too. Listening to these activists' testimonies, I began to think more critically about the cognitive, affective, and physical or bodily labour involved, not only for those who have had to travel abroad to access abortions (a journey which entails substantial emotional, physical, and financial burdens), but about the work involved in researching, planning, and preparing oneself for the possibility of having to access a clandestine abortion inside of or outside of Irish borders. Could we conceptualize this form of labour associated with *preparing* and *planning* to circumvent the law and to access abortion care as itself a distinct and thus far unrecognized form of reproductive work? Eabha's testimony is particularly illuminating in this regard:

'Once I recovered from number two, I knew there couldn't be a number three, under any circumstances. Obviously, I did everything in my power to make sure there wouldn't be, but that's not always enough. So, I did make a decision that were I ever to get pregnant again, I was going to travel. And I knew that I had the privilege, and the money and resources to fly and stay and do it in comfort.'

Two things struck me about Eabha's statement. First, that she had made a very clear decision that she would travel in the event of a third pregnancy and, second, that she had already made specific plans around the logistical elements of this trip. I was particularly intrigued by her proclamation that, if she were to travel, she would "do it in comfort". Her words indicate a further form of reproductive stratification vis-à-vis the modes of travelling available to Irish abortion-seekers. Those with access to systems of economic, social, or perhaps 'reproductive capital', were able to "fly" and "stay over" while individuals without access to passports, or without the necessary economic means, were forced to defer to the often cheaper and less bureaucratic option of ferry transport, and to travel over and back again in the same day to avoid the costs of overnight accommodation.

Sociologist Andrea Bertotti coins as 'fertility work' the 'labor and responsibility associated with navigating a couple's fertility', including the work of adopting, managing, and planning contraceptive methods (Bertotti 2013, 13). This concept has been taken up and further elaborated by Katrina Kimport (2018), who argues that gender inequality is reproduced when the responsibility of preventing pregnancy (and the responsibility of 'fertility work', more broadly) is unquestioningly and disproportionately assigned to women. Kimport argues that 'fertility work' includes not only the 'physical burdens of contraception' but also 'the associated time, attention, and stress' (Littlejohn 2013 and Bertotti 2013 in Kimport 2018, 2). Reflecting on the testimony of Irish abortion activists explored here, I propose the concept of 'abortion work', to encapsulate the cognitive, emotional, and physical, bodily labour which is unequally imposed on women and those who may become pregnant, as they anticipate, plan, and prepare for the possibility of needing to acquire or navigate access to abortion, in contexts where abortion is illegal or practically inaccessible.

By designating a framework which encapsulates the distinctive form of embodied and affective labour associated with anticipating, planning, and preparing for the possibility of having to negotiate access to a clandestine abortion, this analysis reveals a unique form of reproductive labour which has thus far been excluded from feminist theorizations. As Duffy (2007) notes, the category of 'reproductive labour' was first elaborated by feminist scholars and activists in the 1970s 'with the goal of naming and analyzing a category of work that had previously remained virtually invisible within sociology and economics: women's unpaid work in the home' (Duffy 2007, 315). The historic devaluation of reproductive labour is regarded as integral to the perpetual subordination of women in society (Duffy 2007). In the same way, the concept of 'abortion work', as a thus far untheorized category of reproductive labour, offers empirically grounded insight into how women and people who may become pregnant are cognitively, emotionally, physically, socially, and financially burdened by anti-abortion policies and regulations.

Theorizing the 'Five Faces of Oppression', feminist theorist Iris Marion Young (1990) writes that 'the oppression of violence consists not only in direct victimization, but in the daily knowledge shared by all members of oppressed groups that they are liable to violation' (62). Young describes how 'living under the threat of attack on oneself or family or friends deprives the oppressed of freedom and dignity and needlessly expends their energy' (Young 1990, 62). Young's framework is useful to analyse the experience of reproductive oppression in the Irish context then, as it provides us with the tools to understand how anti-abortion laws enact a form of reproductive violence which oppresses women and gestating people, not only in the moment wherein access to abortion is withheld. Instead, as the testimonies of these activists illustrate, the structures of reproductive violence instantiated under Ireland's constitutional abortion ban oppressed women and people who may become pregnant by forcing them to live with the daily, visceral, embodied knowledge that they *might* at some point be forced to travel to a foreign country alone to access abortion care, that they *might* find themselves suffering with sepsis after an incomplete miscarriage and be 'stuck' in hospital, at the mercy of medical gatekeepers who can choose whether to let them live or die, and that they *might* be forced to resort to throwing themselves down the stairs to try to end an unwanted pregnancy.

The temporal politics of 'abortion work': the disciplinary force of anticipation

'Abortion work' can be compared both to 'fertility work' and to the 'mental load' of organizing and managing domestic work, in so far as it is also an unacknowledged and untheorized form of reproductive labour and in so far as it is also generally unequally distributed across the lines of gender, 'race', and class, among other axes of identity. Predominantly, it is women who are burdened with 'abortion work', and 'abortion work' is more complicated for migrant women, for example, who must think about how to navigate visa applications or additional language barriers as part of putting together their 'abortion contingency plans'. 'Abortion work' may be more burdensome for working-class women, too, many of whom must contend with the additional burden of navigating the substantial economic cost of travelling abroad to access abortion care, for example. Moreover, just as the 'mental load' brings with it 'negative implications for women's well-being and mental health' as Reich-Stiebert et al (2023, 466) explain, 'abortion work' can entail an intensive and longitudinal experience marked by stress, anxiety, and fear.

Perhaps what marks out 'abortion work' from 'fertility work' or the 'mental load', then, is its distinctive affective quality. In the case of Ireland, women like Eithne and Sadbh are burdened by quotidian experience of fear and anxiety, the product of going about their daily lives with the 'life-threatening risk' of the 8th amendment constantly hanging over them (Connolly 2020). At the same time, we can conceptualize 'abortion work' as a form of reproductive labour with a distinctively subversive quality. Through the doing of 'abortion work', women and people who may become pregnant engage in various forms of mental, emotional, and physical labour to resist state-mandated regimes of compulsory pregnancy. As evidenced in Sadbh's account, through the doing of 'abortion work', women and people who may become pregnant transform their relationships to their bodies. While on the one hand we might view the imposition of 'abortion work' onto women as emblematic of the state's efforts to discipline or punish those who become pregnant outside of the normative frameworks, we can also see through the doing of 'abortion work' a method by which these individuals reappropriate their embodied labour to preserve and defend their bodily integrity.

Through the concept of 'abortion work', we can see how for those living under the jurisdiction of the 8th amendment, their everyday embodied experience entails not only a particular spatial and affective orientation, but a specific temporal orientation too. Activists like Eabha exist in an *anticipatory* state vis-à-vis the potentiality of needing to acquire an abortion. The idea that one's reproductive body or experiences may be organized according to a specific temporal politics is not new; reproduction itself has long been understood as having an 'essentially temporal dimension' (Bock von Wülfingen et al 2015, 2). By capitalizing on what has been described by queer theorists as our inherent 'compulsion to embrace our own futurity', contemporary politics appropriates and deploys 'the future' – enshrined in 'the figure of the child' – as an organizing principle to mandate a particular heteronormative (reproductive) life-course (Edelman 2004, 21).

Vincanne Adams, Michelle Murphy, and Adele Clarke write that the 'defining quality of our current moment' is not the future but *anticipation*, that is, a characteristic state of 'thinking and living toward the future' (Adams et al 2009, 246). Adams et al explain how this characteristic state of anticipation implies both an *affective* and a *temporal* orientation. Anxiety and fear (tied to 'unpreparedness' and an unknowable future) become important 'political vectors' to 'interpellate and govern subjects' (2009, 249). Adams et al (2009) coin the term 'injunction' to describe the 'moral imperative' to 'characterize and inhabit states of uncertainty' and develop the term 'abduction' to describe the labour associated with the 'requisite tacking back and forth between futures, pasts, and presents' (249). Of chief concern for this analysis, they describe the moral imperative to characterize and live with/in various states of uncertainty as itself a mechanism of *disciplining* the subject-body (Adams et al 2009). The injunction to anticipate, they explain, is a 'requirement to be obedient' which 'demands action' (Adams et al 2009, 254, 256).

Adams et al (2009) claim that anticipation has become a 'lived affect-state of daily life' which 'shapes regimes of self, health and spirituality' (247). They depict the 'biomedical' sphere as an 'exemplary site of anticipatory practice', citing the work of feminist technoscience scholars whose research, they contend, has illustrated the various ways in which 'anticipatory modes reach before birth to fetal management and yet further back to conception, as active domains of the present that allow tactical interventions to prevent and/or enable imagined futures' (Adams et al 2009, 251). Edmée Ballif's (2023) research on Swiss prenatal care regimes, for example, reveals how the behaviours of women intending to become pregnant are surveilled and controlled in the interests of safeguarding the 'anticipated foetal subject' (483).

It is possible then through the concept of 'abortion work' to illustrate how these 'anticipatory modes' reach back before conception, and even before the period of anticipated pregnancy, expanding in their scope to shape and transform the intimate, affective, reproductive experiences and the everyday embodied practices of women and people who may become pregnant (Adams et al 2009; Ballif 2023). Wagonner coins as the 'zero trimester' the 'months or years prior to conception in which women are urged to prepare their bodies for a healthy pregnancy' (2). The 'zero trimester', Wagonner explains, implies the extension of 'maternal responsibility' into the 'pre-reproductive years' (2017, 4). In similar terms, the concept of 'abortion work' reveals a new temporal space of 'pre-abortion' which is part of the reproductive life course for women and people living under strict anti-abortion regimes, during which they are expected to take responsibility for and make a concerted, labour and time-intensive effort to 'take care' of their abortion needs by themselves and without recourse to the state. Aoibhinn, a social worker in her early 40s, explained how living in this 'pre-abortion' space brought with it specific financial burdens. She described how she would try to regularly siphon off money to what she called an "abortion fund" which would allow her to be able to 'travel' on short notice, if required:

'Before the campaign, before I always had the abortion fund in the bank, or the ability to get that loan out of the credit union. If I needed to go to England, and you're talking about €2,000. I always tried to have that money, money you couldn't spend. And I was afraid, so many of us were afraid, so many of us were. For ourselves and for each other.'

Here, Aoibhinn contrasts how before abortion was legalized in Ireland in 2018, she "always had the abortion fund in the bank" or "the ability to get that loan out of the credit union". Her 'abortion fund' consisted of money that she "couldn't spend" and which was earmarked for the sole purpose of travelling to England to access an abortion there. In her forthcoming research, O'Halloran-Bermingham explores how many working-class Irish women created communal 'abortion funds' which would sometimes consist of monies borrowed from their children's First Holy Communion collections. Through the creation of the 'abortion fund', then, we can see how 'abortion work' requires a long-term investment of material resources. As O'Halloran-Bermingham explains, for economically marginalized groups, the collation of these resources is often contingent on community-based solidarity and cooperation.

Discussing the idea of 'anticipatory regimes', Adams et al (2009) describe how the future 'creates material trajectories of life that unfold as anticipated by those speculative processes' (248). In this sense, 'anticipation' becomes another direction; a material trajectory or line of discipline that women and potential abortion-seekers in Ireland are asked to follow (Ahmed 2006; Adams et al 2009). Adams et al (2009) explain that 'anticipatory regimes' work through the 'logics of expansion' (250). Anticipatory regimes, they claim, constantly 'expand their scope of inclusion, elongate their reach in space, and time' (Adams et al 2009, 250–251). Importantly, Adams et al describe how 'as an affective state', anticipation is 'not just a *reaction*, but a way of actively orienting oneself temporally' (Adams et al 2009, 247, my emphasis). The effects of 'living under anticipatory modes of engagement' affect us 'physically, mentally, and emotionally', they say, in ways which we are only now beginning to understand (Adams et al 2009, 251). In the Irish context, living in this 'pre-abortion' space affects women and people who may become pregnant by demanding an investment of their emotional and physical labour and, in addition, by demanding the longitudinal investment of their time.

As Elizabeth Cohen (2018) argues, 'time is widely recognised as one of the most precious and finite resources required for the accomplishment of human purposes' (1). As political subjects, Cohen (2018) says, we are constantly confronted with the 'myriad ways' in which our time is 'structured, valued, appropriated, or freed, by the State' (2). Time is assigned political value, Cohen describes, and this becomes particularly obvious in the sphere of reproductive rights when we think about the contention which surrounds abortion regulations, including mandatory waiting periods. In these examples, Cohen insists, we see how the state 'can and does command the time of its subjects' and how particular rights and privileges are contingent on the passing of durational time (2018, 3). Through the concept of 'abortion work', we can see another way then in which reproductive politics operates via the organization and appropriation of the discretionary time of women and people who may become pregnant. The injunction to dedicate time to planning and preparing oneself for clandestine abortions reveals another dimension of the temporal politics of contemporary anti-abortion regulations.

To conclude, this analysis exemplifies how the regulation of abortion in Ireland was historically constituted not only through the criminalization of abortion in the law, but through the spatial, affective, and temporal orientation of bodies in space. This system of regulatory forces operates as a mode of *disciplining* the embodied, reproductive subject. The 8th amendment, which further copper-fastened the criminal status of abortion in Ireland, entailed not simply a *prohibition* of rights but an *imposition* of structural vulnerability in the body. It produced in the gestating subject a system of thought-patterns which always already 'turned' them away, which mandated the *movement* of the aborting body across borders, and which produced an affective state of fear and vulnerability, as Irish women labour to 'take care' of unplanned pregnancies before they are even conceived.

Acknowledgements

Parts of this chapter are adapted from my article, O'Shaughnessy, A. (2024) 'On the Embodied Experience of Anti-Abortion Laws and Regulations: The Gendered Burden of "Abortion Work"'. *Body and Society.*

3

Tracing the 'Embodied Infrastructure' of the Movement to Repeal the 8th Amendment

Encountering 'pro-life' imagery: the 'Abortion Tears Her Life Apart' campaign

Scholars, activists, and social commentators have cited 2012 as a pivotal year in the consolidation of abortion rights movement in Ireland (Connolly 2020). It was in October of this year that the Irish Choice Network – which would later go on to become the Abortion Rights Campaign (ARC), a grassroots activist group which advocates for free, safe, legal abortion across the island of Ireland – was formed (Carnegie and Roth 2019). In the same moment that the Irish Choice Network was founded, Ireland's abortion laws were once again being thrust into the centre of national and international debate after the death of Ms Savita Halappanavar on 28 October 2012. Ms Halappanavar, a dentist who had migrated to Ireland from India, was 17 weeks pregnant when she self-referred to Galway University Hospital, complaining of unbearable lower back pain. Ms Halappanavar was suffering from sepsis due to an incomplete miscarriage but was denied a life-saving abortion (McCarthy 2016). Ms Halappanavar's death sparked mass outrage and unleashed waves of political protest by abortion rights campaigners, both in Ireland and abroad.

Just months before Ms Halappanavar's death, another event took place which would play a crucial role in mobilizing abortion activists and in the consolidation of the Irish pro-choice campaign. In June 2012, Youth Defence – a 'pro-life' organization originally founded in 1986 during the contentious 10th amendment referendum, to campaign against the legalization of divorce – launched its now infamous 'Abortion Tears Her Life Apart' campaign. The campaign entailed a series of visual advertisements which appeared as billboards and posters on or outside public transport hubs across the country. The campaign included two variations of the same advertisement: one featuring an image of a tearful woman's face and the other showcasing a foetus sucking its thumb. Both images were overlaid with the text 'Abortion Tears Her Life Apart. There's Always a Better Answer' (Morse 2012). In the weeks following the launch of the campaign, the Advertising Standards Agency of Ireland (ASAI) received almost 70 complaints relating to the adverts. Speaking at a Senate debate, Labour Party leader Ivana Bacik described the campaign as 'offensive', 'misleading' and as 'amounting to false advertising' (O'Connell 2012). In particular, Bacik contested the usage of imagery depicting 'a foetus at more than 18 weeks' (O'Connell 2012).

Following Bacik's comments, debates around 'censorship' quickly ensued. In an op-ed, Niamh Ui Bhriain (2012) of the Life Institute (another anti-abortion campaign group) wrote that the posters served simply to 'bring the reality of abortion into focus' (Ui Bhriain 2012). Although the ASAI was ultimately unable to act on the Youth Defence campaign – which as a non-commercial organization fell outside of its remit – the publication of the 'Abortion Tears Her Life Apart' campaign served as a hugely important moment in the development of the Irish pro-choice movement, as individuals perturbed by the Youth Defence campaign banded together to make complaints to the advertising authority. Interviewing abortion activists in 2019 and 2020, I was curious to find out what exactly it was about the Youth Defence campaign which worked so effectively to mobilize this community of individuals, many of whom had not been previously involved in any form of political organizing. Saoirse explained her memories of the 'Abortion Tears Her Life Apart' billboard campaign as follows:

'So, I got involved in 2012 when Youth Defence put up their abortion campaign posters. I hadn't been involved in abortion activism before that, but they really pissed me off. I found some like-minded people on Facebook, and we started having these demos outside the Dáil, just saying "Who the hell are these people?", making complaints to the advertising authority. We were basically just saying "Who are these people?" and actually what is the situation? So, we set up ARC, as the Irish Choice Network.'

Saorise, by this point a seasoned abortion rights organizer, worked in higher education. We met for our interview at an activist space on a late January afternoon in 2020. When I arrived for our interview, she was busy finishing up a meeting and asked me to wait downstairs. While I waited, I occupied myself observing the various types of activist paraphernalia strewn about the lobby, including pro-choice posters and LGBTQIA+ pride flags. Moments later, Saoirse came tumbling down the stairs, rousing me from my reflection. She apologized for keeping me waiting and offered me something to drink. In the meeting room, she cleared some space for me to sit down. I asked

TRACING THE 'EMBODIED INFRASTRUCTURE'

her what it was about the Youth Defence billboard campaign which had affected her so intensely. She explained:

'I remember exactly the first time I saw one. I was standing on Crowe Street on the train platform, I was on my way to work. And there's this billboard, a full-sized billboard and a stock photo of woman crying, and the caption says, "Abortion tears her life apart" and then there was these other ones saying, well they had pictures of foetuses in utero saying something like "Don't murder me", or something like that, it was in the "voice" of the foetus. I had no experience myself of abortion. But I had a good friend who had gone through it. So, I only tangentially understood what it might have been like. It just hit me the wrong way, and I was so tempted – there was like a peeling corner, and I was just so tempted to just rip the poster down and I knew obviously, it's a train station, there's cameras everywhere. Nowadays, I absolutely would. But I didn't know if I was on my own feeling that way because this was all brand new.'

The 'new-ness' of the Youth Defence campaign was reiterated by Mairead, who also became involved in pro-choice activism after the publication of the 'Abortion Tears Her Life Apart' billboards. Mairead was in her late 30s and was born and raised in a rural townland in the south of the country. Prior to the Repeal campaign, her "only activism" (as she described it) was her involvement in the local youth club. She described how she met other pro-choice activists through a Facebook group which was set up in opposition to the 'Abortion Tears Her Life Apart' campaign entitled 'Unlike Youth Defence, I Trust Women'. Describing the members of this coalition as "just a group of angry men and women who got annoyed at a billboard", Mairead explained how from the first protest against the Youth Defence campaign – which comprised around 50 participants – the first annual 'March for Choice', which saw 1,000 pro-choice activists take to the Dublin streets, was born:

'When the Youth Defence billboards went up, the ones that were like "Abortion Tears Her Life Apart" and that kind of thing, I hadn't been involved in any abortion activism but there was something about when the billboards went out. Nobody in the country was talking about abortion. There was nothing to do around the 8th, there was nothing to do around the legislation. There was nothing going on and then these billboards just popped up everywhere. There was a massive one that popped up outside the train station and it annoyed me every day on the way into work. I was just like "Nobody has said a thing about looking for abortion in this country". And there was a few of

45

my friends who I was saying this to … I was like "Have you seen these billboards?", "What is going on?" and then a few of us went out one night for a few drinks and we were saying "We should do something, we should have some sort of a march about it or let them know we're annoyed".'

It appears then that the publication of the Youth Defence campaign was a deeply significant event in the development of the Irish pro-choice movement. In her study of AIDS activism in the United States, Gould (2009) describes the 1986 *Bowers* v *Hardwick* ruling which criminalized private consensual sex between same-sex couples as a seminal 'event' which restructured the 'emotional habitus' of the queer community. Gould draws here upon the work of William Sewell who defines 'an event' as 'an occurrence that is remarkable in some way – one that is widely noted and commented on by contemporaries' (Sewell 1996 in Gould 2009, 134). Sewell (1996) describes events as 'occurrences that have momentous consequences, that in some sense "change the course of history"' (842). For Sewell (1996), an event results in the 'transformation of structures', a 'rupture of some kind' or a 'surprising break with routine practice' (843). Sewell explains that while events can sometimes be 'neutralized, reabsorbed' or even 'forcefully repressed', they may also 'touch off a chain of occurrences that durably transforms previous structures and practices' (1996, 843).

As Gould describes, in affective terms, events can spark a 'change in tone and sentiment' or an alteration of normative 'feeling states' or in the 'emotional habitus' of individuals and communities (Gould 2009, 133). Gould defines the 'emotional habitus' as 'embodied, axiomatic inclinations towards certain feelings and ways of emoting' (2009, 31). While the gay and lesbian liberation movement of the 1970s remained relatively conservative, adopting a 'respectability politics' approach, Gould describes how the *Hardwick* ruling unleashed a wave of anger and indignation as LGBTQIA+ individuals were confronted with the 'extent of their outsider status' (2009, 135). The collective anger, indignation, and despair experienced by the queer community reconfigured their emotional habitus, Gould explains (2009). Left feeling as though they had nothing left to lose, AIDS activists henceforth adopted a far more confrontational, direct-action approach.

Coming back to the Youth Defence campaign, it is clear that these billboards provoked intense feelings of anger and indignation, as is evidenced in the testimony of Saoirse and Mairead. In doing so, the 'Abortion Tears Her Life Apart' billboards appear to have challenged and reconfigured the 'emotional habitus', particularly of young women, living under Ireland's anti-abortion regime. Building on Bourdieu's theory of the 'habitus', Gould explains how living within a particular social context or 'field' one develops a 'practical sense of "things to do or not do, things to say or not say"' (2009,

33–34). Referring to the 'emotional habitus' then, Gould (2009) explains how one develops a similar (only partially conscious) 'bodily knowledge' about 'how and what to feel' and about the socially acceptable 'modes of expression' (Gould 2009, 33–34). Clarifying how, at the time of the launch of the Youth Defence billboard campaign, "nobody had said anything about looking for an abortion in this country", Mairead appears to imply some sort of tacit pre-existing understanding that feeling or expressing any sort of contentious or confrontational opinions or emotions in relation to Ireland's reproductive laws would be deemed as socially unacceptable and may, in fact, be actively discouraged within this particular social context.

Pointing to the absence of a cohesive direct-action abortion campaign during the period when the Youth Defence campaign was launched, Mairead clarified how, when the 'Abortion Tears Her Life Apart' posters were published "there was nothing to do around the 8th" and that "Nobody had said a thing about looking for abortion in this country". What Mairead seemed to be implying here then perhaps was some sort of unspoken agreement with regards to the mutual silence of abortion-seekers and the anti-abortion lobby in Ireland. Her words reminded me of Ann Rossiter's (2009) description of 'Ireland's hidden diaspora' who return home after accessing abortions in England to 'never speak' about their 'ordeal' again (35). I wondered whether, perhaps, the return for the complete silence of Irish abortion-seekers was implicitly understood as some degree of political safeguarding from the most aggressive of the 'pro-life' campaigning? In which case, this tacit agreement was blown apart by the publication of the Youth Defence billboard campaign in 2012. Mairead explicates:

> 'I think it was just the thing of "Abortion Tears Her Life Apart" and I was kind of going, well I've never had an abortion, but I have friends who had. Every so often it would be like "Oh, so-and-so had to get the boat" or "Somebody's gone to England" or something like that. And it just, it sort of triggered something like ... Why are you putting up anti-abortion posters when the hoops that somebody has to jump through to get one are so hard that by the time somebody got to England, they were set in their decision? It was only later that we found out the amount of money they would have for these billboards and that sort of thing, and it was just kind of like, everyone was just going along with life and abortion was just this thing that we swept under the carpet and people went over to England. And then suddenly it's like "No to abortion!" but it's like, "Well, nobody can have an abortion!".'

Borrowing from the work of French philosopher Jacques Rancière, geographer Sydney Calkin (2019) argues that politics can be conceptualized as an 'aesthetic regime' in so far as it 'divides up the world and its people to limit what can be sensed, seen, said, or acted upon' (5). In the Irish case, Calkin (2019) expounds, the political narrative of 'abortion-free Ireland' was maintained through a system of 'manufactured invisibility' of reproductive life (5). Through the systematic institutionalization of women and pregnant people in Magdalene Laundries and 'Mother and Baby Homes' and by 'offshoring' and 'displacing' abortion-seekers to access services in England and beyond, the Irish abortion ban worked as a 'geopolitical aesthetic' that served to 'maintain moral and political claims about Irishness' (8). Within this 'aesthetic regime', I argue that the Youth Defence posters can be understood as representing a 'dislocation of normal life' in that they symbolically reinserted abortion and the aborting body into the social landscape (Sewell 1996, 846; Calkin 2019, 5).

Sewell (1996) indicates how events bring about 'new conceptions' of 'what is possible' and, in this way, constitute a 'cultural transformation' (861). The publication of the Youth Defence poster campaign can be conceptualized then as an important event in the formation of the Irish pro-choice campaign, which, as a 'rupture' to the normative aesthetic regime, redrew the boundaries in terms of what could be seen, heard, spoken about, or *felt* in relation to abortion politics in Ireland at the time. In simple terms, the 2012 Youth Defence campaign materialized the possibility of speaking out about and *mobilizing* around abortion as a political issue. Additionally, by organizing in opposition to the Youth Defence campaign – and through the creation of their Facebook page, in particular – activists like Saoirse came to understand that they were not "on their own" in their feelings and political motivations. The collective identity of the Irish abortion rights movement was thus fortified through this shared contestation around the 'Abortion Tears Her Life Apart' campaign.

Social movement theorist Verta Taylor (2000) defines 'collective' identity as the 'shared definition of a group that derives from its members common interests and solidarity' (222). Polletta and Jasper argue that, while the study of collective identity has often been treated as 'residual' in social movement scholarship, it is only by analysing collective identity formation that we can better capture the 'pleasures and obligations that actually persuade people to mobilise' (2001, 284). Importantly for this analysis, Polletta and Jasper define 'collective identity' as 'perception of a shared status or relation, which may be imagined rather than experienced directly' (2001, 285). Equally, they explain how one of the lesser studied objectives of social movements may be the transformation of collective identity, that is, to change how these groups both 'see themselves and are seen by others' (Polletta and Jasper 2001, 284).

Perhaps then, the reason that the Youth Defence billboard campaign worked to solidify the collective identity of the Irish abortion rights movement was not only because it reconfigured the 'emotional habitus' of Irish women, and specifically, fomented anger and indignation which could be put to use in more confrontational forms of direct action, but because, through these posters, women and people who may become pregnant in Ireland came to recognize themselves as sharing a particular embodied experience of objectification and vulnerability, an embodied condition which they now collectively sought to actively transform. In this vein, the bodily encounter of activists with the Youth Defence billboard campaign must be analysed in more detail to understand how this experience worked to mobilize Irish activists in their droves. The testimony of Muireann – an activist in her mid 40s who worked in the civil society sector – was particularly illuminating in this regard.

Muireann prefaced our interview by telling me that "growing up in Ireland" she was "kind of anti-choice by default". She recounted how her feelings began to "stir" during the 2002 referendum, when a proposed amendment to explicitly remove suicide as grounds for legal abortion was narrowly defeated (Smyth 2016). Her feelings changed further, she clarified, when she found herself assisting a friend in accessing an illegal abortion on a business trip overseas. Although she had no experience of abortion previously, she explained how there was "no question" for her other than to "support" her friend. She revealed how the experience helped her to realize that she was "quite pro-choice as it turns out". Muireann recalled being concerned about how the Youth Defence posters would affect her friend – the one she assisted in accessing an abortion abroad – who came to visit her in Ireland around the same period that the billboard campaign was launched:

> 'So, then she came to visit me in Ireland, when all those horrible Youth Defence posters and billboards were going up all over the place and I remember ringing her and saying "I'm so sorry that you are gonna have to see all these horrible things … like, I'm so sorry that you're going to have to see that" because, it feels like judgement, it feels like constant judgement.'

Feminist scholars have analysed at length the role of visual media in (anti-)abortion campaigning. Social historian Barbara Duden (1993), for example, has argued how the publication of Swedish photographer Lennart Nilsson's exposition on 'intrauterine development' in *Life* magazine in 1965 facilitated 'a new kind of seeing' which implied 'the disappearance of the frontier between visible things that are visibly re-presented and invisible things to which representation imputes visibility' (16). Although, as Duden (1993) describes, Nilsson's images constituted a 'pervasive illusion' – in that they featured foetal remains as opposed to live, in vitro foetuses – the result was 'misplaced concreteness' about the ontology and teleology of foetal development (25). Through the proliferation of foetal imagery, anti-abortion campaigners have largely succeeded in substantiating ideas around 'foetal personhood' by 'making the foetus a public presence' (Pollack Petchesky 1987, 264).

Arguably, what remains understudied in feminist scholarship on abortion politics is how abortion activists experience the *encounter* with graphic foetal imagery and other 'pro-life' protest objects, on an embodied and affective level. The question here is not simply whether these images are accepted by abortion activists as scientifically accurate depictions of abortion or pregnancy development – they generally are not, as Senator Bacik's comments illustrate – or even whether they facilitate the same affective attachments to foetal 'life'. Rather, I am interested in how women and gestating people – the very people whose bodies these images purport to represent – experience these images in terms of their content *and* intent, as well as how they experience the embodied encounter with these posters (or billboard campaigns) as material protest objects in public space. Muireann's testimony offers important clues in this regard. She explained:

'I used to walk down the canal every day and there were obviously posters ... most of the posters were like a pregnant belly or a womb or disembodied floating kind of embryo. So, that was the only representation you saw of yourself for all those months, was a womb. Not even a pregnant person, just a belly, you know. And it was like they were looking down on you, the judgement, and the shame. And again, the echoes of these decades of how women were viewed and how our bodies were policed, just looking down on you from these posters.'

Describing how "the echoes of these decades of how women were viewed and how our bodies were policed" were "just looking down on you from these posters", Muireann illustrates how these posters served as a manifestation and extension of the historic, systematic, and violent surveillance of gendered, reproductive bodies in Ireland. In their discussion of anti-abortion aural rhetoric, Lentjes et al (2020) describe how, although such rhetoric is not 'legally characterized as true threat, incitement or assaultive speech', the noises and sounds made by anti-abortion activists outside clinics and doctors' offices are often perceived as 'intimidation and harassment' by women and pregnant people passing through these spaces (423). Borrowing from Berlant's framework of 'crisis ongoingness', which aims to move the analytical focus beyond instances of 'large-scale trauma or crisis' towards 'everyday scenarios', the authors describe how during the otherwise mundane experience of 'walking down the sidewalk', women are subjected to the sounds of anti-abortion protestors as a form of 'non-consensual listening', which, the authors argue, can itself be experienced as a form of 'violence' (Berlant 2011 in Lentjes et al 2020, 424).

Lentjes et al (2020) characterize anti-abortion protestors as possessing 'acoustical agency', deploying sound 'as a verbal expression of their embodied, patriarchal, political agency' (437). In this vein, such speech acts are experienced as 'upsetting', they emphasize, not only because of the 'content' of what is being said but because of its 'intent' (Lentjes et al 2020, 437). Lentjes et al's (2020) framework is useful here in helping us to understand the embodied experience of activists like Muireann with the Youth Defence posters which are conceptualized and felt as an 'objectifying' and 'invasive' force which assumes public 'ownership of feminised ears' and eyes (425, 423). In their research on anti-abortion clinic activism in the United Kingdom, Lowe and Hayes (2019) offer a similarly helpful contribution. Drawing upon Goffman's (1963) theory of 'focused versus unfocused interaction', Lowe and Hayes (2019) contend that the failure of anti-abortion activists to extend 'civil disattention' to women and abortion-seekers works as a form of 'public harassment' (335).

It is important to consider then how the existence of anti-abortion visual imagery campaigns like the Youth Defence billboards can *shape* and *transform* public space and particularly the embodied and affective experience of women and abortion-seekers as they move throughout these environments. Describing the terms of her encounter with the Youth Defence posters as material objects in public space, Muireann invokes the significance of their spatial configuration and highlights the significance of the literal placement of the posters – which often hang at the top of lampposts or electricity poles. As Muireann takes her walk along the canal, she describes how she experiences the posters "looking down" on her from above, emanating "judgement" and "shame". The placement of the posters, in an elevated location, thus works to remind Muireann of the authoritative and supposedly 'superior' moral stance of the anti-abortion lobby and, by extension, implicates the 'lowly' and 'immoral' position of the aborting subject.

In terms of the content of the posters, Muireann interestingly indicates a positive form of *identification* with these images. Describing the billboard campaign as "the only representation you saw of yourself for months", Muireann explains that she sees herself represented (however inaccurately) in these images. She takes issue with the specific 'representation' of embodiment these posters depict, however, obfuscating or erasing the "pregnant person" who becomes "just a belly" or "womb". Reflecting on the 'emotionality of politics', Reed (2015) describes social movements as 'nurturing sites of counter-hegemonic subjectivity' which make 'belief orientations palpable and contentious politics viable' (942). Applying Reed's ideas here, perhaps we can reconceptualize abortion rights movements as 'nurturing sites' not only for the production of 'counter-hegemonic subjectivity' but of *counter-hegemonic embodiment* instead (2015, 942). For example, Muireann's testimony illustrates how her encounter with the Youth Defence billboards fostered a process of critical self-reflection in terms of her own understanding of and relationship to her reproductive body. The impetus behind her politicization into the pro-choice movement can be understood as being closely informed by her desire to challenge the highly objectified image of the feminine reproductive body in the Youth Defence posters, but also by a desire to transform hegemonic understandings and representations of the feminized, gestating body within Irish society and culture at large.

Urging us to move beyond a traditional focus on the 'organisational and institutional' dimensions of social movement organizing, Reed (2015) argues that an analysis of emotion/affect, culture, and stories is integral to permitting a 'more nuanced appreciation of the processes associated with agency' (947). Explaining how 'political action is embodied by how we feel, not just by what we think', Reed proposes that factors like the 'emotional habitus' and 'affect' comprise the 'subjective infrastructure from which a culture of political activism is animated' (Reed 2015, 947). Building on Reed's concept, I want to propose the framework of the 'embodied infrastructure' of political activism which incorporates a focus not only on the function of 'affect' or 'emotional energies' in social movement organizing but which emphasizes more explicitly the relationship between bodies and power, and which explores the role of a range of everyday bodily experiences and encounters in politicizing individuals and activating collective protest movements (Reed 2015, 947).

Applying this framework of 'embodied infrastructure' to the movement to repeal the 8th amendment then, it can be argued that activists' shared bodily experiences and encounters with the Youth Defence billboard campaign were hugely significant in politicizing individuals and propelling them into the space of collective organizing. In terms of their embodied encounter with these billboards as material objects in social space, activists sought to contest the culture of reproductive coercion and surveillance which the billboard campaign exemplified and reproduced, and to challenge the material and symbolic domination of the anti-abortion lobby in public space. Identifying (with) the fragmentation of their reproductive bodies depicted in these posters, activists like Saoirse and Muireann come to experience a sense of *embodied solidarity* with all of those whose bodies are violently objectified under the photographic gaze, and more importantly are moved by a desire to nurture and make visible alternative conceptualizations and representations of their gendered, reproductive bodily lives.

The death of Savita Halappanavar: the role of anger and (middle-class) indignation

Four months after the publication of the Youth Defence billboard campaign, on 21 October 2012, Ms Savita Halappanavar self-referred to the gynaecology ward at University College Hospital Galway, complaining of pain in her lower back (McCarthy 2016, 14). Ms. Halappanavar, who was 17 weeks pregnant at the time, was initially sent home from the hospital without a diagnosis. She returned to the hospital later that same day, however, reporting 'unbearable pain' (McCarthy 2016, 14). At this point, doctors diagnosed her with 'an inevitable/impending pregnancy loss' (McCarthy 2016, 14). Throughout the week-long management of her miscarriage, Ms Halappanavar's membranes ruptured, causing her to contract sepsis. Her requests to be induced were denied on the grounds that a foetal heartbeat could still be detected. As a result, and considering the sanctions imposed by the 8th amendment, no interventions which would potentially harm the foetus could be made. Her condition continued to deteriorate and Ms Halappanavar died on Sunday 28 October 2012, in the early hours of the morning. A subsequent report into her care by the Health Service Executive identified an 'over-emphasis on the need not to intervene until the fetal heartbeat stopped' and an 'under-emphasis on … managing the risk of infection and sepsis in the mother' (HSE 2013a in McCarthy 2016, 15).

Social movement scholar Linda Connolly (2020) explains that Ms Halappanavar's death was a 'key turning point' that shifted the focus of Irish pro-choice activism 'from the rights of mobile women with means forced to discontinue their unwanted pregnancies in Britain' to 'the 8th being a life-threatening risk and danger to pregnant, immobile, and incarcerated women in Irish maternity hospitals' (51). The Association for the Improvement of Maternity Services Ireland would go on to describe the 8th amendment as a 'spectre' hanging 'over the Irish maternity services', affecting 'everyone who takes decisions related to women's care' (AIMS Ireland 2017, para 3). Following her death, Ms. Halappanavar became the 'widely accepted symbol of the harm the Eighth Amendment can cause to women' (Rivetti 2019, 184). Her 'economic status' as a middle-class dentist, political scientist Paola Rivetti (2019) argues, resonated particularly with 'neoliberal Ireland' (184). Investigating the role of racism in Ms Halappanavar's death, Rivetti critiques how 'pro-choice state elites and policymakers … consumed her as the icon of why the Eighth had to go' while simultaneously 'silencing … the fact that she was a migrant' (Rivetti 2019, 184). This critique was echoed by Eithne, a young migrant activist who was involved in reproductive justice organizing:

'What was really frustrating and still is, is the use of Savita's image. It's just so disturbing on all fronts because they don't give a shit about migrants, they still don't, and they continue to use that image. You have people who are like "class analysis is the only analysis" and it's like, Savita was very middle class, class didn't save her. So, from all sides, your analysis is super reductionist.'

Chakravarty et al (2020) describe the contention around the 'easy cooption' of Ms Halappanavar's image by a largely White, middle-class abortion rights movement which 'failed to engage meaningfully with her background and racialised status as a migrant woman in Ireland' (181). Despite contestation around the use of Ms Halappanavar's image, there seems little doubt that her death mobilized a new cohort of abortion activists in Ireland. More than half of the participants I interviewed cited Ms Halappanavar's death as having catalysed or concretized their involvement in the campaign to repeal the 8th amendment. Indeed, Ms Halappanavar's death was another hugely important event in the formation of the Irish abortion rights movement, constituting what social movement theorists might term a 'moral shock', defined by Jasper (1997) as 'an unexpected event or piece of information [which] raises such a sense of outrage in a person that she becomes inclined towards political action' (106).

Moral shocks, Jasper (1998) explains, are often 'the first step toward recruitment into social movements' (409). Whether triggered by 'highly publicized events' or 'personal experiences', moral shocks often induce a 'state of shock' or a 'bodily feeling on a par with vertigo' (Jasper 1998, 409). Jasper (1998) explains that while some people who experience a 'moral shock' simply 'resign themselves' to their situation, for others, they 'channel' the experience into 'righteous indignation and political activity' (409). Many of the activists I spoke with described their intense feelings of shock and disbelief when they first heard the news about Ms Halappanavar's death, which was only made public in mid-November 2012. Ailbhe described her memories of learning about Savita's death as follows:

> 'I remember really well hearing about Savita Halappanavar. I remember I was at home; I was going to a meeting in the Townsend Hotel. I remember hearing it on the radio and I was cycling into town, I couldn't get it out of my head. I remember arriving at this hotel and telling people that I worked with that this was after happening and people were like "Oh my God". That was a huge turning point for me, it was like a bolt of lightning suddenly back into "This cannot happen". But I think it was just such a body-blow for a lot of women in Ireland. You know, just like "My God". I had a friend who was working in the hospital that night, and it really hit her.'

Ailbhe had become involved in abortion activism through leftist politics, socialist feminism, and trade union organizing. Ailbhe was a teenager when the 8th amendment was inserted into the Constitution in 1983. She described her memories of the 1983 referendum and recounted how, at the time, "there was no question that you were anything other than pro-life". She explained how her own feelings around abortion had changed in her early 20s when a friend experienced an unplanned pregnancy overseas and was able to access an abortion on a college campus. She told me how hearing about an abortion "in context", it "wasn't such a big deal". After taking what she described as a hiatus from activism to raise her children, she became involved in pro-choice organizing again in 2012. When I asked her about her motivations for coming back into the movement, she recounted the significance of Ms Halappanavar's death.

The language Ailbhe used to describe the experience of learning about Ms Halappanavar's death – describing it as a "body blow" for Irish women, and as having "really hit" her friend who was working in the hospital that evening, implies the 'visceral' and 'bodily' nature of the 'moral shock' (Jasper 1998, 409). Her description of Ms Halappanavar's death as a "bolt of lightning" indicates the 'disjunctive' quality of the moral shock which 'jars you into a state of disbelief' and 'forces you to reconsider your habitual going-along' (Gould 2009, 134–135). Coming back to the idea of the 'embodied infrastructure' of the Repeal the 8th movement, Ailbhe paints a picture of a dramatic, *embodied* consciousness change, catalysed by a violent act of institutional misogyny and racism, which propelled her into confrontational direct action. Describing her memories of a vigil which was held for Ms Halappanavar in her local town, Eabha described the atmosphere at the event as one of palpable "anger" and "rage":

'She was so young and every single one of us knows that that could have been fucking avoided. Every one of us. Every parent, every sister, every brother, every person who has ever met a woman in their lives knows that that young woman should have been saved. There's no reason that she should have died. And therefore, every one of us who could be pregnant ourselves or has a person in our lives who could have been pregnant knew that we were in danger. And that's the way it felt, we were in danger. And it felt so unfair. It's terrible that we would not only grieve her but also feel fear for ourselves. ... It felt to me like "This is what they think of women, they don't give a fuck, alive or dead, they don't care. She's nothing, except a container." That was probably the beginnings of rage ... for an awful lot of activists.'

Sewell (1996) describes how historical events are 'characterized by heightened emotion' and are also 'punctuated by ritual' (865, 868). In the days and weeks following Ms Halappanavar's death, huge numbers of demonstrations and vigils were organized in various locations across the country. On 14 November 2012, more than 2,000 demonstrators gathered outside of Government Buildings at Leinster House in Dublin, in an event co-organized by the Irish Choice Network, the United Left Alliance and the socialist, anti-austerity party, People Before Profit. In her speech at the Dáil event, Sinead Kennedy of the Irish Choice Network described how 'anger' at Ms Halappanavar's death would extend 'beyond Ireland' and vowed that if the government refused to act on the issue of abortion, the pro-choice movement would make it their mission to 'bring this government down' (Kennedy et al 2021). Both Sinead Kennedy's words and Eabha's testimony indicates how, following Ms Halappanavar's death, the anger and rage which circulated amongst the women of Ireland became redirected towards the government in a more explicitly confrontational manner.

Both the visceral, bodily experience of the 'moral shock' as well as the intense collective feelings of sadness, anger, and rage can be understood then as constituting important elements of the embodied infrastructure of the Repeal the 8th campaign (Jasper 1998). The anger Eabha describes here is both *relational* and *intentional* in so far as it emerges as a result of the perceived injustice committed against another and involves a particular orientation towards a specific object or social problem (Holmes 2004; Ahmed 2010). In relation to Ms Halappanavar's death then, anger and rage can be conceptualized as productive affective forces which, by physically propelling activist bodies into the space of protest, are translated from embodied energies into concrete social action.

Importantly, Eabha's testimony indicates how *indignation* as well as anger served as an effective mobilizing force in the wake of Ms Halappanavar's death. Gould (2009) describes indignation as a 'variation of anger that revolves around the sense that one has suffered an injustice' (143). The injustice of Ms Halappanavar's death is emphasized by Eabha, who insists that "every one of us knew" that she "should have been saved", that there was "no reason that she should have died". Eabha's words illustrate the 'interpretive quality' of the 'moral shock', where the importance of 'understanding oneself and the world and the relation between the two' takes on greater urgency (Gould 2009, 135).

In other words, what Eabha is explaining here is how Ms Halappanavar's death forced her to reinterpret her own subjective position vis-à-vis the state's reproductive laws. Her astonishment is tangible as she explained to me how she suddenly realized that "they don't give a fuck ... dead or alive, they don't care". In a similar way to how Muireann described how she suddenly identified herself with (the bodies depicted in) the Youth Defence posters, Eabha describes how she and "anyone who could be pregnant" quickly recognized or identified themselves as being "in danger". These shared emotional states and the assumption of a collective sense of bodily vulnerability and solidarity served as an important foundation for activist mobilization then and can be conceptualized, I argue, as fortifying the 'embodied infrastructure' of the Repeal the 8th campaign.

As Gould (2009) indicates, indignation revolves not only around a sense of injustice but is 'a form of outrage that stems from being spurned or rejected after having thought that you were a member of the club and thus entitled to membership rights and privileges' (143). It appears then that Ms Halappanavar's death caught the attention of other middle-class women – particularly White, middle-class women – who, while safeguarded from the violence of institutional racism which contributed to Ms Halappanavar's death, were confronted finally with reality of what could potentially befall them if they were unable to exercise their racial and mobility privilege to seek alternative forms of care outside of the country and found themselves 'stuck' at the mercy of the Irish healthcare system. Ms Halappanavar's death illustrates once again the expansive power of the 8th amendment and the 'chilling effect' it created on healthcare practitioners whose hands were effectively tied in terms of what care they were legally able to deliver under its remit (Carnegie and Roth 2019, 117). This was underlined by Emer, a first-generation, Anglo-Caribbean migrant who worked as a healthcare practitioner:

> 'I think there are lots of other things that stood out and rang home, but I felt, if this could happen to her, you know, who else could it happen to? 'Cause there were other cases of migrant women, or marginalized women and you could kind of explain it as maybe they weren't health literate, maybe maybe maybe … lots of maybes, you know? And it really underscored to me that we were operating a two-tier system. But that ultimately it didn't matter how much money you had, how educated you were, how literate you were, because if you were truly sick and you could not move, you were stuck … and fair play to him, in the middle of all his pain and grief, for agreeing to open this up. I do think that because they were immigrants, I think people were willing to kind of dismiss him and then realized, when he was able to advocate for himself, I think it struck home with some people. And it sounds perverse, but I think it resonated with other middle-income people and young people, like you can't just throw money at this problem.'

Emer emigrated to Ireland from the Caribbean when she was 18 years old to pursue a bachelor's degree. After graduating from university, she decided to stay in Ireland and began her career as a healthcare professional. She explained how, when she arrived in Ireland, she "knew that you couldn't get an abortion on the island". The "actual reality" of the law, she says, only became apparent to her when her colleague got pregnant "in a situation she didn't want to be in". After accompanying her colleague to access an abortion in England, Emer became more interested in the legal and medical regulation of abortion in Ireland and enrolled in a course to learn about the ramifications of the 8th amendment in healthcare provision. She explained how there was a culture of "avoidance" around the 8th amendment in medical circles. The 8th amendment, she says, was a "real big grey stripe" that limited the decision-making and care-giving capacities of medical professionals engaging with pregnant people.

Emer emphasized how Savita's case really resonated with her as she was "so like me", an "educated, financially independent immigrant". Emer's testimony provides a fascinating insight into the intersectional politics of Ms Halappanavar's death. First, Emer alludes to how their identities as migrants played a role in how the news media portrayed Ms Halappanavar's death and the subsequent legal case brought forward by her husband Praveen, explaining how "because they were immigrants, people were willing to dismiss him". She goes on to clarify however that, when the public realized that Mr Halappanavar was "able to advocate for himself" (that is, that he was highly educated and had the social and financial capital to take a legal case against the Health Service Executive for negligence causing his wife's death) that the case "struck home with people". Emer even goes so far as to explicitly state that Ms Halappanavar's story resonated more with "other middle-income people" who realized that they "can't just throw money at this problem", that they too could find themselves "stuck" at the mercy of the system where, as Emer herself described it, "the vagueness of the law hampered delivery of healthcare".

It appears then that Ms Halappanavar's death forced large swathes of the population who might previously have considered themselves shielded from the 'worst' of Ireland's abortion laws to re-evaluate their position vis-à-vis the 8th amendment. The perception of a degree of shared *vulnerability* under the 8th amendment fostered the collective identity of the abortion rights movement and bolstered solidarity between otherwise disparate groups.[1] In relation to the propensity of 'negative' feelings to draw activists into direct action, indignation was specifically relevant it appears in terms of the mobilization of middle-class women (and specifically, middle-class, White women) who were confronted suddenly with life-endangering nature of the 8th amendment and the extent of the government's disregard for the safety and wellbeing of women and pregnant people alike.

Embodying White, postcolonial shame: an affective politicizing force?

I want to conclude this chapter with a consideration of the role of 'shame' in mobilizing Irish abortion activists in the aftermath of Ms Halappanavar's death in 2012. Jill Locke (2007) argues how 'shame occupies a well-established place in the activist toolkit', positing that the performance of 'shaming' works to 'build solidarity', and adding that 'if shame is felt for the *right* reasons, toxic forms of shame may be alleviated' (146–147, my emphasis). In her analysis of the official government apology to the survivors of the

Magdalene Laundries, Clara Fischer (2017) takes a cynical view of collective expressions of shame, which she argues work primarily as a performative mechanism to allow the nation-state to appear repentant without necessarily engaging in any material acts of reparation. Muireann identified how many of the vigils and events organized to memorialize Ms Halappanavar were characterized by a sense of anger and sadness but also by an overwhelming feeling of (collective) shame:

> 'I remember going to the vigil, I was working around the corner, and I thought, I'll just go down to it and see. It was really sad; people were really upset. It was very dignified and very respectful but this simmering feeling of anger and shame. I think just people were so ashamed. And that feeling of like "OK I'm not the only one who feels like this, this is something very collective".'

Explicating the historically important role of shame in Irish reproductive politics, feminist theorist Clara Fischer (2017) describes how in the early 20th century the national and religious identity of Catholic Ireland was built via a process of 'disidentification' with (Protestant) Britain (753). The newly formed Irish Free State constructed itself as morally superior to its Anglian counterpart, with this moral superiority being premised on the supposed 'gendered' and 'sexual purity' of Irish women (Fischer 2019, 38; O'Shaughnessy 2021, 2). In this vein, the criminalization of abortion became synonymous with the 'virtue of Irish women' and subsequently, with the inherent virtuous-ness of the Irish nation-state itself (Fischer 2019, 37). Abortion-seekers, by contrast, were henceforth constituted as 'shameful moral failures incapable of living up to the standards ... required of them as symbols of the nation' (Fischer 2019, 41).

As I have argued elsewhere, the civil society campaign Together for Yes which advocated for a 'Yes' vote in the abortion rights referendum in 2018 appears to have strategically mobilized this national preoccupation with 'shame' and 'shaming', displacing 'shame' away from the figure of the aborting woman and onto the country as a whole, now constituted as '*shameful*' for its lack of compassion for abortion-seekers (O'Shaughnessy 2021, 9). I wanted to know more about this collective experience of 'shame' surrounding Ms Halappanavar's death. During my discussion with Orlaith, an abortion and disability rights campaigner, she explained to me her thoughts about Ms Halappanavar's death and why it was that this case seemed to cause Irish activists to feel so 'ashamed' of their country:

> 'I think it was to do with the fact that this was a woman that was married, and she wanted that baby. One of the things that really struck me as well was the fact that she was Indian, that she wasn't Irish. And

I always kind of told my friends at the time, if the roles were reversed and if this was an Irish woman in India that died because she couldn't access a health service, we'd be going "What a terrible country! What a disgusting terrible country!" We should be applying that here. She wasn't an Irish native. She deserved better treatment than she got. So, I think it was a combination of her being married, wanted pregnancy, the fact that she wasn't Irish. That made it all the more like "Jesus, you came from India to have a better life". And she died here because we couldn't give her treatment.'

Orlaith's explanation that Ms Halappanavar's case attracted public sympathy because she was a "married" woman with a "wanted" pregnancy, as opposed to a "young" person who "got pregnant" through "unprotected sex", exemplifies a type of 'good' versus 'bad' abortions trope typical of contemporary public discourse surrounding abortion rights (Lowe 2016, 66). 'Good abortions' are those where the person in question has a 'good' reason to terminate their pregnancy, such as 'poverty, sexual violence or maternal age'; 'bad abortions' are 'repeat' abortions or those wherein the pregnant person has failed to use contraception (Lowe 2016, 66; O'Shaughnessy 2021, 6). As Orlaith implies, in the case of Ms Halappanavar, her status as a heterosexual, middle-class, married woman who "wanted that baby" facilitated a greater degree of public sympathy in relation to her death – her maternal identity (assumed already by virtue of her 'chosen' pregnancy) making her life inherently more grievable.

Orlaith's emphasis that Ms Halappanavar's case "struck" her because she was not, as she describes, "an Irish native" warrants further analysis. Weerawardhana (2018, para 5) describes that while the deployment of Ms Halappanavar's image in the Repeal the 8th campaign is often touted as an example of 'Irish multiculturalism', this is a deeply flawed and problematic assumption. Wade (2017) describes multiculturalism as the idea that 'notionally separate cultures can interact and mix on equal and inclusive terms, thus increasing democracy and perhaps resulting in an endless and nonhierarchical proliferation of hybrids' (14). Weerawardhana (2018) explains that while Ms Halappanavar's status as a 'well-educated professional with a light skin tone' made her a 'highly marketable' mascot, she remains one of a huge number of migrant women who have died at the hands of a 'misogynistic and white supremacist Irish healthcare system' (para 13).

Indeed, in relation to maternal morbidity, Ireland has historically and consistently reported a disproportionately higher rate of maternal deaths among women of colour in the national maternity system (O'Hare et al 2023). The Confidential Maternal Death Inquiry Report for 2019–2021 showed an overrepresentation of migrant and ethnic minority women who accounted for 31 per cent of maternal deaths but only 23.7 per cent of Irish maternities during the period of 2009–2021 (O'Hare et al 2023, 17). In 2010, Ms Bimbo Onanuga suffered a cardiac arrest and died in the Rotunda hospital in Dublin after being induced with misoprostol to deliver a stillborn baby. As Ronit Lentin (2015) writes, in contrast to Ms Halappanavar's death, Ms Onanuga's death received 'virtually no media attention' because her 'pregnant African body' was constructed as 'the epitome of illegality' (180). With this in mind, expressions of 'shame' in relation to the death of Ms Halappanavar – a "non-native" to Ireland, to use Orlaith's terms – must be further examined.

As I have described elsewhere, the 'morally superior' identity which Ireland constructed for itself in the postcolonial period was contingent not only on its 'virtuous' treatment of 'the unborn' but was predicated on the learned 'racial positioning' of White Irish people as 'saviours' of Black and Brown bodies (Lentin 2004, 303; O'Shaughnessy 2021, 10). Sociologist Ronit Lentin (2004) argues that, owing to the colonialist enterprises of Irish religious missionaries, White Irish people have been conditioned to regard Black and Brown populations, particularly those from the Global South, as 'passive victims' who can 'only be saved by the good offices of the Catholic Church' (303). Orlaith's account indicates that White Irish people continue to deploy this 'saviour' mentality in relation to migrants and communities of colour inside the country today. This is evident in Orlaith's confident assertion that Ms Halappanavar came 'here' (to Ireland) for a "better life". Ms Halppanavar's death then illustrated the failure of the Irish state to live up to its own self-image as a 'compassionate' and 'charitable' country which could offer a 'better future' to migrant women (Lentin 2015, 180; O'Shaughnessy 2021, 10).

Arguably then, public expressions of shame in relation to Ms Halappanvar's death worked at one level to 'recover Ireland's "virtuousness"' and are 'symptomatic of a wider tension with regards to reconciling Ireland's racial positioning and postcolonial identity in an increasingly secular and multicultural context' (O'Shaughnessy 2021, 10). In other words, while the mobilization of White, postcolonial shame certainly appears to have functioned an effective element of the 'embodied infrastructure' of the Irish abortion rights movement, it should not go unnoticed that this strategy relied primarily upon the treatment of racialized women like Ms Halappanavar as 'objects of shame' – whose image can be deployed for political expediency – rather than as autonomous reproductive subjects and agents of reproductive activism in their own right.

Jill Locke (2007) argues that while 'shaming will always be a part of politics', as feminists we should 'focus less on shaming the shamers' and more on 'rewriting the scripts that trigger shame' (149–150). In relation to the campaign to repeal the 8th amendment, then, perhaps a more ethical and useful strategy would have been to dedicate our time and energy in cultivating 'genuine shame' in relation to the effects of structural racism in our healthcare institutions and in Irish society more generally (Locke 2007, 149). Instead, efforts to recognize or dismantle the intersectional nature of misogyny, racism, and classism in our health service were treated as 'optional' extras by the predominantly White, middle-class abortion rights campaign in 2018. As Rivetti explains, efforts to highlight the stories of Traveller women or migrant women in Irish maternity services were ultimately deemed 'unsettling, unpopular and electorally risky' (2019, 186). In the aftermath of the overturning of the constitutional abortion ban, these marginalized groups continue to be 'invisibilised' in Ireland's reproductive law-making processes today (Rivetti 2019, 186).

To conclude, this analysis suggests that the collective experience of shame, anger, and indignation which circulated between and among activist bodies in the aftermath of the death of Savita Halappanavar in 2012 formed an integral element of the 'embodied infrastructure' from which the Repeal the 8th campaign was born. The framework of the 'embodied infrastructure' is important then as it highlights how the specific affective and embodied experiences of activists may provide the impetus for political engagement. In relation to the embodied encounter of Irish activists with pro-life protest objects (specifically with anti-abortion imagery), activists describe feeling compelled to resist the material and symbolic dominance of the pro-life campaign in the social landscape – manifested in the proliferation of anti-abortion billboards and posters – and explain how their identification with the objectified and fragmented representation of the pregnant subject therein catalysed a sense of embodied solidarity with other bodies regulated under the 8th amendment. In this vein, Irish abortion activists illustrate how the movement for abortion rights functions not only as a campaign for access to abortion care, but as the site for the development of 'counter-hegemonic embodiment' too.

4

On the Physicality of Protest: The Politics of Revelation

Mobilizing a movement: 'coming out' for abortion rights

This chapter explores the essential role of women's bodies and of women's embodied protest activity in the Irish abortion rights movement. As many feminist historians and social movement scholars have argued, although the (gendered) body itself has often functioned as an impediment to political engagement (with women historically being conceived as intellectually and physiologically incapable of participating in formalized politics), women's bodies have at the same time remained their core entry point to the political sphere (Parkins 2000). In contexts wherein women have been barred from formal political engagement, their physical bodies have oftentimes been the only 'weapon at their disposal' (O'Keefe 2006, 549). In this chapter, I explore the testimonies of Irish abortion activists to better understand their bodily experience of political engagement. I explore the role of physical protest activities like mass demonstrations, marching, or chanting and ask, how do these collective embodied practices redefine the boundaries of 'legitimate' political engagement? Moreover, how do they transform social norms and cultural codes which have historically served to discipline women's reproductive bodies? And finally, how do activists reconstruct their embodied subjectivities through their protest experiences?

In this vein, this chapter builds upon my analysis in Chapter 3 in relation to the idea of social movements as sites for the nurturance of 'counter-hegemonic embodiment'. In other words, I pay attention here to the ways in which embodied protest activities provide an opportunity for women to challenge or refute stereotypical ideas about their bodily realities, and to put forward alternative imaginings and representations of women's bodily lives. One of the central objectives of this chapter is to make clear that the movement to repeal the 8th amendment began with, was made possible by, and was carried out through the bodily labours and energies of Irish women, predominantly. This is particularly important to reaffirm, I think, and provides a necessary counter-narrative to political discourse which focalizes, for example, the relevance of changing political opportunity structures in the development and consolidation of the Irish abortion rights movement. That is not to say that organizational factors did not play a role in the Irish abortion rights movement, but by refocusing our analysis on the level of embodied and affective experience, I want to restate the centrality of women's bodies as both 'message' and 'instrument' of the campaign to repeal the 8th amendment (Sasson-Levy and Rapoport 2003).

Thinking about the role of women's bodies in the articulation of political protest, my analysis draws upon the work of Latin American feminist scholars, like Argentinian sociologist Barbara Sutton (2007 who deploys the terminology of '*poner el cuerpo*' to describe her understanding of how political agency, in this context, is manifested and constituted through embodied protest activity. Translated from the original Spanish, '*poner el cuerpo*' literally means 'to put the body' and, in English, signals the idea of 'putting the body on the line' or 'into action'. As Sutton (2007) explains, the concept of *poner el cuerpo* emphasizes the significance of 'bodily participation in social change', allowing for a reconceptualization of social transformation itself as an 'embodied, collective project' (Sutton 2010, 130, 177). In Sutton's (2010) study of women's political protest activity in Argentina, she examines the ways in which bodies are 'embedded in and significant to political protest' and, moreover, illustrates how, through their involvement in political activity, women activists challenge and transform hegemonic constructions of gendered embodiment (171).

This chapter begins by analysing activists' initial experiences of physical or bodily mobilization into the Irish abortion rights movement. This is conceived as slightly distinct from the process of 'politicization' (as explored in Chapter 3) and pertains more specifically to initial experiences of becoming actively or identifiably involved with the pro-choice campaign; either by 'coming out' (onto the street/into public space) as part of a physical demonstration or by publicly 'outing' oneself or 'coming out *as* an abortion activist' in a public forum. Following analysis of these initial experiences, I go on to explore the role of embodied protest actions more generally, specifically analysing the role of physical activities like marching and chanting, which I argue function both as space-claiming activities and as 'cathartic' experiences through which activists achieve a feeling of bodily emancipation. Finally, I examine the ways in which Irish activists deploy their bodies as a *symbol* or *text* in protest activity, exploring the political meanings and values created and attached to particular items of clothing. Here, I focus on the launch of the 'Repeal jumper' in 2016 to investigate the role of what I term 'gestural dress' as a uniquely caring, embodied protest activity which fosters a sense of intimacy, solidarity, and goodwill among the community of abortion activists.

I begin with this idea of 'coming out' as a physical action and/or a speech-act which individuals perform or engage in, as part of their induction into abortion activism. Before delving into activist testimonies, I want to first pause to reflect on the political history and contemporary usage of the terminology of 'coming out' itself. The term 'coming out' emanates originally from the culture of elite debutante balls and was later borrowed by the queer community to describe the process 'by which people reveal their sexual identity' (Stambolis-Ruhstorfer and Saguy 2014, 811). Sexuality studies scholars argue that there is no 'singular' experience or meaning of 'coming out' (Guittar 2011). Individuals may come out to themselves, to others, or to family/friends, in different ways, and there may be different meanings attached to each of these experiences, at different times (Guittar 2013, 184). Some people may in fact have no interest in disclosing their sexual or gender identities openly; while for others, particularly for those whose gender expressions are consider 'non-normative', 'coming out' is not a choice but an unavoidable reality of their everyday lives. Queer theorist Eve Sedgwick (2008) coins the term 'the glass closet' to describe the experiences of gender and sexually nonconforming individuals who are considered 'visibly queer' and who are generally identified as such, regardless of whether they have ever 'outed' themselves.

In sexuality studies literature, 'coming out' is generally understood to be a 'transformative' process which entails some sort of significance in terms of 'identity formation and maintenance' (Guittar 2011, iii). As an individual experience, 'coming out' is generally understood as the pursuance of a desire to 'have one's authentic self recognised and valued' (Saguy 2020, 2). Generally, being 'in the closet' is associated with feelings and experiences of shame and hiding, while coming 'out' is considered as a rite of passage for those who wish to proudly claim their sexual/gender identities (Saguy 2020, 2). The idea of 'coming out of the closet' involves making oneself plainly *visible* and implies the possibility of 'casting off secrecy, shame and marginality by affirming one's gay or lesbian identity' (Stambolis-Ruhstorfer and Saguy 2014, 811). In this way, 'coming out' is understood as a method to transgress or refuse social norms. For members of the LGBTQIA+ community, it is understood to imply a 'refusal' to hide one's identity or to 'pass' as straight (Stambolis-Ruhstorfer and Saguy 2014, 813). As a political strategy, identity-based movements have historically advocated for 'coming out' as a method to defy negative stereotypes and promote social acceptance of sexual minorities (Saguy 2020).

Recent sociological scholarship has explored how the term 'coming out' has become a sort of 'master frame' for a range of contemporary social movements, that is, it has become a popular 'way of understanding the world that is sufficiently elastic and inclusive, that a wide range of social movements can use it' (Saguy 2020, 3). For example, the #MeToo movement has encouraged women to 'come out' as victims of sexual violence and assault and has asked women to 'out' their sexual abusers (Saguy 2020, 3). The term 'coming out' has even been adopted by fundamentalist Mormons, who, while remaining socially conservative in other ways, have found it 'politically expedient' to connect their advocacy for legalized polygamy to the struggles of LGBTQIA+ groups across the world (Saguy 2020, 7). In his research on lesbian motherhood and gay fatherhood in Great Britain, sociologist Robert Pralat (2021) has posed the question of whether the term 'coming out' could be used to describe the 'reproductive orientations' of queer people. Pralat explains how, similarly to the ways in which people express their sexual identities, queer individuals also 'come out' regarding their reproductive orientations. That is, they 'come out' or disclose their desires or intentions regarding having or not having children. Interestingly, in Pralat's research, he explores the experience of 'coming out' as a process by which *feelings* about parenthood are made explicit.

Despite this wealth of scholarship on the extended usage of the terminology of 'coming out' in a diverse range of social movements, there has been little theorization of the operation of the concept in abortion politics. Interestingly, in my own research on the abortion rights movement in Ireland, the phrase was used widely by activists to describe their initial entry into abortion-related political campaigning. Listening to these individuals recount their experiences, I began to conceptualize the process of 'coming out', as they described it, as an embodied protest activity with two distinct but interconnected valences. In the first instance, 'coming out' can be understood as a speech-act or a form of storytelling; wherein individual actors speak about or *disclose* their own personal abortion experiences, or wherein they 'out' themselves as abortion activists by verbally confirming their political orientation. In the second instance, 'coming out' involves the physical transition and mass assembly of activist bodies in public spaces. Both modes of action rely on a politics of visibility where activists take public ownership either of their abortion experience or of their 'pro-choice' identity.[1] Here, Orlaith tells me about her decision *not* to 'come out' about her abortion experience to other members of the deaf community to which she belonged:

> 'I haven't really told a whole lot of people in the deaf community, even though it happened 11 or 12 years ago. I still haven't come out to the deaf community about the fact that I had an abortion, even though I was so strongly involved in the Repeal campaign. Because I know what they're gonna say about me "That's the only reason she fought for Repeal, because she had one herself", you know? So, the deaf community were kind of lagging on … because the deaf

community don't have that incidental access to radio. You know, you go into a supermarket, you hear music in the background, your brain is taking in all this information without you knowing you're taking it in. Deaf people don't have access to that same incidental-those debates happening on TV, Joe Duffy Liveline, there's none of that. They don't have access to that. ... And this is the other thing as well. ... Any information, any workshops were all face to face. And then, because the deaf community is small, everyone knows each other. My parents are both deaf as well. If I tell someone, they might tell their mother and their mother might tell my mother. It's just a very small community.'

Orlaith had an abortion in 2009 using pills she ordered online from Women on Web. At the time of her abortion, Orlaith was a student, and was supporting herself financially via her disability allowance. She describes the moment she realized that she couldn't afford to "go to England" and decided instead to "order these dodgy pills off the internet". As Sydney Calkin (2020) explains, medication abortion pills have radically transformed the 'abortion access strategies' of Irish women (73). Between 2012 and 2016, 3,328 abortion pills which were ordered online by Irish abortion-seekers were confiscated by Irish customs officials (Power 2017). Like many abortion-seekers in the Republic during this period, Orlaith had the pills delivered to a friend in Northern Ireland, who then posted them to her. She told me how she never disclosed this experience to her mother, who died shortly after Orlaith had her abortion. When I asked her why, she explained that it was because of "the shame and secrecy that was put upon me, because of the fact that it wasn't allowed". In this way, Orlaith seems to imply that the stigma attached to abortion kept her 'in the closet' regarding her own abortion experience. At the same time, she felt reticent about 'coming out', as this could make her vulnerable to further shaming and discrimination within her community.

Despite the risks associated with it, 'coming out' can operate as a 'strategy for social change', as Nancy Whittier (2012) describes (3). Recounting the history of the gay liberation movement in the United States, Whitter (2012) explains how, in the 1970s, queer activists began to 'come out' both as a 'celebration' of their identities but also to challenge 'invisibility, stigma, and assumptions about the nature of homosexuality' (2). Importantly, Whittier (2012) underscores how gay and lesbian activists in the United States drew inspiration from 'Black Power, American Indian, and Chicano movements' who 'fostered the idea that pride in one's identity was a means of challenging a dominant culture that denigrated one's group' (3). As a social movement strategy, Whittier (2012) explains, 'coming out' points to 'the political nature of "identity politics" as well as to the interplay between individual and collective identities' (7). On the individual level, Whittier (2012) explains, 'coming out' enables activists to 'feel a sense of self, of ownership over their own experiences' (17–18). In this sense, 'coming out' entails an 'emotion-laden individual transformation' of identity (Whittier 2012, 2).

On the collective level, Whittier (2012) clarifies, 'coming out' works as a strategy to influence and change culture and policy. By 'coming out' activists transform 'internal group definitions of collective identity' but also impact external perceptions and beliefs about the group at hand (Whittier 2012, 2). 'Coming out' thus serves as an 'antidote to shame' for individuals who have been marginalized and stigmatized, but moreover, by engaging in collective 'coming out', activists deploy what Whittier (2012) describes as a 'visibility politics' to transform the 'attitudes and feelings of others' (15). During my interview with Saoirse, she indicated how a similar 'politics of visibility' worked in the Irish abortion campaign. As activists came forward and publicly disclosed their own abortion stories, those close to them were forced to see the 'social conditions and concrete situations' in which abortions take place (Pollack Petchesky 1990, 360). In this vein, 'coming out' became an important political tool which helped abortion activists to reconceptualize the morality of abortion in terms which were more practical and accessible to the wider community. Saoirse explained this strategy as follows:

> 'I think a lot of people who had had an abortion who never told people before, quite a few of them decided to open up to people, people they were close to … we heard a lot of those kinds of stories, where people were essentially "coming out" and telling people. I suppose it's all very well thinking "oh well they were being slutty and went off and got pregnant" but then it's different when it's you. You know, you're my cousin. You have to know a person to understand it. And that makes me grossly uncomfortable, for women, you know the fact that I have to be known to be seen. There is something about that, but also, that is reality.'

Interestingly, Saoirse's statement points both to the advantages as well as to the limitations of 'coming out' as a political strategy. Through 'coming out', activists rely on a type of visibility politics, wherein individuals who have had abortions attempt to make themselves (and their experiences) visible – to "be seen", as Saoirse describes – as a means of achieving 'representational power' (Phelan 1993, 140). In establishing 'representational visibility' as its goal, however, the abortion movement thereby contributes to the reification of the 'hierarchical relationship between the visible and the invisible' on which the patriarchal regulation of reproduction depends (Phelan 1993, 139). As American feminist scholar Peggy Phelan writes, there is a 'fraught relationship between visibility, invisibility and reproduction' (1993, 130). Phelan explains how it is precisely the hyper-visibilization of the pregnant woman's body which has historically made her susceptible to subjugation by the law.

There are advantages and disadvantages then to sharing one's personal abortion experience as a form of activism. In 'coming out' with their abortion stories, activists contribute alternative imaginings of abortion which have the powerful potential to destigmatize abortion and promote social acceptance. On the other hand, by making representation a primary goal of the abortion movement, pro-choice activists inadvertently contribute to the cultural surveillance and hyper-visibilization of women's bodies, which makes them more susceptible to social control. In other words, through 'coming out' with their abortion stories, activists inadvertently reify the idea that, to be granted social acceptance, people who have abortions must open themselves up public scrutiny and investigation. In addition, through the telling of abortion stories, we unintentionally propagate the idea that women's bodies and emotions should be available for public consumption. Finally, by relying on the use of 'abortion stories' to garner public acceptance, we confirm the patriarchal idea that only those women who can make themselves identifiable *in relation* to the men in their lives (this is usually achieved by presenting the aborting subject at the centre of the story as a 'mother', a 'sister', 'a daughter' or a 'wife'), are worthy of being granted dignity, safety, and autonomy in their reproductive lives.

Despite these challenges, the fact remains that 'coming out' and the telling of 'abortion stories' functioned as a highly effective strategy in the Repeal the 8th movement, specifically in the period between 2012 and 2018 (Darling 2020). In 2015, writer Roisin Ingle and comedienne Tara Flynn both 'came out' with their abortion stories via articles published in the *Irish Times*. Both stories garnered intense public scrutiny and brought increasing attention to the burgeoning Repeal the 8th movement. Flynn and Ingle were not the first women to make public their abortion experiences in Ireland, however. In 1990, during political debate over the 'X case', singer and activist Sinead O'Connor 'came out' publicly about her two abortions and demanded a meeting with Taoiseach Albert Reynolds to discuss Ireland's abortion laws (Smyth 2016). This act of naming and acknowledging one's abortion experience publicly has also been used as a tool by pro-choice activists across other historical moments and contexts. In what is now regarded as a vital moment in the French abortion rights movement, 343 women signed a manifesto in 1971 stating that they had illegal abortions, drawing a tide of media coverage and political attention to the pro-choice campaign which would culminate in the legalization of abortion under the *Loi Veil*, four years later.[2]

Reflecting on the risks and benefits of utilizing 'abortion stories' as a campaign strategy, Orlaith Darling explains how this strategy took an intense physical and emotional toll on Irish activists. Darling (2020) confirms how, in sharing their 'abortion stories', activists risked exposing themselves and their bodies to violent public inquiry (para 16). She describes how, while telling one's story may be cathartic for some, publicly disclosing one's abortion experience is also a 'radical act of vulnerability' which runs the risk of 're-entrenching women's role as the suffering body' (para 5). Darling (2020) concludes that is precisely women's embodied and emotional pain that elevates the abortion experience to the status of a 'story' as opposed to 'other female bodily experiences' like 'smear tests or periods' (para 6). Despite contestation over the ethics of 'coming out' as a campaign tool, it seems irrefutable that it was through the embodied vulnerability of those who first shared their abortion stories that the pro-choice campaign in Ireland began moving the public body to consider voting 'Yes'.

It is important to remember however that the call to 'come out' is also a *call to action*, as American sociologist Abigail Saguy (2020) describes. Saguy outlines how Harvey Milk, a prominent activist in the US Gay and Lesbian Liberation Movement urged fellow queers to 'come out, come out' to defeat a California proposal to ban LGBTQIA+ teachers from working in state schools in the 1970s. Milk supposed that if Californians realized that 'they had friends, co-workers and family members who were gay' they would oppose the initiative 'out of solidarity' (Saguy 2020, para 16). As a social movement strategy, then, 'coming out' mobilizes a politics of visibility which operates on both the *discursive* and *material* level. Activists seek to counter stigma and shame attached to marginalized identities by 'coming out' as a member of the oppressed group, and by physically 'coming out' onto 'the street' where they take public ownership of their collective identity, engage in an act of embodied solidarity, and reassert their political agency. In the latter case then, 'coming out' implies the *literal movement of bodies in space*. Here, Deirdre – an activist working in the civil society sector, who had become involved in abortion activism during her time at university – describes the process of 'coming out' as an explicitly embodied experience which requires "actually coming out" onto the streets:

> 'Someone once said to me, "Well, when's the moment you become an activist?" It's the moment you step off the pavement and onto the street. And I think that really resonated with the March for Choice. People really felt like they were doing something. I think the March for Choice worked on two levels. People really felt like they were becoming visible, stepping out of the shadows. On one level you were calling for a referendum, but on another level, you were rebuilding your own society. Like, you actually felt like you were changing the communities and the world that you lived in. You felt that by actually coming out, you were breaking down stigma and opening eyes.'

As described in Chapter 3, the first annual 'March for Choice' took place in September 2012, with numbers increasing exponentially in the following years, from about 5,000 attendees in 2014 to an estimated 40,000 in 2017 (Holland 2014; RTÉ 2017). Deirdre's testimony illustrates how by "coming out" and "stepping off the pavement and onto the street" as part of the annual March for Choice, activists increased both the visibility of the movement as well as the perceived legitimacy of its political claims. As Judith Butler describes, 'political action takes place on the condition that the body appear' (Butler 2015, 76). By 'coming out' into the streets, activists are 'posing their challenge in corporeal terms' (Butler 2015, 83). As Butler explains, 'the claim of equality is not only spoken or written but is made precisely when bodies appear together' (2015, 88–89). In this vein, 'coming out for abortion' can be understood both as a speech-act which may or may not entail a transformative affective experience (and which oftentimes requires offering up the emotional and physical body to public scrutiny) *and* as a physical movement of the body (or of massed bodies) into contested public space.

As described in Chapter 2, abortion politics in Ireland has historically been contingent on the spatial regulation of gendered, reproductive bodies. Thus, through their physical occupation of public space, activists not only make themselves visible, thereby increasing their representational power; moreover, they disrupt the geopolitical status quo, making a 'public claim to political agency on behalf of abortion-seekers whose collective power is diffused by social stigma and political marginalization' (11–12). While I want to emphasize the importance of the gathering of massed bodies in public space (as Deirdre describes it) as politically disruptive, I want to be careful to highlight that public space is not equally accessible to differently gendered, classed, racialized, and disabled bodies. In correlating political subjectivity with bodily action, I do not mean to indicate that the recognition of political subjectivity be contingent on the public making-present of bodies. As Butler (2015) argues, 'the capacity of the body to move depends upon instruments and surfaces that make movement possible' (72).

Finally, Deirdre's testimony illustrates the active or doing nature of 'coming out' as an embodied movement or transition. Deirdre explains how "by actually coming out" (the 'actually' here presumably indicates the *physical* act of coming *outside* – inserting one's body in public space) – activists succeeded in "breaking down stigma and opening eyes". Deirdre describes how, through their experience in collective physical demonstrations like the March for Choice, activists came to feel that they were "rebuilding your own society" and "changing the communities and world that you lived in". Deirdre emphasizes how through the act of 'coming out' onto/into the streets, activists reconceptualize their bodily and political agency, and enact their physical involvement in the reconstruction of their own society. Perhaps then, by 'coming out' onto the street then, these activists engage in a politics of 'revelation' (rather than a politics of visibility). I distinguish between visibility and relegation here through a focus on the quality of movement, inherent to the act of 'revealing'. This politics of revelation reaffirms the political salience of representation but foregrounds this in the need to pose the political challenge in corporeal terms, by physically and verbally (re)inserting the body and reaffirming one's political agency in what has historically been highly contested public space.

Transforming bodies/performing politics: the role of collective action

In July 2016, four years after the first annual March for Choice, the Irish government announced that a Citizens Assembly would be held to consider the issue of the 8th amendment and to make recommendations with regards to possible legislative change. Comprised of 100, randomly selected members of the Irish public, the Citizens Assembly was intended to 'provide a representative sample of the Irish population' (Field 2018, 614). Convening over the course of five sessions between November 2016 and April 2017, the Citizens Assembly heard contributions from 'medical, legal and ethical experts' and considered 'pre-recorded personal testimony ... from women affected by the Eighth Amendment', as well as deliberating over 'written submissions from members of the public' (Field 2018, 614). In a shock move, the Citizens Assembly concluded with 87 per cent of members voting against 'retaining the Eighth Amendment of the Constitution as it currently exists' and recommending that the government legislate for the provision of unrestricted abortion up to 12 weeks of pregnancy and up to 22 weeks for 'socio-economic reasons' (McGreevy 2017).

Perceiving the Citizens Assembly as a 'delay tactic' emblematic of the government's desire to pass the buck on the abortion issue, members of the Irish pro-choice campaign came together to protest the Citizens Assembly's activities and to demand that the government simply call a referendum on the 8th amendment outright (Conroy 2016; Cahillane 2018). Inspired by the 2016 'Black Monday' protest which saw thousands take to the streets across Poland to oppose an almost total-ban on abortion by the Polish government, Strike 4 Repeal – an 'ad hoc, non-affiliated group of activists, academics, artists and trade unionists' – proposed a similar event in Ireland for March 2017. Strike 4 Repeal released a statement demanding that the Irish government call a referendum on the 8th amendment, before International Women's Day. If a referendum was not called by this date, the organizers vowed that they would request a non-industrial strike on 8 March 2017 to 'show solidarity for those forced to travel for abortion that day, and everyday' (Strike 4 Repeal 2017). Sadbh recounted her memories of the 2017 event as follows:

ON THE PHYSICALITY OF PROTEST

'2017 I feel was the year that everything felt most heightened. I kind of felt the most sense of power. We were moving towards the referendum, but it still wasn't definite. They still could kick the can down the road so there were a lot at stake. There was the Strike for Repeal in March and that had a very big turnout, we shut down O'Connell bridge and there was a really great sense of power then. I know the *gardaí* had to stop traffic and everything which they weren't expecting so there was this sense of "We've caught them on the hop" and then the March for Choice that year was really powerful as well. I remember when we were coming in past government buildings, there wasn't this sense of hopelessness where you're having a rally but there's nobody watching you or people are laughing at you, it felt like, we're actually a force to be reckoned with now.'

Sadbh's testimony indicates then how collective physical actions (such as the annual March for Choice) operate as important sites where activists begin to redefine their bodies not as objects of shame and stigma but as sites of agency, strength, and even pride. As Sadbh indicates, the huge numbers that lined the Dublin streets for the Strike 4 Repeal on the evening of 8 March were largely unexpected by event organizers and media alike. As Sadbh explains, through their collective presence alone, the protestors were able to "shut down O'Connell bridge" and "stop traffic". In bringing the capital city – the seat of government – to a complete standstill during rush hour, Strike 4 Repeal activists demonstrated, to themselves and to the public, that the pro-choice movement was indeed "a force to be reckoned with", both literally and figuratively speaking. Fionnula, an activist from the rural southeast, narrated her experience of the Strike 4 Repeal in similar terms, emphasizing the size of the demonstration and the importance of the activists' "amplified voice":

'I remember there was one march in particular, it was the Strike 4 Repeal march which was on in the evening. I can't remember, I think it was International Women's Day. I think that's March? It was on in the evening time, and it was quite dark, but we marched through Dublin City Centre, and the atmosphere at that was amazing, it was electric. There was this amplified, anger and amplified voice. Myself and a friend had travelled up on the train to Dublin in the evening to join the march, the actual Strike 4 Repeal. I know a senator personally and I was chatting to them afterwards and they said "I saw that march, and it was the largest march I'd ever seen outside the Dáil". They were able to go undercover a certain degree because they're not very well known. They walked by and they just said there was just swarms of young women in their 20s roaring abuse at politicians, chanting slogans. I can't even describe it. It was so electric.'

Fionnula's emphasis on the size of the Strike 4 Repeal demonstration – which her Senator associate described as "the largest march I'd ever seen outside the Dáil" – illustrates the significance of this event in terms of the *number of bodies* which gathered to protest. As Barbara Sutton explains, 'massed bodies' constitute 'tangible sources of power' in political protests (Peterson 2011 in Sutton 2010, 174). Goodwin and Pfaff (2001) argue that 'mass gatherings' can produce 'something like a Durkheimian "collective effervescence"' which they define as a 'collective feeling of unusual energy, power and solidarity' (289). Contrasting the "dark" evening with the "electric" atmosphere produced and circulated by the gathering of activist bodies, Fionnula's description of the Strike 4 Repeal takes on an almost visceral quality. Her testimony invokes the idea of activist bodies as individual voltage points which, when connected to one another, produce a powerful energetic charge which powerfully lights up the night sky.

Describing how activists were "chanting slogans" and "roaring abuse at politicians", Fionnula's testimony illustrates the importance of oratory practices as mechanisms by which activists encourage one another and cement their collective identity (Goodwin and Pfaff 2001). Describing the 'democratic' nature of the voice as an instrument, bell hooks (1995) writes that 'voice' can be used 'by everyone, in any location' (211). While hooks (1995) speaks specifically about the significance of spoken word for African American activists 'in the process of decolonisation in white supremacist capitalist patriarchy', her arguments in relation to the importance of 'claiming voice', 'asserting one's right to speech' and transgressing the boundaries of 'accepted speech' provide important lessons for activists challenging other forms of structural violence (212). hooks (1995) emphasizes the importance of voice specifically where 'institutional structures' are unavailable to oppressed groups (212). The "amplified voice" of abortion activists at the Strike 4 Repeal is particularly important then both as a source of energy and as a tool by which activists enact and reinsert their political agency in an environment which has traditionally marked their voices and bodies as grounds for political exclusion.

As Wendy Parkins (2000) illustrates, embodied activity and particularly high-risk physical action has been central to the success of many historical women's movements. In the case of the British suffrage movement, Parkins (2000) describes how during this period and according to the liberal political tradition, political agency was derived from the possession of property rights. Those without property were not regarded as citizens and thus were not eligible for participation in the political sphere. Parkins (2000) explains that through embodied protest the suffragettes 'refigured political agency as based on performance, rather than entitlement' (63). Parkins continues, explaining that such performances worked to keep the suffragettes' cause 'at the forefront of public attention' and to imbue activists with 'a powerful sense of their own bodily capacities' (2000, 63). In the case of the Irish abortion rights movement then, it appears that physical protest activities like the Strike 4 Repeal played a similar role in maximizing the public visibility of the movement and forcing increased political attention upon the campaign. More importantly, as Muireann indicates, these events offered activists the opportunity to *move*, *feel*, and *relate* to their bodies in a manner which contrasted radically with their typical embodied experience:

> 'That physical presence, noise, taking up space is so important. I think for anyone who had been impacted by the 8th amendment in any way, which you could argue is any person whose lived in Ireland is impacted in the 8th amendment in some way, to feel that they're not alone and to feel that solidarity I think is so important. I think the fact of, the horrors that have been inflicted on women by the Irish state – that we're still only learning about – there was definitely a sense of like "Fuck that shit, that's not who we are, we want to cast that off" and again I don't think it's something you were actively thinking about all the time but it was definitely in your DNA and in your responses and for something like reproductive rights, which is a very physical thing, 'cause it's a feeling of not having control over your body and a feeling of your body being owned, and written into the constitution. So, being able to get out and march, and march alongside other people and shout is very cathartic and really really important. It also can't be ignored; they can't ignore 30,000 people on the street making a load of noise.'

In her testimony, Muireann discusses the importance of the explicitly embodied aspects of protesting – particularly those wherein activists are making "noise" and "taking up space". Like Fionnula, Muireann emphasizes the importance of the number of bodies that gather to protest, reminding us how "30,000 people on the street making a load of noise" can't be "ignored". Interestingly, Muireann describes the importance of these embodied activities as a mode of catharsis for all those who have been "impacted by the 8th" (which she clarifies, interestingly, as "any person who lives in Ireland"). The word 'catharsis' has several meanings, including describing a process of bodily purging or cleansing, by which one's body becomes purified, or *open*.[3] Explaining how "being able to get out and march ... and shout" operates as a form of 'catharsis' which works to offset the effects of having the body "written into the constitution", Muireann illustrates the importance of collective bodily protest activities as arenas for the transformation and reconstruction of embodied subjectivity.

Muireann's description of how the withholding of reproductive rights in Ireland wasn't something that she would necessarily "actively think about" but rather, felt "in your DNA and in your responses" again indicates how

Ireland's system of reproductive governance was so deeply formative to the quotidian embodied and affective experience of women and gestating people in Ireland. Her testimony reaffirms the expansive power of Ireland's abortion laws – which not only imposed additional reproductive labour upon women and pregnant people (in the form of 'abortion work'), but which literally shaped, limited, and constrained the everyday experience and movement of the reproductive body, by "writing" the gendered body "into the Constitution". In this vein, the bodily experience of protest takes on an additional relevance for Irish activists as it provides them an opportunity to physically enact an alternative modality of embodiment. Through physical protest activities, the body is released (or releases itself) from its boundedness and enacts a sense of expansiveness and liberation. Aoibhinn recounted a similar experience, which she described in the following terms:

Aoibhinn: I guess, from a young age, I didn't feel that my body was mine and I think a lot of people are like that. So, I feel very strongly even now, like kids don't have to hug you … you ask a child for consent before you touch them. So, even at 12 and 13, I was getting shit said to me and that included members of my own family. More than one member and on more than one side of my family. It was so grand and normal to say things about women's bodies. So, my body always felt to me something more like a target than me … I literally felt hands on my body.
AOS: How does that translate then to when you're on a demo or on a march? In terms of the feeling of it?
Aoibhinn: It literally feels like you're wrenching off the hands with your hands. It gives you so much energy. When you're in it, like I was when I was younger, you don't even know that you're so contained… I shout a lot, I'm very loud at marches. Not angrily, I shout nice things, and sing, and whatever. The liberation … the bodily freedom that I experienced. They went hand in hand with the ability for me to say "No, fuck off. Get off my body." They happened at the same time for me, for the same reason.

Having been "recruited" into the anti-abortion organization Youth Defence as a teenager, before leaving and becoming active in the pro-choice movement in the 2010s, Aoibhinn explained to me in no uncertain terms how growing up in Ireland, under the 8th amendment, affected her feelings about and relationship to her body. Aoibhinn described how as a young girl, she felt that her body didn't 'belong' to her. She explains how she experienced her body as a vulnerable object, as something akin to a "target". In light of this, she explained how the physical experience of protesting took on an extra layer of significance as an opportunity for her to "wrench off" what she felt were "hands on (her) body". There is an interesting resonance then between Muireann and Aoibhinn's accounts. While neither report being explicitly aware of Ireland's abortion laws and its effects as young women, both describe feeling or experiencing a type of "containment" within or in relation to their bodies which, through their involvement with reproductive rights activism, they have come to be able to name and resist.

As I described in Chapter 2, Ireland's system of abortion governance affected the quotidian embodied experience of Irish women by literally regulating the mobility of the reproductive body within and across geopolitical space. Muireann and Aoibhinn's accounts then illustrate how the system of reproductive governance in Ireland worked to constrain and restrict the movement of the gendered body at the level of *intentional experience*. Through marching, singing, and shouting at demonstrations and rallies, activists like Aoibhinn 'actively embody, manipulate and change' social norms as they exist and relate to gendered reproductive body (Inglis 1997, 16). Not only does Aoibhinn experience a sense of bodily "liberation" or "freedom" at these protests, which stands in direct opposition to the sense of 'containment' she previously described, but her phenomenological experience of her body in *relation* to the world and to others is transformed too. Being able to "get out and march and … shout" – through the physical reconstruction of her embodied experience – Aoibhinn literally enacts her bodily emancipation.

'Gestural dress' and the case of the Repeal jumper

In early 2016, Anna Cosgrave launched the Repeal Project; a partnership with the Abortion Rights Campaign, designed to 'give voice to a hidden problem' (O'Connor 2016). Cosgrave's project sold plain black sweatshirts with the word 'Repeal' in large, white, block capitals emblazoned across the front (O'Connor 2016). With proceeds from the sale of the jumper, Cosgrave and colleagues sought to raise money for the Abortion Rights Campaign and to start discussion about 'the need and want for free, safe, and legal access to abortion in Ireland' (O'Connor 2016). Cosgrave was a student at Trinity College Dublin in 2012 when Savita Halappanavar died. In an article she wrote after the launch of the Repeal project, Cosgrave explained how she felt 'powerless, haunted, and outraged' after Ms Halappanavar's death and wanted to 'do something' to help those affected by Ireland's abortion laws (Cosgrave 2016). The idea to create the Repeal sweatshirts came to her, she explains, after seeing pictures of American activist Gloria Steinem wearing a t-shirt reading 'I Had An Abortion'. Cosgrave envisioned the Repeal jumper as a 'stigma-buster' which would work to open and broaden the conversation on abortion in Ireland (Cosgrave 2016).

The black-and-white Repeal jumper would quickly become one of the most recognizable elements of the material culture of the Irish abortion rights campaign. Analysing the material culture of the second-wave feminist movement, Bartlett and Henderson (2016) describe four categories of 'feminist objects' used in political protest: corporeal things (which draw attention to and/or are worn on/consumed by the body), world-making things (textual, aural, and verbal objects which 'bring into being a feminist world', including booklets, photographic exhibitions, and so on), knowledge and communicative things (including newspaper articles or newsletters), and protest things (including badges, banners, and posters) (Bartlett and Henderson 2016, 162–165). Objects can belong to several of these classes, they describe, although they will generally have one 'primary association' (Bartlett and Henderson 2016, 162). Clothing, Bartlett and Henderson explain, belongs to the category of 'corporeal things', which 'highlight the feminist use of the body to promote feminist issues' (2016, 163). Indeed, as Irish journalist Niamh Cavanagh (2016) explains, through the wearing of the Repeal jumper, Irish abortion activists moved away from making 'fringe political statements' using small badges, tote bags, and so on, to directly projecting its message onto the bodies of Irish activists.

I was curious to know more about the function that the Repeal jumper played in the abortion rights movement in Ireland. Was its role purely to serve as a political communication device? Or did the act of wearing of the Repeal jumper itself also serve some sort of embodied or affective function? And how is the Repeal jumper similar or different to other 'corporeal' protest objects used in abortion activism across the globe, for example, the green *pañuelo* for abortion rights which has become so emblematic of the struggle for reproductive justice in Latin America? Interviewing Irish activists, it quickly became clear how the Repeal jumper was important not simply as an element of the material culture of the Irish abortion movement, but that the action of wearing the black-and-white sweatshirt itself functioned as an integral element of the movement's (embodied) protest activity. One of the first public actions involving the Repeal jumper to garner widespread media attention took place in September 2016, when six politicians from the leftist party Anti-Austerity Alliance/People Before Profit wore the Repeal jumper during the 'Leader's Questions' session in the Dáil (O'Cionnaith 2016). Ailbhe described the importance of this "stunt" as demonstrating the "power" of collaboration between grassroots activists and politicians and for increasing the visibility of the movement through the international media attention it garnered:

'I think one thing that Repeal did very well was show the power of effective collaboration between some TDs and a grassroots movement.

So, it showed when they worked in harmony, the impact. When they wore the Repeal jumpers in the Dáil in 2016, that was an incredible stunt. That was as powerful as the March because it got international attention.'

It is clear then that the black-and-white Repeal jumper served first as an important communication device, as a 'communicative thing', which worked to clearly and effectively articulate the political demands of the abortion rights movement (Bartlett and Henderson 2016). As Ailbhe describes, wearing the Repeal jumper generated increased awareness of the campaign among the Irish public and internationally. This was particularly true in instances where the jumpers were worn by a group of activists in an organized political action, as described here. As Ailbhe explains, in these types of direct actions, the collective wearing of the jumper served as a "powerful" material strategy, manifesting as a symbol of hope for an alternative political future. In this vein, the collective wearing of the Repeal sweatshirt functioned as a unique and novel form of embodied protest, much like the *pañuelazo* in Latin America. A '*pañuelazo*' is a specific form of protest action wherein large numbers of abortion activists come together and hold up their green scarves to create one huge '*pañuelo*' (Vacarezza 2021b). Thinking about the affective function of the Repeal jumper, I was keen to learn more from Irish activists about how they felt when wearing this item of clothing. Speaking to Emer over Skype in January 2021, she describes the launch of the Repeal jumpers as the moment when "the Repeal movement kind of took off". She recounted:

'I had lived through Savita and all the repercussions about Savita, all the ramifications and all the talk about Savita. And I realized how many people didn't think about it or were almost willfully ignorant. As I had been! You know? So, I got the jumper. And it was funny because the jumper was really comfortable. I was going to wear it anyway but it was really cosy so I would wear it and reach for it all the time, you know, not just when I was going to a protest. I think with the first batch, it was a little frustrating 'cause you saw celebrities wearing it and getting it and I was like "I ordered mine weeks ago, where is it?" and when it arrived and you saw people wearing it, and you saw it on a Saturday morning when somebody had obviously just popped into the shop to get milk. When you saw it at the gym when somebody pulled it on after they had done their workout. And you know, it became like this little nod. Like, this little wink you know? And I would wear it every time I flew. Every time I flew I wore it … You know, the feeling of … not necessarily fear but secrecy and I felt that by wearing it, it made my position clear. I hoped that for people who were also in secret, and maybe couldn't be open, that it said "There's somebody who's in my favour".'

When I asked Emer about the Repeal jumper, she began by reflecting on the time when she was "almost wilfully ignorant" about Ireland's abortion laws, before contrasting this with the moment when she "got the jumper", which she describes as having a transformative, radicalizing, consciousness-raising effect. According to Emer's description, the procuring and wearing of the Repeal jumper itself appears to function as part of the process of becoming an abortion activist, as an important step in the process of becoming a part of the Repeal the 8th movement. In this vein then, the sweatshirt can be reconceptualized itself as a mobilization device, or perhaps as an activist-making device. Listening to Emer speak, I reflected on how the wearing of the Repeal jumper might have been connected in some way to this process of 'coming out' as an abortion activist, which I described earlier on. What seemed clear was that, for Emer, the act of wearing the jumper gave her an opportunity to *do something*, to participate in feminist politics using the primary weapon at her disposal, her body.

Because of how "comfortable" it was, Emer explains how she found herself "reaching" for the jumper "all the time", not only when she was "going to a protest". She recounts the experience of seeing other people wearing the jumper when they had "just popped into the shop to get milk" or "at the gym when somebody pulled it on after they had done their workout", illustrating how the jumper worked to foster the collective identity of the abortion movement. In addition, Emer's testimony exemplifies how political dress, as an embodied practice, creates additional spaces for political participation. By wearing the Repeal jumper "at the gym", or in "the shop", activists like Emer reconstitute these spaces as sites for 'nonviolent resistance' (Yangzom 2016, 629). Again, this is particularly important in a geopolitical context where women have historically been excluded from formal political opportunity structures. In this vein, resonances can be traced between the Repeal jumper and the orange 'voting hand', which was the first principal symbol utilized to establish a recognizable political identity for the abortion rights movement in Uruguay (Vacarezza 2021b).

I wanted to know more about Emer's decision to wear her Repeal jumper "every time" she flew. Why was this so important to her? And what kind of political or personal purpose did this serve? When we first met, Emer had described to me one of the things which first drove her to become part of the abortion rights movement, which was her experience of having to accompany a friend to England to access an abortion there. Reflecting on her memories of that journey to England, Emer explained how subsequently she chose to wear her Repeal jumper every time she travelled, to make her "position clear" and to indicate to other 'abortion travellers' that there was someone on board that airplane who understood and supported their actions and who recognized the injustice of the journey they were having to make. Describing the wearing of the Repeal jumper in these cases as a "little wink", Emer indicates this specific bodily protest activity worked both to increase visibility and awareness of the movement, but also served as an important embodied *gesture* whereby abortion activists conveyed their feelings of care, solidarity, and goodwill to other women and abortion-seekers.

From the 15th-century Latin *gestura*, the word 'gesture' signifies a 'manner of carrying the body' or a 'mode of action'.[4] It exemplifies a 'movement of the body or part of the body intended to express a thought or feeling'. More contemporary definitions conceptualize a 'gesture' as an action taken to illustrate an attitude or feeling, as is explicit in the common phrase 'a gesture of goodwill'.[5] Thinking about the act of wearing the Repeal jumper as a form of 'gestural dress', we can conceptualize this action as an effort to transmit care to abortion-seekers or, in fact, as a type of care work or caring labour, in itself. As Himmelweit and Plomien write, care has long been a key concern for feminist theorists, given the gendered inequality in the division of care work and the universal lack of recognition for and undervaluation of caring labour (2014). Care work is important, they describe, as it 'enables people to do what others can do unaided' (Himmelweit and Plomien 2014, 1).

This is a particularly relevant distinction in relation to the Irish example then, wherein the wearing of the Repeal jumper as a form of *gestural dress* can be conceptualized as an act of caring labour wherein activists provide emotional support to abortion-travellers as they negotiate access to abortion care abroad. Himmelweit and Plomien describe care work as a form of 'emotional labour', where the 'attitudes and emotions of the caregiver are fundamental to what she provides' (2014, 2–3). Indeed, through wearing the Repeal jumper, Irish activists make explicit their feelings of goodwill towards women and pregnant people who have been effectively abandoned by their own government and medical providers and, sometimes, by their own communities and families as well.

Analysing abortion care activism in Peru, Duffy et al (2023) explore the work of abortion *acompañantes* – that is, people who accompany individuals navigating access to abortion care, in this highly restrictive legal context. Duffy et al explain how the infrastructure of *acompañamiento* in Peru is underpinned by a 'feminist ethic of care' where care is provided 'beyond the state' and is 'holistic' as well as 'collective' (585). Duffy et al argue that activists' work in abortion accompaniment in Peru functions to disrupt the 'state of uncare', which they define as a 'context where state-led systems of care and care policies are orientated towards restricting abortion and where those who access abortion and those who facilitate it face reprisals' (586–587). Whilst I do not want to conflate the multi-faceted, complicated and highly laboursome nature of abortion accompaniment (particularly in legally restrictive contexts) and wearing the Repeal jumper, I do want to argue that the act of 'gestural dress' can be conceptualized as a specific type of protest activity wherein Irish activists use their bodies to disrupt the 'state of uncare' in relation to abortion provision in Ireland (Duffy et al 2023). By wearing their Repeal jumpers, activists deploy their bodies to convey solidarity, care, and goodwill to abortion-seekers, to support Irish abortion-seekers in a way, albeit from a distance.

In the Irish context, the act of 'gestural dress' did not come without risk, however, and as has so often been the case throughout history, the attachment of these mostly young, female activists to what was perceived as a mere item of clothing was used as evidence of the frivolity of the movement and the political ineptitude of Repeal activists by those seeking to keep abortion rights campaigners outside of the sphere of legitimate politics. Comedian Oliver Callan called the Repeal jumper a 'too cool trend' and wrote that, within the 'ranks' of the Repeal movement, there was 'little discussion ... beyond constantly sharing the daft Repeal the 8th logo'.[6] When I spoke to Ciara, who lived in a rural, agricultural community in the south of the country, she told me how there was a "backlash against the Repeal jumpers" and "what they were associated with". When I asked her to clarify what she meant by this, she explained:

> 'Yeah, someone was going on about the "blue-haired feminists in their Repeal jumpers", that kind of stuff. Some of the fun stuff, girls posing in the news with the statue of Mary. Most of that was dismissed, it was whatever, there was a little bit of outrage but mostly people didn't care. The girl who appeared on the Pat Kenny show, anyway she was talking, and the next day I ran into three or four people who said, "Oh my god, she shouldn't be allowed anywhere near the campaign." One woman said to me "I don't know what it was about her, she just got on my goat." People were so judgmental about these young, attractive women being totally unapologetic. Which I think is a great thing. But for some people, it was that reaction of "They're not taking this seriously enough at all".'

As Ciara describes here, the Repeal jumper quickly became associated with "young, attractive" and "unapologetic" female activists. It was these same "blue-haired feminists in their Repeal jumpers" who attracted intensive media attention for their engagement in what might be construed as a more unconventional repertoire of playful, creative, and subversive protest activities. In 2017, for example, in a particularly contentious move, a group of abortion rights activists in Dublin placed a Repeal jumper on the altar of a local church, subsequently sharing pictures of the scene on social media. The picture soon went viral, sparking intense online debate; with conservative political commentators deeming the move as reckless, disrespectful, and even blasphemous (Fenton 2017). The 'scandal' caused by these activists draping the jumper across the altar demonstrates how the Repeal jumper itself had taken on the status of a 'disobedient object' – serving as a material manifestation of the movement's indictment of the church–state apparatus' historical maltreatment of women and pregnant people (Flood and Grindon 2014 in Orozco 2017, 357). In affective terms, the Repeal jumper became what I term an 'incendiary object', as illustrated in the testimony of Laoise, below:

> 'I remember there was one year, one Christmas I had just gotten my Repeal jumper so it was whenever they came out and I wore my Repeal jumper home and my mammy was like "Take that off" or whatever, she was like "We're going down to granny's, you can't wear that in granny's." I was like "Honestly, granny's not gonna know what Repeal means." No one knew what repeal meant back then, you know. But mammy was like "Take it off, take it off!" and then the time I came home with my "Free, Safe, Legal" bag, she was like "Oh, free, safe, legal what?" and I was like "Abortion!" She was like "Oh my god!", she nearly had a stroke, like.'

Returning to her hometown in the midlands for Christmas, Laoise describes her mother's intense discomfort and unease at her daughter's arriving home in the black-and-white Repeal sweatshirt. Listening to Laoise's description of her mother fussing anxiously about the jumper, urging her to "Take it off, take it off!", the incendiary quality of the garment again comes to light. In my mind's eye, I see Laoise's mother trying to pull the jumper off her daughter's body, throwing it the ground and stomping upon it repeatedly, attempting to douse the sparks that if left to burn, might ignite her kitchen into full-blown, all-encompassing flames. Reflecting on Laoise's story, then, it becomes clear how the Repeal jumper serves not only as the manifestation of activist consciousness, but the wearing of the jumper constitutes an act of situated, bodily resistance – one that becomes even more intolerable by virtue of the fact that it is predominantly "young, attractive ... unapologetic" women engaging in this activity.

While wearing the Repeal jumper constituted an act of resistance, it also entailed, by the same virtue, the assumption of a degree of bodily vulnerability. This contradiction was explained to me by Blathnaid, a young social justice campaigner in her late twenties, living and working in the southeast. During my meeting with Blathnaid, she spoke at length about the lessons she learned from activist colleagues who had been mobilizing around the abortion issue in the 1980s. She narrated a story of the 1983 anti-amendment campaign, recounting the particularly violent tactics of the Society for the Protection of the Unborn (SPUC), whom she described as "like Youth Defence on acid". Blathnaid told me about reading an article which described how the anti-amendment/pro-choice campaigners were "pelted with stones" and "beaten up" by SPUC activists. She compared the "self-consciousness" she felt wearing her Repeal jumper with the explicit violence that activists in the 1980s experienced. Her testimony illustrates her expectation that, as part of her involvement in the abortion rights movement, she might be required to *'poner el cuerpo'* or to put the body on the line in similar ways (Sutton 2010). Wearing the Repeal jumper was one way in which she regularly put her body on the line, as she explains here:

> 'I felt self-conscious when I bought a Repeal jumper and I wore it only a couple of times but one of the times was when Pope Francis came to Ireland and there were the survivors of the Magdalene Laundries and you know Colm O' Gorman, he had a big march about it. And I know a lot of people who wanted to wear the Repeal jumper and they did, and I did because I wanted to get across that message of like, that public ownership of it. I remember the amount of comments I got in public, derogatory comments, misogynistic comments, etc. But for people who were like very much so in the public realm, whether you're a politician or a leader of one of the coalitions or whatever, how tiring must that be.'

Pope Francis's visit to Ireland occurred three months after the successful abortion referendum in May 2018, meaning that Blathnaid's decision to wear her Repeal jumper during the counter-protest was perhaps motivated by a desire to "get across that message of public ownership" of the pro-choice victory. Again, even though the 8th amendment has successfully been repealed at this point, she recounts receiving "derogatory" and "misogynistic comments" about the sweatshirt from members of the public. Indeed, the Repeal jumper proved to be an increasingly incendiary object in the run-up to the 8th amendment referendum. In April 2018, a young gay man was viciously attacked in Dublin 'for wearing a "Repeal" jumper' and sustained serious physical injuries (Berry 2018). In her research on Argentina which focalizes this concept of *poner el cuerpo*, Sutton (2010) illustrates how women's political resistance in this context 'connotes risk, courage and struggle' (180). Defying the 'status quo', Sutton (2010) explains, means exposing the body to 'potential jeopardy' (180). Blathnaid's statement then points to the complex and sometimes contradictory potential of the Repeal jumper as an incendiary object, which at once works to stimulate and energize activists (and the movement at large), while at the same time functions to reconstruct the activist body as a site of vulnerability and risk.

To conclude, the testimonies put forward here by Irish activists illustrate that activist practices are not only happening 'through the body', but that, through these embodied activities, activists in fact reassert their political agency and reconstruct their embodied subjectivities, too. For these activists, then, the protest body is the vehicle, agent, and *outcome* of political resistance. The embodied experience of Irish activists must be considered in order to understand how political resistance operates in this context, but also to understand the varied and nuanced *objectives and consequences* of the abortion rights movement. The campaign to repeal the 8th amendment can thus be reconceived not only as a movement for the legal provision of abortion access, but as a campaign to reconstruct and reconfigure the quotidian embodied experience of women and gestating people inside the country at large.

5

Embodying Respectability: The Politics of Concealment

A softer, gentler movement for abortion rights: the 2018 referendum

In July 2016, a resolution was passed by the Irish government to convene a Citizens Assembly to deliberate on the issue of repealing Ireland's 8th amendment (Field 2018). The Assembly, which would meet over the course of five sessions between November 2016 and April 2017, was comprised of 99 randomly selected citizens who heard submissions from members of the public and special interest groups, including medical professionals, lawyers, and theologists, on various issues relating to Article 40.3.3 of the Constitution. In an unexpected turn of events, the Citizens Assembly overwhelmingly agreed that Ireland's constitutional abortion ban should be removed. The Citizens Assembly also made a series of liberalizing recommendations regarding the parameters of any forthcoming legislation relating to abortion provision. In September 2017, the Joint Oireachtas Committee (JOC), a special government committee, was established to consider the findings of the Citizens Assembly. The JOC would accept the majority of the Assembly's findings, apart from the proposition that abortion be allowed up to 22 weeks' gestation, on request; and in the case of pregnancies with severe (rather than fatal) foetal anomalies (Field 2018).

Following the conclusion of the JOC, the Irish government announced in January 2018 its intention to propose a referendum on the 8th amendment (Bardon 2018). The Referendum Bill was passed in the Dáil on 21 March 2018. A week later, the Minister for Health Simon Harris confirmed the date for the referendum as 25 May. The day following Minister Harris's announcement, on 22 March 2018, Together for Yes – the national civil society campaign which would advocate for a 'Yes' vote in the forthcoming referendum on abortion in Ireland – was formally launched (NWCI 2018). Nominally an 'umbrella network' for over 100 different pro-choice organizations, Together for Yes was coordinated by three individuals representing the three primary constitutive groups; Grainne Griffin, founding member of the Abortion Rights Campaign, Orla O'Connor, director of the National Women's Council of Ireland, and Ailbhe Smyth, convenor of the Coalition to Repeal the Eighth Amendment.

There can be little doubt that the Together for Yes campaign was an astounding success, with 66.4 per cent of voters electing to repeal the 8th amendment and legislate for abortion access in Ireland in the May 2018 referendum. In the months following the referendum, however, it became clear that many of the activists who had campaigned on behalf of Together for Yes were dissatisfied with the organization's messaging and tactics. In particular, debate about the perceived 'conservativism' of the 'Yes' campaign ensued. These tensions were further stoked by the publication of exit poll data which indicated that the majority of those who voted in favour of repeal did so based on their belief in the right to choose (a theme which was not centralized in the messaging of the pro-choice side in their pre-referendum campaigning); demonstrating that a substantial liberalization of abortion attitudes in Ireland had already taken place prior to 2018 (Reidy 2019).

Reflecting on the referendum campaign, abortion activist and disability rights campaigner Emma Burns (2018) described the launch of Together for Yes as signalling a changeover from 'a purely grassroots, homegrown, diverse, feminist' movement to a 'slick, centrally directed, professionally run campaign with strict messaging and zero tolerance for deviation from the messaging booklet' (para 24). Burns describes how the public 'didn't hear from the messier edges' of the movement where 'multiple oppressions occur to squeeze people of their rights' (2018, para 25). Notably, she says, migrant women, Traveller women, and trans men were generally excluded from high profile or leadership positions. Emma Campbell, co-chair of Alliance for Choice Belfast (a Northern Irish abortion campaign group), critiqued 'the cost of the emotional labour' which was paid by those who volunteered as part of the 'Yes' campaign, the majority of whom were women and members of the LGBTQIA+ community (Campbell 2018, para 6).

Continuing my analysis of the role of the body in the Irish abortion rights movement, I want to turn in this chapter to investigate the emotional and embodied experiences of activists as part of the official referendum campaign between March and May 2018. I explore how the 'Yes' campaign required activists to embody a particular type of 'respectability' and analyse the bodily and emotional costs to activists of having to perform respectability on the campaign trail and 'on the doorsteps' of prospective voters. This analysis indicates a distinct transformation in the modality of embodiment between the grassroots and the official referendum campaign; wherein the former was predicated on the radical potentiality of 'coming out' or *revealing* the reproductive body, the latter appears to be contingent instead upon processes of covering up or covering over (aspects of) the activist body (or certain groups of activist bodies, in some cases).

I situate this analysis in relation to existing scholarship on 'race' and 'respectability politics', and on the intersections of class, gender, and respectability (Higginbotham 1993; Skeggs 2002). Coined in 1993 by Evelyn Brooks Higginbotham, the term 'respectability politics' was first devised to describe the tactics of the Black Women's Baptist Church movement – a group of anti-racist organizers active in the United States in the early 20th century – who utilized code-switching, emotional labour, and impression management techniques as part of their activist strategizing. By consciously dressing and speaking in ways that White America would find acceptable, members of the Black Women's Baptist Church movement asserted their claim on respectability, allowing them to initiate a 'process of dialogue' between Black and White society (Higginbotham 1993, 196). In short, respectability politics can be conceptualized as a subversive political strategy which encourages members of a social movement to speak, act, and behave in ways that might bolster their social acceptance by the dominant social group.

Higginbotham's work keenly illustrates how respectability functions as a device of social control which works in tandem with the regulation of 'race' and class, and which in fact illustrates the social construction of these categories. In the case of the Black Women's Baptist Church movement, the performance of respectability allowed these activists to challenge Social Darwinist ideas about the inherent 'uncleanliness' of Black people and provided them with the opportunity to 'define themselves outside of the parameters of prevailing racist discourses' (Higginbotham 1993, 190–192). In the UK context, Beverly Skeggs (2002) explains how respectability functioned as a central mechanism through which the concept of class emerged in the late 19th and early 20th centuries. In British context, Skeggs argues, it is the working class which has been consistently 'classified as dangerous, polluting, threatening, revolutionary, pathological, and without respect' (Skeggs 2002, 1). In both historical contexts and cases, respectability works as a marker of racial and or class hierarchy which is inscribed and performed primarily through women's bodies.

Drawing upon the work of Black feminist scholars like Higginbotham (1993) on the emotional and aesthetic labour of respectability politics, and on Beverley Skeggs' (2002) research on respectability as a form of capital which working-class women are compelled to aspire to through the performance of 'responsible' reproductive and domestic labour, I conceptualize respectability politics here as a form of body politics. Respectability politics is a form of body politics, I argue, in so far as the performance of respectability requires a particular type of bodily performance, including the adoption of speech patterns, emotional management, and expression strategies, as well as the undertaking of contextually specific forms of aesthetic labour.

In addition, I argue that respectability politics are always already a form of body politics, in so far as 'respectability politics' strategies require women to distance themselves from or to deny their sexuality/sexual bodies to acquire 'respectability' (this is particularly true for women from racialized and colonized populations, as well as for working-class women, who have historically been constructed as 'hypersexual' and therefore 'disreputable', as illustrated earlier).

Before beginning my analysis of the embodiment of respectability in the 'Yes' campaign, I want to further contextualize the development of the Together for Yes organization and to review existing literature on the tactics and outcomes of the 2018 referendum campaign. One year after their historic victory which saw the Irish electorate vote to overturn Ireland's abortion ban by an astounding 66 per cent majority, the leaders of the Together for Yes campaign published a book entitled *It's a Yes! How Together for Yes Repealed the Eighth and Transformed Irish Society* (Griffin et al 2019). In this book, the three Together for Yes coordinators explain how the organization was developed as well as how the decision was made to structure the 'core arguments' of the 'Yes' campaign around three pillars of 'care, compassion, and change', which would come to be known as the 'three C's' strategy (Griffin et al 2019).

Explaining the thinking behind the 'three C's' strategy, the Together for Yes leaders explain how the public would be asked to vote 'Yes' to enable 'care' for pregnant women 'in their own country' (Griffin et al 2019). As I have argued elsewhere, with this discourse, the 'Yes' campaign successfully mobilized a type of postcolonial, nationalist sentiment, by urging Irish voters to provide *care* for pregnant women in 'their own country', as opposed to forcing them to travel abroad (notably, to England) to access medical care (O'Shaughnessy 2021, 4). Second, voting 'Yes' was constructed as an act of '*compassion*', particularly towards those couples or families who are obliged to travel abroad to secure abortion care after receiving diagnoses of severe or fatal foetal anomalies during pregnancy. Finally, Together for Yes cast a 'Yes' vote as the only pragmatic choice which could possibly *change* the clearly dysfunctional status quo. Abortion was already a practical reality of women's lives in Ireland, it was argued, as evidenced by the large volumes of abortion pills entering the country daily (Calkin 2020, 73).

In *It's a Yes!*, Griffin et al describe the origins of Together for Yes and how the campaign strategy was developed. In 2015, stalwart feminist activist and organizer Ailbhe Smyth – acting on behalf of the Coalition to Repeal the Eighth Amendment – approached the advertising and design agency Language, commissioning them to undertake research to 'get a sense of specific tactics and how they would play out with the Irish public' in a hypothetical referendum on the 8th amendment (Griffin et al 2019, 50). A subsequent research plan was developed, they explain, in conjunction with the Irish Council for Civil Liberties, the National Women's Council of Ireland, Amnesty International, the Abortion Rights Campaign, the Irish Family Planning Association, and the Unions of Students in Ireland. This research, the results of which would go on to inform the Together for Yes messaging, collected data through a series of focus groups.

Two focus groups (each consisting of a two-hour session) were carried out in Dublin, and 'to get a real sense of how people were feeling outside of Dublin – "the pro-choice bubble"', two additional focus groups were carried out in Mullingar, Co. Westmeath, and two in Tralee, Co. Kerry (Griffin et al 2019, 49). Mullingar (the third most populous town in Ireland's midlands region) was chosen as a focus group location on account of 'its proximity to Roscommon' (the only county to vote 'No' in the same-sex marriage referendum in 2015), while Tralee was selected to give an 'urban ... but also rural' perspective (Griffin et al 2019, 49). No details are provided of how many participants were involved in each focus group, or how they were recruited. Nor was any information given in relation to the demographic background of participants.

The book argues that this research demonstrated that the people of Ireland wanted the outcome of the abortion referendum to be 'caring and humane' (Griffin et al 2019, 51). It refers to opinion polls which demonstrated that 'the majority of Irish people ... would only support the provision of abortion in certain, restricted circumstances' (Griffin et al 2019, 50). Referring to a 'centre ground', the 'Yes' campaign coordinators explain how this group 'was thoughtful and caring and realistic about the need for change, but ... felt emotionally torn on the issue' (Griffin et al 2019, 51). They maintain that this 'muddled middle' would not support abortion without restrictions (Griffin et al 2019, 51). The book explains that the public 'wanted a safe space to listen, think and talk', but 'tended to withdraw' if the debate 'turned angry' (Griffin et al 2019, 52). It resolves that, despite the campaign leaders having their own 'reservations about expressing abortion as a need rather than a right', a consensus was reached that 'a softer, gentler, reasoned approach' was, in fact, the best way forward (Griffin et al 2019, 51, 55).

As alluded to earlier, in the months following the referendum, academic research, blog posts, and newspaper articles offering critical reflections on Together for Yes began to circulate. Analysing the relationship between respectability politics and the 'racialised politics of representation', Chakravarty et al critique the overwhelming 'Whiteness' and 'Eurocentrism' of the referendum campaign (2020, 170). Describing the 'Yes' campaign as 'intersectionally tone-deaf at best, purposefully exclusionary at worst', Chakravarty et al (2020) critique the 'easy cooptation of "diverse" images', like that of Savita Halappanavar by this group of predominantly 'white, Irish, middle-class feminists' who failed to engage meaningfully with the significance of Ms Halappanavar's background as a migrant woman. This failure to interrogate the role of racism in Ms Halappanavar's death, they argue, is symptomatic of a more systematic failure of intersectional praxis in the Irish pro-choice movement (Chakravarty et al 2020, 174).

Political scientist Paola Rivetti offers a similar critique of the 'middle-class identity politics' of the referendum campaign and the coterminous 'invisibilisation in the law of those people who represent the "other" to the Irish population' (Rivetti 2019, 186). Specifically, she contends, 'traumatic stories relating to abortions carried out in Direct Provision centres' or 'episodes of racism carried out against Traveller women or women of colour in maternity wards' were excluded (Rivetti 2019, 186). By contrast, Haughton et al (2022) argue that narratives of 'respectable' and 'responsible' womanhood which centralized the experiences of middle-class, White, heterosexual, married, Anglophone women, deserving of 'empathy' and 'trust', were utilized to convince the 'middle ground'. Interestingly, Haughton et al conceptualize 'respectability' not as a form of embodied capital or as a marker of class or racial hierarchy (as I do here) but as the 'absence of stigma, the freedom from shame, the warmth of assured collectivity via community' (2022, 3).

In the following sections, I investigate the *embodiment of respectability* in the referendum campaign, through the analysis of activists' testimonies surrounding their affective and bodily experience as part of Together for Yes. A key question I want to address here is who shouldered the costs of this 'respectability politics' strategy? Etymologists have established a link between the words 'shoulder' and 'to shield'. To 'shoulder a burden', then, means to literally shield someone/something from harm by taking the burden onto one's body. As described earlier, respectability politics have an implicitly bodily valence. How, I wondered, were the respectability politics of the Together for Yes campaign embodied? And what were the embodied effects on campaigners of having to toe the line of this arguably assimilatory strategy?

Speech politics, emotion management, and clothing in the 'Yes' campaign

It was a windy Wednesday evening in mid-April when I joined up with my local Together for Yes group to participate in my first door-to-door canvass. I was campaigning in my home county of Carlow, the second smallest county in the country, located in Ireland's southeast region. The county is largely rural and boasts a strong agricultural community, while 40 per cent of the inhabitants reside in the town of Carlow itself which lies to the north of the county, close to the border with Kildare. With a population of more than 27,000, it would take our relatively small canvassing group several weeks to knock on every single door in Carlow town. For my first outing, I was paired up with a more experienced canvasser. She would take charge of the first few doors, as I followed tentatively, listening and learning. As we made our way from house to house, I made note of the various talking points and the types of language my colleague used. She spoke at length about the importance of privacy, the role of doctors, and the injustice of forcing women abroad, 'turning our backs' on our sisters, cousins, friends, in the moments when they were most in need of care.

Over the course of the next few evenings, I noticed how the word 'abortion' itself was rarely used on the doorstep. Neither was the terminology of 'choice', 'bodily autonomy' or 'reproductive rights'. I was confused, disappointed, deflated. For me, this whole referendum was about bodily autonomy, my bodily autonomy and the bodily autonomy of every woman and person in the country who was directly affected by the constitutional abortion ban. It was about having my family, my neighbours, my community recognize and respect my agency, my sexuality, my life. It was about having these people acknowledge that I matter. Why were we not talking about any of these things, I wondered? After the campaign was over, many of the activists I interviewed described feeling similarly confused about the terminology and talking points that the mainstream referendum campaign had chosen to focalize. Oonagh, an activist and student in her early 20s, recounted feeling unsure about what language she was 'allowed' to use on the campaign trail. She told me about a tense exchange with a co-campaigner which ensued on her first day of door-to-door canvassing where she utilized the word 'abortion' in a conversation with a prospective voter:

> 'Oh yeah, I remember one of the first days knocking on a door and using the term abortion and one of the other campaigners ate me because she said we're not allowed use the term abortion, we have to only talk about women's rights. Which is a real skirting around the issue. So, there's a few standout moments, that was one of them. So, trying to figure out, should we continue to skirt around this issue, or should we come out with it? 'Cause they can always slam the door in your face, which happened a few times.'

Oonagh provides important clues here as to the 'speech politics' of the 'Yes' campaign, when she describes feeling conflicted between her desire to "come out" with the word 'abortion', and the injunction laid upon her by her fellow campaigners to continue "skirting around the issue". As described in Chapter 3, the term 'coming out' designates a process of *revelation* (Stambolis-Ruhstorfer and Saguy 2014). To 'come out' as an abortion activist, I explained, implies an act of bodily resistance but also the assumption of a state of embodied vulnerability. Here, Oonagh describes her uncertainty as she wrestles with the decision to simply 'come out' with the word abortion on the doorsteps, thereby revealing the 'reality' of the issue. Again, the instructions given to her by her co-canvasser indicate how the bodily experience of the referendum campaign can be characterized by this impetus towards *concealment*, which stands in stark contrast to the body politics of the grassroots abortion campaign which utilized radical acts of bodily *revelation* to great political effect.

On the other hand, Oonagh explains how the decision to "come out with it" (to 'come out' as an abortion activist) implies a degree of physical *risk* – of having the individual "slam the door in your face", for example. Her other option then, as she describes it, was to "skirt around the issue", or perhaps to put a skirt around the issue? To wrap the word abortion in a 'softer', more 'feminine' cloak. To paraphrase feminist theorist Sara Ahmed (2017), Oonagh's story indicates how the demand to be respectable is 'lived as a form of body politics, or as *speech politics*: you have to be careful of what you say, how you appear' (para 30, my emphasis). As Ahmed describes, the goal of respectability politics is to 'maximise the distance between yourself and their idea of you' (2017, para 30). I wondered whether by wrapping the idea of abortion in a softer, more feminine cloak – specifically, by obscuring it in the language of "women's rights" – the goal here was to 're-feminize' abortion-seekers, to circumvent the idea that abortion-seekers are somehow un-womanly? In my conversation with Saoirse, it became increasingly clear that the language selected by Together for Yes elicited strong, often conflicting feelings among activists. Saoirse explained her thoughts on the chosen terminology as follows:

'It was very pathologized, I'd agree with that. It was a very particular set of words that were picked. I think it was focus groups they used. The buzzwords were compassion and care. And it worked, I guess is the most important thing. I think what's frustrating for some activists was realizing that the campaign was not designed to appeal to us. It was designed to appeal to the moveable middle, and it did. It was not appealing to me to see this plastered on smile on it all. That it always had to be abortion care, and never just an abortion. As if the word "care" somehow kind of softened it – like, "Don't forget there's a hug at the end!" I found it quite jarring that a lot of the people who shared their stories, the overwhelming narrative was of suffering and tragedy relating to abortion. And that of course was the strategy and it made people stop thinking about murder of babies and start thinking about "who needs this"?'

The "buzzwords", as Saoirse labels them, of 'care, compassion, and change', proved particularly divisive among campaigners. As I have documented elsewhere, the word 'compassion' comes from the Latin *'compassionem'*, which includes the stem 'pati' meaning 'to suffer' and 'com' which means 'with'

(O'Shaughnessy 2021, 8). The idea of having compassion for someone then literally translates into suffering *with* them (O'Shaughnessy 2021, 8). Saoirse describes as "jarring" this "overwhelming narrative" within the official referendum campaign of "suffering and tragedy in relation to abortion". Despite her own negative feelings about this discursive register, however, she acknowledges the success of this "strategy" in shifting the focus away from "the murder of babies" and onto the idea of abortion as a 'need'. Interestingly, Saoirse's testimony here indicates the *fluidity* of moral discourse in relation to abortion and highlights again how the 'Yes' campaign sought to ground itself in a 'practical morality' which focuses upon the real-life situations in which people find themselves needing to access to abortion care (Pollack Petchesky 1990).

Describing the contemporary emotional construction of abortion, Australian sociologist Erica Millar (2017) notes that the popular tendency to emphasize experiences of 'suffering' and 'tragedy' in relation to abortion works to construct abortion as 'inherently productive of grief and shame' (3). This particular 'emotional script', Millar explains, operates such that, even in cases where women and pregnant people have the legal 'choice' to terminate their pregnancy, abortion will nevertheless be constructed – in emotional terms – as an inherently 'damaging experience' (Millar 2017, 3). In the Irish context, as I have argued, the discursive focus on 'compassion' and 'suffering' in relation to abortion is emblematic of efforts to mobilize religious and postcolonial gender logics which conflate the suffering Irish mother both with the suffering Virgin Mary and the suffering Motherland; thereby, ultimately reinscribing the apparently 'sacrificial' nature of 'Irish femininity' (Martin 2002 in O'Shaughnessy 2021, 12).

As I listened to Saoirse, I was struck by the disjuncture between the image she described – standing on a doorstep, with a "plastered on smile" – and the way she appeared in front of me in that moment, almost seething with anger and visibly holding back tears. Saoirse's testimony designates how, for campaigners like herself who toed the line of the 'Yes' campaign's referendum strategy, canvassing entailed not only intense physical work but also required an intensive investment of emotional labour. In her ground-breaking book *The Managed Heart: Commercialization of Human Feeling*, American sociologist Arlie Hochschild (2012 [1983]) coins the term 'surface acting' to describe the process whereby people adopt specific types of body language or facial expressions to outwardly display particular emotional expressions (36). In 'surface acting', Hochschild (2012) clarifies, facial expressions are 'put on' but not experienced as an authentic 'part of' the subject (36).

Hochschild (2012) describes how women, as well as those working in the service industry, are most often required to perform this 'emotional labour' in line with normative expectations of their gender(ed) role. Discussing the emotional labour of social justice activism, Sara Ahmed (2017) explains how smiling is a particularly important instrument in the emotional labour toolkit. Smiling works to 'soften' one's appearance, particularly where one is perceived as 'too hard' (Ahmed 2017, para 25). Ahmed (2017) discusses how smiling is particularly helpful for social justice activists or diversity workers who may otherwise be perceived as 'aggressive' or 'hostile', facilitating their efforts to 'pass' into institutions of power (para 25). As Muireann explained to me, the management of emotions and in particular, the expression of 'positive' emotions was integral to the strategy of the referendum campaign and was, in her opinion, designed to distinguish the approach of the 'Yes' activists from that of the anti-abortion movement:

> 'You know, I think the tone that was decided really early on of, we're gonna be positive, we're not gonna get into mudslinging with the antis, we're gonna respect people's opinions, we're not gonna shout, we're gonna be the approachable friendly people. And I remember at canvassing training, people being like "What?! I don't want to have to be really nice if somebody is telling me they don't think women should be having sex", or whatever. And that was really hard and that really took a toll on people, having to swallow that stuff every day, because you just need that person to vote Yes. And I think that has taken me a very long time to process, what that actually does of saying "I understand what you mean, I understand your question, I understand your concern", when they just don't trust women. Like, I don't understand! So, I think that Together for Yes did that really well, of like, if you were looking in from the outside, you're going to want to side with the smiley, friendly people who aren't shouting things into a megaphone about murder and who are going to say "OK, yeah no I can understand that". People are gonna respond to that, they're not gonna respond to shouting.'

Like Saoirse, Muireann spoke at length about the utility of smiling on the campaign trail; explaining that members of the public would be more likely "to want to side with the smiley, friendly people who aren't shouting things". Analysing the gendered politics of smiling, Ahmed (2017) defers to Betty Friedan's landmark text, *The Feminine Mystique* (2010 [1963], 5), on the 'problem which has no name', that is, the unexplainable yet pervasive dissatisfaction of the bourgeois suburban housewife in the United States, post-Second World War. Ahmed describes how Friedan's work 'exposed a rotten infection underneath the smile of the housewife' (2017, para 18). Ahmed (2017) analyses representations of Friedan's object of study, explaining how in images of the White, bourgeois housewife in mainstream media, for example, she always appears smiling (para 18). This smile becomes 'evidence',

Ahmed explains, that the housewife is 'happy' to do the unpaid, reproductive labour in the home (Ahmed 2017, para 18).

Moreover, smiling is a 'feminine achievement', Ahmed (2017) explains, and exemplifies the housewife's successful performance of hegemonic gender roles (para 24). As Muireann explains, neither herself nor her fellow campaigners were 'happy' to take on the very specific emotional labour that the 'Yes' campaign required of them. Recounting a conversation at canvassing training, Muireann recalls a colleague's reaction towards the instruction to "be nice" to voters who espoused sexist or misogynistic views on the doorstep. Again, demonstrating the explicitly bodily valence of the 'respectability politics' strategy, Muireann explains the toll this took on activists having to "swallow" such comments. As she spoke, Muireann contorted her face as though recalling the unpleasant taste "that stuff" left in her mouth.

During my interview with Ciara who was canvassing in the rural southwest, she explained how the injunction to "present ourselves as respectable" necessitated not only the assumption of particular ways of speaking and specific emotional expressions but the adoption of a distinctive 'uniform', as well. Returning to the 'respectability politics' strategies critical to the history of the Black organizing tradition in the United States, Tanisha Ford (2013) demonstrates how clothing and uniforms became a particularly important 'cultural and political tool' in the civil rights movement (627). In the early 20th century, Black women activists were encouraged to dress as if they were 'going to Church', Ford (2013) explains (629). By performing 'respectable' womanhood, through their 'conservative' clothing, these women sought to 'publicly articulate their moral aptitude', Ford clarifies (2013, 629). Here, Ciara recounts a similar politics of dress at play within the referendum campaign in 2018:

> 'There was no place in our campaign for blue hair or Repeal jumpers. We could wear our badges, it was only at events we could put on our shirts, 'cause then you're crew. And sometimes I would wear it if I was on a street stall, I might wear my jumper then, 'cause then you're a walking billboard. But when you're out walking in the town and you're meeting people on their lunch, we had to take a different strategy, we had to present ourselves as respectable. Our message had to be respectable, but still we'd managed not to compromise too much on the content. But we had to present it in a certain way.'

Reflecting on the launch of Together for Yes, Ciara complained that "rural perspectives weren't included" in putting together the referendum campaign messaging. Moreover, Ciara alleged that some of the Together for Yes media spokespeople "had a detrimental effect down the country." As Mary McGill (2019) has explored, as both 'geography and imaginary', rural

Ireland occupies a 'distinct space in the Irish landscape' characterized 'by the region's assumed conservatism' (109). Both national and international media commentary constructed the abortion debate as neatly divided along the lines of rural versus urban (McGill 2019). In reality, almost every county in Ireland delivered a landslide 'Yes' vote in the 25 May referendum. In Wicklow, the 'Yes' side secured a 74 per cent victory, with voters in Roscommon (assumed as one of Ireland's most conservative rural enclaves) delivering a victory of 54 per cent for the pro-repeal campaign (Henley 2018).

While rural Ireland ultimately proved itself as less conservative than was perhaps assumed by the 'Yes' campaign, Ciara's testimony indicates a culture of misogyny which continues to be pervasive in rural Ireland and which had to be deftly circumvented by pro-choice activists. Canvassing in rural Ireland required a "different approach", Ciara clarified, which entailed the adoption of an alternative sartorial presentation. As I illustrated in Chapter 4, while the black-and-white Repeal jumper played a hugely important role in the consolidation of the Repeal the 8th campaign after its launch in 2016 – as a tool to foster collective identity, as a symbol of hope, and as a mechanism of 'gestural dress' – the jumper had to be thrown out by certain factions of activists during the referendum campaign, particularly as it appeared to signify a type of non-normative and 'disrespectable' femininity, and thereby prevented these activists from successfully embodying and *proving* their moral worth. Ciara explained:

> 'There's this whole thing about respectability that really went through our campaign as well, with the jumpers and everything. As my partner in crime would say, "We have to put on our church clothes when we're going to canvass". When she's doing street stalls, she'd have her nice dress on, she'd have her hair done and her make-up on and good shoes and she'd stand there in her good coat. People would be like "Oh who are you now?" and like, you could be from MACRA. Like, wholesome. You had to put on the middle-class persona, you could be picking your kids up at the school or you could be on a lunchbreak from the solicitor's office.'

Analysing Ciara's account, it becomes clear how clothing became an integral element of the 'Yes' campaign's 'respectability politics' strategy. Referencing 'MACRA', a voluntary organization set up 1944 to provide young (male) farmers with training and an outlet for socializing in rural areas, Ciara indicates how she sought to embody a particular version of 'traditional' Irish femininity (Macra Na Feirme 2022). Echoing Ford's (2013) analysis, Ciara explains how through donning her "church clothes", activists like herself and her colleagues in the rural southwest sought to prove their moral aptitude. Explaining how they needed to look like they "could be picking (their) kids up from school", or "be on a lunchbreak from the solicitor's office", Ciara's testimony indicates how, for rural women in particular, the endowment of respectability was contingent upon on socioeconomic or class status, as well as upon the assumption of traditional, maternal roles (2). Laoise elaborated on how this reinscription of conservative gender roles and the coterminous concession to classism formed integral elements of the 'Yes' campaign's strategy from the outset:

> 'Behind the scenes, they were doing canvasses in 2013, 2014 ... all in the run up to the campaign. They had gone and they had tried different messaging. They had tried taking, you know "Trust women" and unfortunately, Irish people don't trust women, that was not working on the doors. The whole human rights thing, just not buying human rights or whatever. They came back and they were like "Well, what's working, people trust doctors", yeah, I think it just ... this private decision with a doctor. Irish people like privacy, they're really private. I think it did work for that older generation. Now, the younger generation and the activist in me, wanted to scream out "It is my body and it is my choice!" but that's not gonna work on the door, you know. I took to the streets, and I did scream that many a time. But when you're door to door, face to face with someone, you have to see where people are at as well.'

Referring to the focus group research started by Smyth and colleagues in 2015 – which Laoise describes here as the "canvasses" that "they were doing" – Laoise matter-of-factly explains to me how this research had demonstrated that "Irish people don't trust women" and that this message was apparently "not working on the doors". Skating adeptly over this pronouncement of inherent (and apparently unchallengeable) cultural misogyny, Laoise clarifies that the same research confirmed that Irish people "trust doctors". As Erica Millar (2017) notes, this prioritization of medical 'expertise' in political debate around abortion – which often comes at the expense of the testimony and experiences of women and abortion-seeking people – is not new. In contexts where abortion has become medicalized, Millar (2017) argues, a 'web of gendered power relations' operates to construct the idea that abortion should be a 'medical doctor's, rather than a woman's decision' (14–15).

In her analysis of the role of the 'collective, pro-choice medical voice' in the Repeal the 8th movement, Sadie Bergen explains that Doctors 4 Choice – a small, physician advocacy group set up in 2002 to advocate for legalized abortion in Ireland – effectively leveraged their 'cultural authority' and 'social position' to fight for reproductive autonomy (2022, 1). Bergen explains that Doctors 4 Choice sought to 'distance itself from a legacy of physician authority over reproductive decision-making' and sought instead to emphasize 'patient autonomy as a pillar of medical ethics' (2022, 3, 14). Bergen describes how members of Doctors 4 Choice found themselves 'marginalised within the broader medical profession' because of stigma related to abortion provision and also because of various structural barriers which prohibited activist engagement (2022, 8). Bergan concludes that physician advocates played an important role in the 2018 campaign, albeit while remaining on 'safe political ground', which framed abortion according to a health-based, rather than 'rights-based' model (2022, 15).

The decision to centralize the voices of doctors in the Together for Yes campaign certainly feeds into a wider effort to shift the terms of the debate; to 'depoliticize' abortion, to construct abortion as a legitimate healthcare issue, and thus to make abortion a more palatable concern for 'on-the-fence' voters. Analysing the testimony of activists like Ciara and Laoise, however, it appears that the decision to prioritize the voices and experiences of doctors – instead of those of abortion-seekers themselves – may speak to deeper intersecting structures of misogyny, classism, and paternalism at play within Irish society at large – structures which the 'Yes' campaign chose not to challenge but to simply circumvent. Moreover, the prioritization of 'medical expertise' in the referendum campaign has culminated, I argue, in a post-Repeal policy landscape which continues to hierarchize medical evidence over lived experience in the development and regulation of abortion provision (O'Shaughnessy et al 2023).

By encouraging campaigners to adopt a 'positive, non-reactive' tone, by asking them to 'skirt around the issue' of abortion (to use the term 'women's rights' instead of 'abortion'), by compelling activists to 'swallow' the sexism they encountered on the doorsteps, and by prioritizing a discursive register which focalizes the 'suffering' of aborting women, the 'Yes' campaign sought to establish a connection with the voting public on the basis of a collective, conservative interpellation of gender, and a shared culture of paternalism and class hierarchy. Centralizing the experiences of 'respectable', White, middle-class, heterosexual women (and couples) whose pregnancies involve fatal foetal abnormalities, the 'Yes' campaigners could by association prove their own moral aptitude and social value as charitable, respectable, bystanders, concerned with the welfare of these suffering women and their families.

Higginbotham (1993) describes 'respectability politics' as entailing a 'highly conscious' concession to hegemony. The question remains, I argue, as to whether the reproduction of paternalistic tropes within the 'Yes' campaign signals a *conscious* (and potentially subversive) concession to or appropriation of misogynistic logics, or whether this exemplifies a more cynical conservativism at the heart of the referendum campaign. While the embodiment of 'respectable' dress allowed activists like Ciara to initiate the process of dialogue with conservative voters, the costs of this 'assimilationist' strategy are less clear (Higginbotham 1993, 187). In addition, we are compelled to ask, by colluding in the reproduction of a classist, heterosexist performance of gender, (how) did the 'Yes' campaign reinscribe the idea of the 'disrespectability' or moral *inaptitude* of activists who did not successfully embody these norms?

"The rage has yet to come out": White femininity and the fear of anger

Reflecting on the emotional politics of social justice organizing, feminist theorist Sara Ahmed (2017) describes how being 'part of a cause' is often 'assumed to require getting over your misery: getting over it; getting over yourself' (para 1). Ahmed (2017) recounts how the idea that one must put one's emotions aside to successfully engage in diversity or social justice work – exemplified in the popular expression 'don't agonise, organise' – has become a commonly accepted refrain (para 2). Ahmed (2017) takes issue with this notion, complaining that there is 'something wrong with the idea that there is a right way to feel when protesting' (para 3). By contrast, Ahmed clarifies that 'protesting is messy' and 'there are times when we arrive and leave with grief in our hearts' (Ahmed 2017, para 4).

In this way, Ahmed (2017) keenly observes the 'complicated' and 'sticky' nature of emotion work in activism. The activist may 'smile and be plotting', she explains; they may appear to be 'working in agreement in order to work *against an agreement*' (para 32, my emphasis). Taking forward Ahmed's words, I want to pause here on the term 'agreement' and reflect upon its various etymological meanings. From the French verb *agreer*, meaning 'to please', the phrase to be 'working in agreement' could signify the idea of trying to 'please' or even 'placate' others. Working 'in agreement in order to work against an agreement' might then indicate a process of concession to the status quo, to ultimately overturn the very same system. In French, the word *agreement*, however, also signifies the idea of 'mutual understanding'; in this case, to be 'working in agreement' should imply a process of *working together* based on formal, mutual comprehension or consensus.[1]

While there is an argument to be made that the 'Yes' campaign's appropriation of 'respectability' was motivated by subversive ends – that the campaign sought to establish commonality with the voting public on the basis of shared understandings and values around gender and class, for example, in order to eventually overturn established norms – the question of whether and in what ways this strategy was conceived of or supported by the collective campaign remains unclear. The lack of detail around the public relations research conducted by Together for Yes preceding the referendum, combined with the fact that this research contradicts exit poll data in relation to public attitudes towards abortion in Ireland begs the question of where this injunction to embody respectability might have come from? Returning to Saoirse's testimony, it becomes increasingly clear that the respectability politics strategy came at a great cost for activists on the ground. Saoirse describes how toeing the line of the Together for Yes strategy had left activists with a great deal of "rage" and "anger" which had yet to "come out":

> 'This is the nature of a referendum campaign. We had to appeal to everyone. And that's awful because suddenly you're tone policing yourself. I'm not allowed to be angry because that's what people think we are. You're not allowed to demand your rights. You have to beg for them, and I think a lot of people felt like the sacrifice they made on the doorstep, it was the indignity of having to ask and ask with someone else's words was just really really hard for people. Immensely hard emotional work that people were doing. Canvassing wasn't just hard because its brave and you're knocking on strangers' doors. Which is in itself kind of mind-blowing, just the idea of approaching someone else's space is quite intimidating. It's really not easy to do so, to do that in a sort of forced, kind of, subjugated isn't the right word but in a pleading kind of a way, it was the indignity of it was just shocking and it really exhausted people. And we were asking the most educated, the most brilliant, the most empowered people to kind of beg for their lives. No wonder people are angry. I don't think we've started to deal with that yet. The absolute rage that's still in the back of people's minds ... it's yet to come out.'

Saoirse points to how the "indignity", as she describes it, of having to "beg for your life" was compounded by the fact that she "wasn't allowed to be angry" about it. As Saoirse explains, having to suppress her anger constituted "immensely hard emotional work". Hochschild (2012) terms as 'deep acting' this labour whereby one attempts to subdue or induce authentic or 'real' emotions in oneself (35). 'Deep acting' differs from 'surface' acting, Hochschild (2012) explains, as it implies intervening in the 'inner shape of feeling', as opposed to simply 'shaping the outward appearance of one' (36). Again, demonstrating how she and other activists struggled against this mandate to *conceal* their true emotional selves, Saoirse reinvokes the terminology of 'coming out', in reference to the "rage" which has "has yet to come out" after the conclusion of the referendum campaign. Listening to Saoirse's account, I was reminded of the words of feminist activist and writer Soraya Chemaly, who describes anger as being 'like water'; 'no matter how hard a person tries to dam, divert, or deny it', Chemaly explains, '[anger] will find a way, usually along the path of least resistance' (2018, 31).

Drawing on the work of Black feminists like Audre Lorde (1981) who described anger as a 'powerful source of information and energy', Chemaly (2018) proclaims that anger is what keeps us 'invested in the world' (Lorde 1981, 8; Chemaly 2018, 32). Explaining the positive, productive nature of anger and rage, Chemaly (2018) agrees with Lorde that anger plays a hugely important role in social justice work and feminist organizing. Anger 'bridges the divide', Chemaly argues, between 'what *"is"* and what *"ought"* to be' (2018, 31, my emphasis). Indeed, as Audre Lorde (1981) contends, translating anger into action 'in the service of our vision and our future' is 'a liberating and strengthening act of clarification' (8). As I described in Chapter 3, emotions like anger, rage, and indignation worked as hugely important affective forces in the mobilization of activists within the Repeal the 8th campaign.

As evidenced by the testimony of activists laid out here, with the changeover from the grassroots campaign to the official referendum strategy however, campaigners were encouraged to enact a very different emotional repertoire. As activists like Saoirse describe here, her involvement in the 'Yes' campaign required intense emotional work including both 'surface' and 'deep acting'. In concrete terms, as part of the Together for Yes campaign, activists were encouraged to suppress their anger and, instead, to approach the canvass with calmness and 'compassion'. Dorsey and Chen (2020) explain that such 'in-group policing' is characteristic of respectability politics strategies wherein members of the 'marginalised groups' are not 'afforded the nuance of individual personalities' (para 17). I asked Saoirse to expand on the experience and consequences of having to consistently 'swallow' her rage, as she described it:

> 'Some people are so burned out that they'll never come back to activism. They're done. And I don't blame them ... mentally and physically. Because it's not good for people to kind of carry that trauma around, and it is trauma, mentally or otherwise. I think some people have diverted it into other kinds of activism. I think people are just very brittle and they're arguing and they're fighting and they're looking around at other activists, and they're fighting with other activists. There's a massive sense of betrayal. A sense of "this wasn't what we agreed on". But nobody agreed on any of it. We are all angry and so the ontology of whose anger is prioritized ... there's already narratives emerging about whose especially angry, I can't blame them. I think anger is an important thing, especially in Ireland, especially for women ... I don't know what's gonna happen to all that. Because I think people are hoping for a resolution, but it's not there, it's not available. Nobody has it, they're looking around the room, to other activists who've also gone through it. But to a lesser extent, or more

depending on the person, they feel similarly betrayed or traumatized and are just wrecked. Nobody has the answer. The shock waves are still going.'

Explaining how activists have been left "very brittle" in the aftermath of the campaign, Saoirse's words provide a sharp illustration of the various ways in which power 'gets right to the bone' (Ahmed 2014, para 25). Her description of how herself and her comrades have been left "carrying (trauma) with them" speaks to the idea of an unreasonable degree of (bodily) sacrifice – or what Barbara Sutton (2007) might term 'bad' *poner el cuerpo* – which was required of pro-choice campaigners in the 2018 campaign. For Sutton, the term *poner el cuerpo* signifies the idea of putting the body 'on the line' as an activist, for example by engaging in specific forms of bodily protest, by performing emotional labour (either by managing the inner nature of one's own feelings, or by enacting a specific repertoire of outward emotional expression), or by engaging in reproductive or domestic labour related to caring for oneself or for one's activist colleagues. One of Sutton's interviewees distinguished between 'good' *poner el cuerpo*, which entails giving of one's body 'in a more or less equitable way', and bad *poner el cuerpo*, which invokes 'an unwarranted sacrifice' (Sutton 2007, 146).

I was struck particularly by Saoirse's description of the anger and the "massive sense of betrayal" around the 'Yes' campaign's adopted strategy which, as Saoirse explains, "wasn't what we agreed on". There was a particular sense of anger then, it seemed, both in relation to the selected tactics and approach of the 'Yes' campaign, and in relation to the intensive emotional work that was required of campaigners to enact and perform this particular strategy. Having to mediate their language and behaviour for such a long period of time had left activists feeling estranged from themselves and their feelings, and from the movement at large. This sense of alienation became more evident to activists like Aoife who, instead of feeling "elated" after the campaign victory, instead found themselves facing a "difficult transition":

'It was really rough. And I think there was this idea afterwards that we should feel elated. But I think there was something to do with the way we ran the campaign and the compromises that made us feel … there was a difficult transition afterwards. I couldn't really reconcile some of what happened during the campaign. Everybody just wanted to sweep everything under the rug until we had won. But in that, we compromised on our core foundation, which was bodily integrity and respect for people. Within five months of the referendum, I had had a full breakdown. I don't think my experience is unique. I think I was possibly out and about more than the average campaigner. But it was a hugely emotional campaign and just extremely draining and I'm still not over it. I can't be involved in any activism at the moment. And so, it was quite hard because all the organizations ended up fighting. We compromised a huge number of our values as a campaign. And it was done through fear not through principle ... I think we were scared. Scared about everything and scared of how quickly we might lose and this idea that if we did lose, we wouldn't have another chance for years.'

Aoife had gotten involved in abortion activism while she was studying in the United Kingdom but moved home to Ireland just prior to the Citizens Assembly taking place in 2016. In the run-up to the 2018 referendum, she spent much of her time travelling around the country giving "mini values clarification" workshops on abortion rights. As she spoke about the official referendum campaign in 2018, her disappointment both with regards to the 'compromises' made and with the fact that she didn't *feel* how she thought she would feel after the referendum were palpable. Sara Ahmed (2017) describes how 'anger' is often the emotion which 'fills the gap' between the 'promise of a feeling and the feeling of a feeling' (para 23). Similarly, discussing what we might term the embodied costs of emotion work, Hochschild (2012) argues that 'maintaining a difference between feeling and feigning over the long run leads to strain' (90). The separation of 'display' and 'feeling' leads to a process of 'emotive dissonance', Hochschild continues (2012, 90). The performer is forced to 'remove the self from the job' and in the process, the 'self becomes smaller' (Hochschild 2012, 135). In asking activists to assimilate to the 'respectability politics' strategy then, Together for Yes required more than 'surface acting'; it required campaigners to engage in a process of affective alienation, to distance themselves from their feelings, to make themselves smaller.

To come back to Dorsey and Chen (2020), when engaging in respectability politics strategies, it is important to acknowledge 'why' and 'who' we are performing for. As Aoife explains, there appeared to be an implicit understanding among certain segments of the campaign that the concessions being made by Together for Yes were motivated (or perhaps, legitimized) by "fear". Aoife explained how herself and other 'Yes' campaigners were "scared ... scared about everything and ... scared about how quickly we might lose". Listening to Aoife's testimony, I began to wonder about the relationship between *fear* and *anger*. I wanted to know whether or how this pervasive sense of 'fear' related to the ways in which the 'Yes' campaign sought to manage or mitigate the 'anger' which circulated among and between activist bodies both before and after the referendum. My conversation with Shauna, a Southern European migrant who campaigned on behalf of Together for Yes provided some important clues in this regard.

'So, as a migrant, we fought, we sent emails asking them to change "women of Ireland" for "pregnant people". We fought for Savita's face not to be used as the "good migrant"... We were told we were problematic, we were aggressive, we were unable to represent the campaign. Like, what the fuck do you want me to do? You're silencing us. We're literally fucking dying. And you are OK with this? To what? Benefit the Minister for Health? The National Women's Council? Labour? So, of course I'm fucking angry. On top of the campaign, how strenuous it was, it was that sense of anger and despair. We had no resources, we had no funding. We worked and worked till the end and then when it finished, we kept going. It was an awful lot of friendships lost, comrades lost, abuse ... let us celebrate, we did the best we could ... sorry, it's a little bit sore.'

The activist group in which Shauna was engaged was made up primarily of migrants and women of colour. She described how after various attempts to approach White colleagues in the pro-choice movement, to discuss intersectional politics and the use of the image of Savita Halappanavar (among other issues), her and her comrades were dismissed, branded as "aggressive" and as "unable to represent the campaign". Listening to Shauna, and thinking about the pervasive sense of fear described by Aoife and other activists in relation to the 'Yes' campaign, I began to wonder what exactly it was that the 'Yes' campaign was afraid of? Was the 'Yes' campaign afraid solely of 'losing' the referendum, or was the decision to run a conservative 'respectable' campaign also motivated by a fear of being perceived as 'angry'? By a fear of anger, in itself, perhaps? More importantly, why, if anger was such an important mobilizing force for the campaign, did the referendum campaign choose to quash it?

Chemaly (2018) argues that 'when a woman shows anger in institutional, political, and professional settings, she automatically violates gender norms' (25). She continues, explaining that 'gendered ideas about anger make us question ourselves, doubt our feelings, set aside our needs, and renounce our own capacity for moral conviction' (31). In choosing *not* to be angry then, the 'Yes' campaign decided to lean into normative ideas around 'gender appropriate' emotional expressions. In essence, the 'Yes' campaign chose to prioritize the comfort of the Irish public and of (male) politicians by keeping their (female) anger under wraps. As Audre Lorde describes, women have been socialized to understand that 'the anger of others was to be avoided at all costs', since there was 'nothing to be learned from it' apart from 'a judgement that we had been bad girls, come up lacking' (Lorde 1981, 9).

As Shauna's testimony indicates, however, some women – specifically, women of colour – were already being perceived and admonished for being 'angry', 'too angry', in fact, to represent the campaign. In this sense, we can understand how, in this context, the experience and expression of anger contravenes strict, conservative gender norms, and in addition, carries with it a distinctly racializing function. As Wendy Ashley describes, in the 19th century White patriarchal constructions of femininity ascribed virtue, domesticity, and piety as emblematic of 'good' womanhood (2014, 29). Since enslaved Black women were sexually brutalized, they were excluded from the category of 'virtuousness' and, as such, enacting 'religious faithfulness' and 'impassivity' became their only route to enact 'successful' femininity (Ashley 2014, 29). The trope of the 'Angry Black woman', Jones and Norwood describe, would conversely become the 'physical embodiment' of the 'worst negative stereotypes of Black women' (2017, 2049). It is one of several 'controlling images' used to make racism appear 'natural' as Hill Collins writes, and to punish Black women for daring to challenge the status quo (2009 [1990]).

When Black women use their voices to draw attention to injustice, the trope of the 'Angry Black woman' is used to displace blame, Jones and Norwood argue (2017). That is, it allows the 'aggressors' to 'deflect attention from their aggressive acts and to place blame for these encounters on Black women' (Jones and Norwood 2017, 2055).[2] At the core of this mechanism, Accapadi (2007) explains, is a racialized hierarchy of appropriate gendered behaviours, and specifically, of acceptable emotional expressions, which privileges 'crying, lower tones of voice, and direct eye contact' and punishes 'anger' and 'raised voices' (214). The former behaviours are often associated with Whiteness (and White femininity specifically), Accapadi argues, while the latter 'problematic' behaviours are often assigned as characteristic of the emotional expressions of women from 'communities of colour' (Accapadi 2007, 214). Accapadi contends that for White women to acknowledge their racial privilege, they must acknowledge this privilege is 'not only about our social identities' but the 'associated behaviours which are normalized within those social identities' too (2007, 214).

Perhaps then, this fear of anger within the 'Yes' campaign was motivated not simply by the concern that, through the display of negative emotions like anger and rage, activists might violate heterosexist gender norms, thereby incurring the wrath of paternalistic power upon whose 'benevolence' the success of the campaign – and by extension, our lives and wellbeing – depend. Perhaps, by seeking to present themselves as *not* 'angry', the 'Yes' campaign sought to distinguish itself from activists like Shauna and from the supposedly "aggressive", "problematic" approach her and her comrades exemplified? In this way, it could be argued that the 'Yes' campaign sought to lean into a particular version of White femininity which was premised on emphasizing the innate 'goodness' and non-confrontational 'nature' of (White) Irish women.

Returning to Higginbotham's (1993) avowal that respectability politics invariably entails a concession to hegemonic values, I would add that while 'respectability' takes on different meanings across cultural and historical settings, it is always already entangled in and (re)productive of contextually specific, racist, sexist, and classist logics. As Beverley Skeggs (2002) argues, 'respectability contains judgements of class, race, gender and sexuality and different groups have differential access to the mechanisms for generating, resisting and displaying respectability' (1). For the Together for Yes campaign, the 'respectable' woman – that is, the morally apt woman – is the White, middle-class, 'professional' mother who is never angry, but instead smiles consistently through suffering and sacrifice.

Analysing the differential experiences of activists within the Together for Yes campaign provides some important clues then, I argue, which might allow us to move beyond reductive, binary analyses which situate 'respectability politics' strategies as *either* subversive of or concessionary to hegemonic norms and values. The testimonies of Irish activists put forward here illustrate, I contend, that our time might be better spent – as activists and academics – not in deciding whether 'respectability' narratives are radical or assimilationist, but in examining the racialized hierarchy of appropriate gendered behaviours, as well as the *embodied costs* and the *affective outcomes* that respectability politics strategies entail, for activists positioned differently across gendered, classed, and racialized groups. The emotions which circulate between and among activist bodies in the aftermath of campaigns can be reconceptualized then as important sources for feminist knowledge production and for meaningful intersectional feminist praxis.

Soraya Chemaly (2018) argues that anger is 'an assertion of rights and worth … it is the demand of accountability' (692). Ignoring our anger, she says, 'makes us careless with ourselves and allows society to be careless with us' (Chemaly 2018, 692). When we take seriously our anger, we make it clear that we 'take ourselves seriously', Chemaly explains (2018, 34). Perhaps, then, one of the most important lessons we need to take away from this analysis of the 'Yes' campaign's respectability politics strategy is the value and importance of anger. In this post-Repeal landscape, it is imperative to think about what might be gained for activists to acknowledge and sit with their own anger and the anger of our activist comrades, which may look, sound, and feel very different to our own.

In her keynote address to the National Women's Studies Association Conference in June 1981, entitled 'The Uses of Anger', Audre Lorde wrote that 'your fear of anger will teach you nothing' (1981, 7). Indeed, I would argue that for the Irish abortion rights campaign, our fear of anger has accomplished very little. By contrast, and inspired by Lorde's words, I argue that there is much to be *learned* from this fear of anger and from the anger itself which continues to circulate among and between certain groups of activist bodies in the aftermath of the referendum campaign. By analysing this (fear of) anger produced within the 2018 abortion rights campaign, we can arrive at a clearer understanding of how racist, patriarchal power structures continue to shape and influence the emotional politics of reproductive justice activism, as well as the everyday lives of women and abortion-seekers in Ireland, in a broader sense.

6

Changed Bodies? Life after Repeal

Refusing shame and the intersectional politics of cathartic breathing

Uncharacteristically for early Irish summer, Friday 25 May 2018, was bright, warm, and sunny. After a night of broken sleep, I woke early, and immediately turned on the radio to keep a close track of the day's events. The WhatsApp group I shared with my activist colleagues in County Carlow was abuzz with conversation. With nimble, eager fingers refreshing the Together for Yes Twitter page, we spent the morning engaged in a real-time commentary, dissecting each piece of referendum-related news as it slowly trickled through. Around mid-morning, Sinead – one of the local campaigners – shared an image in the WhatsApp group. The picture was of a single white rose and 'Tá' (Yes) badge attached to the outside. After casting her own vote, Sinead had brought the flower to the memorial for the survivors of the Magdalene Laundries in Graiguecullen Park, County Carlow. She placed it on a headstone which read: 'To the memory of all those who passed through the institutions in Ireland: may their injustice never be forgotten.'

Later that day, I travelled by train to Dublin, exchanging warm, anxious glances with fellow travellers sporting 'Yes' paraphernalia. By the time I arrived in Dublin in the late afternoon, there was a tentative but jubilant atmosphere in the city centre. Excitable bodies in Repeal jumpers spilled out from every cafe, restaurant, and bar. Later that evening, I joined my aunt in her home to watch the announcement of the results of the first exit poll which would be broadcast towards the end of the popular Friday-night talk show, *The Late Late Show*. Shortly after 10 o'clock, journalist Paul McCullagh revealed the results of two exit polls, one taken by national broadcaster RTÉ and the other carried out by the *Irish Times* newspaper; both of which reported a margin of victory of 68–69 per cent for the 'Yes' campaign (Leahy 2018). Thirty-five years after its insertion, it appeared that the electorate had chosen to remove Ireland's constitutional abortion ban by a resounding two-thirds majority.

From early in the afternoon on Saturday 26 May, large crowds gathered in the grounds of Dublin Castle – the former centre of colonial administration in Ireland – where the official referendum results were due to be announced. A large stage was set up where the co-directors of Together for Yes gathered to make speeches, joined by public figures like comedienne Tara Flynn and journalist Roisin Ingle (two women who were among the first to 'come out' to the Irish media with their abortion stories in the early 2010s). Peter Boylan (former Master of the National Maternity Hospital), as well as various politicians who had (some, rather belatedly) supported Repeal also joined the group on stage. Final tallies revealed that 1,429,981 votes were cast in favour of the proposal to repeal the 8th amendment, with 723,632 people voting to retain Article 40.3.3 of the Constitution (Leahy 2018).

My own memories of referendum day are a blur of anxiety, nerves, tears, and excitement, followed by relief, happiness, and finally, a deep sense of anti-climax. More than anything, I was completely and utterly exhausted; emotionally and physically. I cried all day on the 25th and the following day, as well. Nothing I did could stem the tears. My body was seeping, overflowing with everything I had been struggling to contain in the previous weeks and months. At the same time, I felt lighter; like somebody had taken a huge weight off my chest. A couple of months after the referendum, I wrote in a blog post for the Abortion Rights Campaign, then I felt my whole body 'decompress ... as though coming out of the brace position' (O'Shaughnessy 2019a). Reflecting on the mixed emotions I felt on referendum day, I was curious to know more about other activists' experiences of that fateful weekend. What did their physical and emotional experiences of referendum day tell us about the significance of the Repeal victory for women in Ireland? And what did their contradictory and sometimes unexpected bodily feelings tell us about the arguably complicated nature of the way in which campaign itself was won? During our meeting in December 2019, Clodagh – an activist in her late 20s who campaigned in the midlands region – recounted her experience of standing in the grounds of Dublin Castle on 26 May, when the official results of the vote were announced:

> 'It was around 6 o'clock because all the journalists on the stage were fidgeting. It was raining. And I'm going to try say this without crying. But this person next to me – everyone was putting their hoods up and this person said "Oh, it's like its washing our sins away" and I just took to sob. It was the most cathartic experience of my life. My friend was like "Do you wanna get under my umbrella?" and I was just like "No, I just wanna stand." ... So, I just stood in the rain, and it was an amazing experience. But I was so angry at the same time, all day, for the women who didn't get to have this. So, I met some friends from TFMR [Termination for Medical Reasons] and they were in great

form. But I remember being so angry for those people, that it was too late for them, you know? It was too late to circumvent their tragedy. So, I was upset for those people. But also happy, and it was a weird kind of happiness because I was so relieved and probably delirious from exhaustion as well.'

I was struck by the very visceral imagery of Clodagh standing in the rain in the grounds of Dublin Castle, an experience she described as one of the "most cathartic" of her life. I paused to reflect on her use of the word 'catharsis' itself, which on the one hand can signify a process of release of repressed emotions, and on the other hand, a process of bodily cleansing, purification, or purging. Listening to Clodagh describe the sensation of listening to the referendum results being read out, and feeling as though the rain was "washing [her] sins away", I began to wonder: what exactly were these 'sins' that Clodagh felt were finally being "washed away" by the rain in Dublin Castle on 26 May 2018?

Diarmuid Ferriter (2009) writes that in Ireland, sexuality has historically existed within a 'thematic of sin' (3). The sexual body was constructed as an object of guilt, secrecy, and shame and the denial of sexuality became central to the creation of the national body in the late 19th and early 20th century. As Ferriter (2009) explains, in the establishment of the Irish Free State, religious and national identity would be premised on the distinctive sexual purity and supposed virtuousness of Irish women, while the rigid control of women's reproduction served as an integral element in economic development. Those who 'lapsed', that is, who failed to perform sexual ascetism, were hidden away in workhouses, asylums, or religious institutions (Ferriter 2009, 5). As Tom Inglis writes, the gendered inequality of this sexual regime was justified by the argument that women were somehow more embodied, more 'saturated with sex' in comparison with their male counterparts (1998, 15–16). This sinful or shameful state could only be overcome for women through their assumption of the role of the 'chaste mother', which existed in diametrical opposition to the figure of the 'whore' (Inglis 1998, 15–16).

While this process of 'learning to interpret the body as a site of shame' may not necessarily be unique to Irish women, and can in fact be understood as part of a broader experience of gendered socialization, as described by feminist philosopher Luna Dolezal (2015, 106), what perhaps sets Ireland apart is the historical and systematic inculcation and weaponization of sexual shame as part of a conservative church–state apparatus intended to incarcerate and oppress women and to tightly regulate their reproductive functions, as part of a broader pro-natalist postcolonial project. Dolezal (2015) argues that the process of 'overcoming shame' is particularly important for women in the 'validation of subjectivity, both personally and politically' (2015, xv).

Coming back to Clodagh's testimony then, and her description of listening to the results of the referendum and feeling as though the water was "washing away her sins", the significance of the Repeal victory becomes clearer. The vote signified the removal (or perhaps, the refusal) of shame, the washing away of the original sin of simply being a woman, in Ireland.

Clodagh's testimony provides clues then as to the various meanings of the repeal victory, the first of which is the refusal of the historical and cultural construction of the gendered, reproductive body as a *shameful object*. Her testimony brings into focus as well some of the additional meanings that the pro-choice victory held across different generations and communities of Irish activists. As Enright (2018) describes, the 'Repeal' campaign existed as a 'floating signifier' that was 'appropriated, not only by campaigners for reproductive justice in the present, but by queers demanding bodily autonomy, disabled women insisting on being seen as adults with sexual and reproductive lives, older women asking for recognition of past historical abuses' (9). Clodagh lamented how the result came "too late" for people like her grandmother, who had spent a large portion of her life incarcerated in a Magdalene Laundry. Clodagh explained how, for her, voting 'Yes' was a way to acknowledge what her grandmother had experienced, even if her grandmother herself "might never make the connection".

Reflecting on the referendum campaign Mairead, too, spoke passionately about the intergenerational nature of Repeal activism (de Londras 2020). She explained how many of the women who she campaigned alongside had mothers who were also involved in anti–8th amendment organizing and activism in previous decades. Mairead explained how, for her, the referendum victory signified the removal of a specific burden that her (future) daughter would no longer be forced to carry. When I asked her about the wider significance of the repeal of the 8th amendment, she describes feeling as though there was a "weight gone off", for her and "for the next generation coming after us". I wasn't entirely sure what Mairead meant when she described this "weight" which was apparently "gone" now that the 8th amendment had been repealed. Perhaps, this word 'weight' was meant to signify the intensive bodily burden of 'abortion work' imposed on women and people who might become pregnant in Ireland under the 8th amendment (a burden which would certainly now be lessened, for many women, although perhaps not completely removed). Or perhaps with the term 'weight', Mairead intended to describe and invoke the specific gendered burden of 'shame' which had historically been forced upon and which worked to limit and constrain the bodies and lives of women and people who transgressed Ireland's strict sexual regime.

Interestingly, both Clodagh and Mairead characterize referendum day as having an almost spectral nature, in so far as it was marked by the 'absent-presence' of previous (and future) generations of Irish women and abortion-seekers (15). American sociologist Avery Gordon (2008) writes that 'spectres or ghosts appear when the trouble they represent and symptomize is no longer being contained or repressed or blocked from view' (xvi). The ghost Gordon (2008) identifies 'is not simply a dead or missing person, but a social figure', the analysis of which 'can lead to that dense site where history and subjectivity make social life' (8). Pertinently for this analysis, Gordon (2008) describes how 'ghostly matters' can 'haunt our bodies' (8). Haunting, she clarifies is 'one way in which abusive systems of power make themselves known ... especially ... when their oppressive nature is denied' (Gordon 2008, xvi). In the following excerpt, Mairead describes how, through the memorial which had been erected in her honour in Dublin city centre, referendum day was demarcated by the spectre of Ms Savita Halappanavar, who died after being denied a life-saving abortion in October 2012:

> 'I remember waking up the next day and just feeling that there was just a weight gone off, that we had done it. 'Cause as I said, an awful lot of the women that I had campaigned with, some of their mothers were campaigners against the 8th amendment when it was coming in. I remember lots of them were saying, I don't want my daughter still to be doing this. So, it felt like a weight off, it felt like we'd done something good for the next generation coming after us. One of my resounding memories of that time was going round to the memorial for Savita Halappanavaar that they had up at that stage. There were just strangers on the street, writing messages, hugging each other, crying and everything. I think it took a lot out of a lot of us, that we didn't realize till afterwards. There was a sense that you'd been holding your breath for too long, and then everything just came out in one flood of emotions. But there was definitely a thing when you sort of realized that, yeah, I'm getting back into my exercise routine, I'm getting back into this or that. And then it's like "Oh, my jaw isn't as sore as it used to be", it was like a tightly wound spring being released like.'

Mairead explains how, in the days and weeks following the referendum she felt a profound sense of relief which she experienced deep within her body as the alleviation of muscular aches and pains. Placing her hands to her face, she explains to me how she had realized that her jaw became less "sore" after the campaign, like a "tightly wound spring being released". Listening to Mairead, I was struck by the contrast between the apparent *temporality* of bodily life pre- and post-Repeal. As I explained in Chapter 3 with my analysis of 'abortion work', before the 8th amendment was repealed, women and gestating people in Ireland existed in a state of *anticipation*, labouring and orienting their bodies always towards the future, towards a potential crisis pregnancy. Mairead's testimony illustrates then how the release from this anticipatory state was experience on an embodied and affective level as a slow and tentative corporeal unfurling which brought with it a set of growing pains, as women like Mairead got used to bodily life released from the burden of the constitutional abortion ban.

Deploying similar terminology to Clodagh who related the "cathartic" experience of standing in the rain in Dublin Castle, Mairead describes the unstoppable surge of feelings flowing through her in the moment that the results of the referendum were announced, recounting how "everything just came out, in one flood of emotions". She explains being struck with the sense that she had, in fact, been "holding (her) breath" until that point. Listening to Mairead recount her memories of referendum day, I paused to think about this idea, as she described it, that she was able to *breathe differently* after the 8th amendment was repealed. This relationship between power and breath/breathing is one which has been intensively explored, particularly by Black and Indigenous feminist scholars analysing the bodily experience of racism (Moraga and Anzaldua 1983).

Reflecting on the 'I can't breathe' refrain associated with the Black Lives Matter movement, Gabriel Apata writes how air plays a central role in the operation of contemporary racism. Apata contrasts how, while under slavery, the Black body was the direct object of explicit violence, degradation, and dehumanization, contemporary racism functions 'from a distance', via 'mediated systems, structures and institutions' which slowly and methodically suffocate Black bodies (2020, 245). Apata explains how 'the lack of basic healthcare provision or Medicare, poor housing, unemployment, inadequate education' together 'make up the social air that suffocates, chokes, strangulates, asphyxiates, and finally kills' Black communities (2020, 246). In his research on the 'suffocating nature of racism', Apata reminds us that 'air is foundational to life' (2020, 242). Not only does air 'represent freedom', Apata explains, but it is also 'the embodiment of freedom – not freedom from something but freedom to be, to live' (2020, 243).

Apata distinguishes between 'different kinds of airs' including 'cosmic or ecological air' which 'is linked to climate change and environmental pollution'; 'biological air' which 'relates to personal health and various pathologies'; and finally, 'social air' which 'revolves around political and socio-economic conditions of life, relating to questions of value opposites that include freedom and bondage or incarceration' (2020, 243). While Apata contends that air may be regarded as a 'universal entity', he urges us to keep in mind that 'some of us breathe a better quality of air than others' (247). Specifically, he argues, 'white people ... breathe a different kind of air: a cleaner, lighter, purer air of inherent privileges that society bestows' (2020, 247). Muireann also deployed air and breathing related metaphors to describe the experience of listening to the announcement of the referendum results. As she spoke, she took a deep breath and exhaled slowly, letting her shoulders drop:

> 'In Head Office ... there was a load of people I hadn't even seen all week 'cause we were all coming and going, so seeing them and just crying. ... It was just like this valve and it was like "gguuuuhhhh". I think that's my abiding feeling, just relief and that it was so definitive ... Everything just hanging on these words that someone is gonna read out and then it was like this valve just opening, it was this [deep breath] "Oh thank god!" ... It sounds a bit woolly but the fact that it was mostly women, nearly entirely women and that feeling that we were all connected in terms of what it meant for our bodies, whether or not we'd ever had an abortion.'

Describing how herself and her activist colleagues were "all connected in terms of what it meant for our bodies", Muireann suggests that the repeal of the 8th amendment would usher some sort of transformation in her everyday bodily life and in the everyday embodied experiences of her activist colleagues. I noted the word 'valve', which Muireann used twice in describing her memories of referendum day. After our meeting, I looked up the definition of the word. The Cambridge Dictionary defines valve as 'a device that controls the flow of air or liquid from one place to another'.[1] Valves work by partially obstructing a passageway, to change or control the amount of liquid or gas that can flow through it. When a valve opens, gas or liquid flows in a direction from higher pressure to lower pressure. For people with respiratory diseases, valves can be inserted into the lungs to reroute away from damaged tissue, helping patients to breathe easier. Etymologically, the English word 'valve' can be traced to the Latin *valva* which indicates one 'leaf' (or section) of a set of double or 'folding' doors.[2]

Describing their joyful inhalation and exhalation on referendum day, Mairead and Muireann's testimonies serve as further evidence of the fact that breathing is 'not just a metaphor' but a 'process that manifests current power relations' (Górska 2021, 116). I was particularly fixated with one detail of Mairead's account; her description of the activists gathering in their droves at the memorial to Savita Halappanavar, erected on a wall near the George Bernard Shaw pub in Dublin's south inner-city. The mural dedicated to Ms Halappanavar had become a focal point for Repeal campaigners in the weeks prior to the referendum, with activists gathering there to write messages of gratitude, remorse, and apology to Ms Halappanavar and her family. Feminist legal scholar Ruth Fletcher (2018) writes that remembering those who had been 'the subjects of reproductive injustices' can operate as a way to 'bring them into the narrative of Repeal as a form of restoration' (249). In relation to the memorializing of Ms Halappanavar, however, Fletcher (2018) cites the words of Emily Waszack (co-founder of the group Migrants and Ethnic Minorities for Reproductive Justice) who poignantly observes that the mural served as a 'visceral reminder' of the 'physical manifestation of white tears' covering over 'a brown migrant woman and her pain' (Fletcher 2018, 242).

Reflecting on the outpourings of grief at Ms Halappanavar's mural on referendum day, Fletcher (2018) pushes us to question why it is that certain (racialized) bodies only 'come into our vision as a sequence of cadavers' (242). Indeed, given the well-documented criticism of the marginalization of the voices and experiences of women and activists of colour in the Together for Yes campaign, there was something deeply uncomfortable, I thought, in the iconizing of this one-dimensional *image* of a dead Brown woman, who, because of her death within a violent, racist, misogynistic Irish healthcare service, was ultimately unable to speak back. Why was it, I wondered, that the campaign seemed comfortable with engaging with women of colour, only when those women existed as objects of grief or pity? Perhaps, the gathering of activist bodies in front of Ms Halappanavar's mural is further evidence of the learned racial positioning of White Irish people, as sociologist Ronit Lentin describes, conditioned to regard Black and Brown people as 'passive victims' who can 'only be saved' (or not saved, in this case) by the 'good offices' of White Irish people (Lentin 2004, 303).

Describing 'feminist breathing' as 'a set of rituals for living through the foreclosure of political presents and futures', queer theorist Jean-Thomas Tremblay (2019) explains how 'feminists train themselves to keep inhaling without the certainty that there will be a world to welcome their exhalation' (94). Contrasting the 'vigorous breathing' of White feminist consciousness-raising groups in the late 20th century with the laboured breathing of women of colour activists confronted with unwelcoming White feminist spaces, Tremblay (2019) reaffirms the connection between racism and the politics of breath (94). Drawing upon the work of Chicana feminist scholar Cherríe Moraga (1983), Tremblay (2019) highlights how 'the ability to experience cathartic breathing' is 'a matter of privilege' (95). The capacity for some women to 'breathe deeply and to laugh, moan and cry, all of which compress and extend the airways', Tremblay (2019) maintains, is often 'contingent on the concealment of the breathing needs of women of colour' (95).

Returning then to the hordes of activists gathered at the memorial wall for Savita Halappanavar on referendum day, we are forced to think again about this uncomfortable juxtaposition of the cathartic breathing of those predominantly White bodies gathered there and the breathlessness of Ms Halappanavar whose death six years earlier resulted directly from the pernicious enmeshment of the 8th amendment inside of a racist, misogynistic Irish healthcare regime. Perhaps this image of the jubilant, ecstatic breathing of White activists outside of Ms Halappanavar's mural gives us a new way to reconceptualize the repeal of the 8th amendment then. Staying with these metaphors of breathing and breath, we can reconceptualize the repeal of the 8th amendment as the opening of a valve – where the valve in question is not simply a device regulating the control of air, but borrowing from the original Latin, a set of doors. These doors open and close to facilitate the movement or *release* of certain bodies. At the same time, they continue to curtail the movement of other (Othered?) bodies, refusing to let these other bodies breathe easily or pass freely through.

Healing the sores of the protest body: challenging activist burnout

> Anyway sometimes changing the world means you end up with PTSD, and sometimes if you have PTSD that means you need to go on a really long walk, for a really long time, with no internet, no instagram or anything, just shut yourself off and get away from all the noise and the posters and the Claire Byrne Live and just be with nature and birds and fresh air, just like heal, you know? Just like, process. Am I allowed to say PTSD … is that even what this is … I'll need to google that. (Needham 2019; reproduced with permission of the author)

So goes the introductory monologue of Irish author and actor Miriam Needham's play entitled *Compostela*, written in 2019. Needham's play explores the aftermath of the repeal of the 8th amendment through the lens of the experience one activist, Dawn, as she walks the length of the Camino de Santiago in Spain. *Compostela* grapples deftly with complicated nature of feminist activism and examines themes including activist burnout and the appropriation of the labour (and victory) of grassroots abortion activists by the political establishment. The sore feet, the fatigue which Dawn struggles against on her hike are emblematic of the challenges of the 'Yes' campaigners, who put their bodies on the line for the pro-choice victory. In particular, Needham wrestles with the sticky emotional politics of the movement and the sense of unease and discomfort which many activists were left with in the aftermath of the vote.

Drawing upon auto-ethnographic data gathered during her own involvement in the student protest movement in Canada in the mid-2010s, Hannah Quinn (2018) describes how activist bodies are 'profoundly changed' through the protest experience (62). Quinn (2018) argues that the 'embodied experience of protest produces and reveals different embodied inscriptions' (58). The 'legacy' of our protest activity remains in the body Quinn (2018) clarifies in a physical sense, as 'scars and wounds, muscles that are quick to tighten under threat, muscles that are tired and sore, dark circles under my eyes' (58, 63). By analysing our protest bodies 'in relation to one another', Quinn (2018) maintains, we can better understand how we 'embody social suffering and violence in distinctly different ways throughout the protest process' (58). Nuala, a lesbian student activist in her mid 20s, recounted the sheer physical toll that campaigning had taken on her body as well as the complicated emotional experience of the referendum victory itself:

'It wasn't a feeling for me anyway, it wasn't a feeling of joy ... it wasn't ... a lot of excitement, it wasn't anything. It wasn't like that. Whereas I suppose marriage referendum would have been all of those feelings. But this was very much ... relief. It was relief and it was exhaustion ... it was "Thank God it's over". Because the day we finished campaigning and canvassing, I ended up at home from complete exhaustion. I got into the car after dinner, after last leaflet drop. I got really sick and had to go to bed when I came home. I got really really sick; I was completely exhausted. And I was dehydrated and everything. So, it wasn't a feeling of joy, or even ... it was very much for me anyway just pure relief that thank God it's over ... like, thank God it's actually repealed and ... you know, if it hadn't have passed, how many years more would we have been waiting for another referendum on it? So, when it came out it was just a feeling of "It wasn't all for nothing".'

Like many of the activists I interviewed, Nuala connected and compared the experience of her involvement in the 2015 same-sex marriage referendum with her experience in the 2018 abortion rights campaign. Nuala, herself a member of the LGBTQIA+ community, recalls the 2015 referendum as entailing great "joy" and "excitement". By contrast, she explains, the 2018 referendum on abortion rights "wasn't like that". Instead, the dominant feelings Nuala recalls are those of "exhaustion" and "relief". The word 'relief', coming from the Anglo-French *relif*, indicates 'that which mitigates or removes' and stems from the Latin *relevare* which means 'to raise' or 'lighten'.[3] Again, Nuala seemed to be pointing to this idea of the experience of the repeal of the 8th amendment as being akin to the removal of some type of weight, or of a burdensome, embodied restriction.

Interestingly, Nuala was just one of several activists who told me how they became "really sick" in the immediate aftermath of the referendum campaign; again, demonstrating how activism entails great bodily commitment and investment, as well as the risk of bodily vulnerability (Sutton 2007). As alluded to earlier, several of the activists I interviewed recounted the intense exhaustion or 'burnout', as some of them described it, which they experienced in the weeks and months following the referendum. The topic of activist 'burnout' is receiving increasing attention in social movement scholarship (Chen and Gorski 2015). Activist burnout is defined by Chen and Gorski as a 'chronic condition' which can result in those 'once highly committed to a movement or cause' losing 'the idealism and spirit' that once motivated their political engagement (2015, 368). Activist burnout can manifest in a multitude of ways, they explain, including through 'depression and anxiety', 'health challenges' such as 'headaches, high blood pressure, and illnesses' as well as 'increased feelings of alienation and despondency' (Schaufeli and Buunk 2002 in Chen and Gorski 2015, 369).

In her 2021 book *Repealed: Ireland's Unfinished Fight for Reproductive Rights*, adult and community education scholar Camila Fitzsimons dedicates several pages to the discussion of burnout in the post-Repeal activist landscape. Via a combination of online surveys and in-person interviews, Fitzsimons's (2021) research gathers testimony from 405 canvassers involved in the Together for Yes campaign to analyse 'their memories of the campaign, their thoughts on abortion services today, and their levels of activism two years on' (208). Fitzsimons (2021) identifies burnout as a key reason why 'one-third' of activists have 'disengaged' from reproductive rights activism in the aftermath of the 2018 campaign (148). Fitzsimons's (2021) participants highlight the damaging effects of trying to live up to the image of 'the ideal activist' who 'is able to prioritize "the cause" over everything else' (150). This idea is particularly impactful for women, Fitzsimons (2021) describes, who are 'supposed to hold down a job, give quality time to kids, be fully in control of their reproductive health and pick up the slack in terms of elder care and domestic responsibilities' (150).

In her testimony, documented here, Eimear recounts the intensity of the 'burnout' she experienced after the conclusion of the Repeal the 8th campaign, explaining that it took her "about a year to recover" from the referendum. Eimear's testimony seems to indicate that part of the reason that activists were so 'burnt out' following the conclusion of the 2018 campaign was due to the divisions which ensued across the activist community and between different groups who disagreed, among other things, with the tactics and strategies adopted by Together for Yes. Eimear explained how a similar split had occurred in 1983, between the more radical faction of the abortion rights movement, as she described it, who wanted to advocate for the legalization of abortion forthright and those who mobilized specifically against the insertion of the 8th amendment. She stated:

'I was exhausted. And I was also very exhilarated. I mean I'm not a leader in my own head and I've never really led a campaign. To have that responsibility of making those decisions, it took me about a year to recover to be honest with you, I'm only now back to myself . I'm disappointed that there was a split. I'm really disappointed about that because its woman against woman. I'm really disappointed about that. And social media, which wasn't there when I was your age … I'm heartbroken actually to see that it's not kind of bringing feminists together. I'm not saying that the campaign split feminism, I don't think it did, but it highlighted differences.'

When I asked Eimear to explain the causes of this split in the abortion activist movement, as she perceived it, she recounted that much of the disagreement was in relation to "things around intersectionality". Indeed, a split did occur (or perhaps widen) after the conclusion of the Repeal the 8th campaign, specifically between those groups who had been directly involved in the design, leading, and management of the official referendum campaign, and other grassroots groups. As described in Chapter 6, Migrants and Ethnic Minorities for Reproductive Justice were vocally critical of the 'Yes' campaign both during and after the referendum, arguing that the proposed legislation and provision system would leave behind many migrant and ethnic minority groups as well as working-class and disabled women and people (MERJ 2019). Migrants and Ethnic Minorities for Reproductive Justice point specifically to the barriers created by the 12-week gestational limit, the lack of second-trimester abortions (which could leave those without the economic means or necessary travel documents forced to continue unwanted pregnancies), and the lack of information and assistance made available to asylum-seekers in Direct Provision centres, among other factors.

In her study, Fitzsimons (2021) explains how the concept of care emerged as a 'controversial area' in the activist community post-Repeal (151). Despite this, she explains how some activist groups have taken steps to address burnout within their communities. During our interview, Shauna described the actions taken by herself and her activist colleagues in the aftermath of the 'Yes' campaign to deal with the intense levels of burnout many of them were experiencing. Within their activist network, Shauna and her colleagues had set up workshops on the topic of "communal aid", to work out resources and strategies for carrying out caring and reproductive labour, in an effort to carve out periods of respite for activists so that they could recover from the burnout they experienced after the referendum campaign:

'Three months after the Repeal campaign, I was in hospital for three weeks. It nearly killed me. You're working, you're studying, daily life, meetings. You keep moving, moving. You're not doing this for appreciation, because you want your name somewhere. The reason you're doing it is because there's someone worse off than you. When someone worse than you reaches out, there's nothing you can do. So, no it's not a choice. We don't have a choice. We take turns and we actually developed these workshops, on communal aid. 'Cause we need each other but we need to be OK. As women, that we take emotional labour, physical labour, caring labour, reproductive labour, we take all the labour in the fucking world and how to say "How are you?", "How can we help for you to come back?" We need your brains, your power. And to be strong with the criticism that comes your way.'

Listening to Shauna explain how the referendum "nearly killed" her, how she had to "keep moving, moving" because there's "someone worse off than you", I reflected upon the 'sacrificial' nature of the activist body as she described it. I wondered whether and in what ways this idea of the 'sacrificial' activist body might operate similarly or differently to the idea of the 'sacrificial' body of the Irish mother-martyr figure (O'Shaughnessy 2021)? Was reproductive activism becoming yet another arena in which women were expected to martyr themselves or to sacrifice their bodies and material needs for some sort of greater good? Studying 'burnout' in social justice organizing, Chen and Gorski (2015) identify a 'culture of martyrdom' which is often present in activist circles and to which activists are expected to 'comply' (379). In many activist spaces, Chen and Gorski (2015) argue, activists are conditioned to believe that engagement in any sort of 'self-care' is self-indulgent and demonstrates a lack of commitment to the cause (379).

Hearing Shauna's testimony, I began to consider how reproductive justice activism itself is not immune to the assumption of unequal reproductive norms. In many ways, abortion activism is yet another area of social life within which the key organizing principle remains the assumed, inherent, and incessant 'corporeal generosity' of women and feminine bodies (Diprose 2002 in Hird 2007, 2). As Hird (2007) explains, however, while processes of 'embodied "gifting"' entail the possibility of 'threatening the integrity of bodies', they equally furnish opportunity for 'opening up new possibilities' in terms of how gendered, reproductive bodies give and take from one another (2). I recalled Shauna's account of the communal aid workshop she had developed with her fellow activists in their reproductive justice organizing group in response to their experience of collective burnout.

Shauna's testimony also serves as an important reminder of how reproductive autonomy continues to be withheld from large swathes of the population, under Ireland's new abortion provision system. On Thursday 20 December 2018, President Michael D. Higgins signed the Health (Regulation of Termination of Pregnancy) Bill 2018 into law, paving the way for the introduction of legal systematic abortion provision for the first time in the history of the state. Services were scheduled to begin as of 1 January 2019, via GPs, family planning services, and at several hospitals across the country. The new law would provide for abortion only on three conditions: up to 12 weeks on request, and up to 24 weeks in the cases of medical emergencies, in cases of fatal foetal anomaly, and where there is a 'risk to the life, or of serious harm to the health' of the pregnant person (Health (Regulation of Termination of Pregnancy) Act 2018).

Ireland's new system of abortion provision was envisioned as a 'community model of care', which would be embedded primarily within 'existing primary care infrastructure' (Mishtal et al 2022, 5). Medical practitioners were invited to 'sign-up' to provide abortion care, which would be delivered predominantly in GP surgeries. This system of allowing practitioners to 'opt-in' quickly produced a sort of postcode lottery of abortion access in Ireland, which primarily disenfranchised rural abortion-seekers (ARC and Grimes 2021). In late 2018, masters of three of the country's maternity hospitals wrote to the Minister for Health expressing concern as to the 'readiness' of the Health Service to successfully implement the new law (McCrave 2019). Indeed, hospital settings were particularly slow about signing-up to provide abortion care. As of March 2024, 17 out of the 19 maternity hospitals in the country offer medical terminations, 12 out of the 19 provide surgical abortion care, and only 3 hospitals in the country offer all three legal methods – surgical, medical, and manual vacuum aspiration (Griffin 2024). Disparities in hospital-based provision are particularly problematic for the delivery of emergency abortion care, as well as later gestational abortions, and creates a knock-on effect for referral services from primary to secondary care settings (Duffy et al 2023).

Writing in early 2020, legal scholar Fiona de Londras (2020) offered a 'cautionary accent to celebratory discourses of Repeal' (35). Explaining the 'shortcomings' of the Health (Regulation of Termination of Pregnancy) Act 2018, de Londras (2020) argued that 'post-repeal abortion law reform was more about managing risk than maximising agency' (33). De Londras (2020) clarifies that the new legislative regime remains 'foetocentric' in nature and that, as a result, pregnant people continue to be exposed to 'constitutional and dignity harms' and to 'lack decisional security' in the post-Repeal legal landscape (33). Mairead Enright (2018) offers a similarly critical analysis of the provisions of the Health (Regulation of Termination of Pregnancy) Act 2018, and reminds us how Together for Yes 'said as little as possible about the legislation or about the possible shape of future constitutional law' during the referendum campaign in 2018 (7).

Drawing upon her own experience as part of the campaign, Enright (2018) clarifies that many activists felt that they were 'over a barrel' – in no position to refuse the proposed law (7). As a result, Enright (2018) explains, 'securing speedy passage' of abortion legislation 'began to take priority over its content' (7). Reflecting on the first year of provision under the Health Act 2018, the Abortion Rights Campaign celebrated that 'the clear majority of those who need an abortion' were able to 'receive this essential healthcare at home', adding, however, that the new legislation 'has left people behind', particularly rural and disabled abortion-seekers, as well as migrants and asylum seekers with limited mobility rights, as well as those with limited access to economic and infrastructural resources (ARC 2020, para 4). In

December 2020, I spoke with Deirdre, who had been involved in the official referendum campaign. I asked her about her views on the Health Act 2018 and the current provision of services. She replied:

'I'm not that well placed to speak to it, because really I'm just repeating what other people have said to me, I'm not actually involved in provision. And I'm not doing any evidence gathering at all in terms of people's experiences of it. But from talking to people, the ground has shifted entirely, like it's wonderful. We've walked into a whole new world in terms of access, it is working. It is working well. I mean, in Ireland, we're so small. You know so we're just never going to have to deal with issues that you're gonna have in much bigger countries or in larger states, you know, where people have to travel hundreds and hundreds of miles, because you just can't do that here. And over the years, we've looked at a lot of global activists and a lot of the problems that they've dealt with so it's with that perspective, we always knew, that even if we only had access in Dublin, that would deal with the vast majority of people. And I mean, that's obviously not good enough, you need to have local access. But with the GP piece, in the main, there is local access available. There are still some pockets, but they're working through them. They are getting there.'

I was struck by Deirdre's assertion that Ireland is "so small" and "even if we only had access in Dublin" that this would be adequate to deal with the needs of the "the vast majority" of abortion-seekers. At the conference I had attended the week previously, organized by the Leitrim branch of the Abortion Rights Campaign, the sparse geographic provision of services had been earmarked as a huge obstacle for rural abortion-seekers, those living in Direct Provision Centres and for people with disabilities unable to avail of the already limited national public transport services.

Listening to Deirdre, it became increasingly evident, not only that the bodily costs of organizing, evidenced for example in the high levels of burnout across the activist community post-Repeal, have been unequally distributed across and between abortion activist groups; but that the repeal of the 8th amendment – while widely celebrated among the various factions of the pro-choice community in Ireland – held radically different meanings and had different practical consequences for these diverse groups.

Indeed, while for many women and people who may become pregnant, the repeal of the constitutional abortion ban was experienced as the removal of a unique 'spectre', of an embodied burden, or of a condition of gendered vulnerability, there is no doubt that for individuals from marginalized backgrounds, there are other 'spectres' or burdens (apart from the 8th amendment itself) which continue to haunt their experience of reproductive healthcare, and which continue to impose on them additional embodied burdens (AIMS Ireland 2017). The spectre of the disproportionate maternal morbidity rate for ethnic minority women, for example, which stands at a fourfold difference for those from Black and ethnic minority backgrounds and at an almost twofold difference for those from Asian backgrounds (Masheti 2021). Or the spectre of criminalization for those who do not qualify for an abortion under the narrow confines of the Health Act 2018, and who do not have the money or documentation required to travel abroad, thus being forced to attempt self-abortion, by purchasing abortion pills.

In this vein, this analysis illustrates the importance of continuing to pay attention to the emotional and physical toll of activism on our differently gendered, racialized, and classed bodies, in order to understand the subjective and collective consequences of concessionary 'respectability' tactics, but also so that we might better appreciate how regimes of reproductive coercion often cannot be dismantled in one fell swoop but, instead, change shape and sustain themselves in more diffuse and nefarious forms, often at the expense of those who already the most marginalized in our communities.

The 'embodied consequences' of abortion activism

In the weeks preceding the 8th amendment referendum, media articles had predicted a 'muted, sombre' acknowledgement in the event of a repeal victory (Finn 2018). Instead, 26 May 2018, saw the grounds of Dublin Castle filled with triumphant activists and voters singing, dancing, and waving flags and placards. Letters sent to the office of the Taoiseach, Leo Varadkar, and the Minister for Health, Simon Harris, in the weeks following the vote expressed outrage at Mr Varadkar's and Mr Harris's participation in what was deemed an 'inappropriate' display of jubilation regarding the introduction of legal abortion on Irish shores (Hourihane 2018). Such efforts to tone-police the celebrations of the 'Yes' campaign continued into referendum weekend. As Muireann discusses, in refusing to pander to demands to hold back on celebrations, activists laid down their intention to throw off the yoke of respectability which they had been burdened with throughout the entirety of the referendum campaign:

'There'd been all this "Oh no you can't celebrate" and "It wouldn't be appropriate to celebrate". And then people just being like "My body, I'll celebrate if I want to!" and this feeling of like, dancing and casting off that restriction that had been there, for the months beforehand but also, for your whole lifetime. Having to be ashamed of your body and having to hide it away and just being like … it totally changed how I felt about my body, in a way I never expected. And it took me a while to figure out afterwards, like … a few of us met up the 27th or

28th and I remember thinking, we all looked different. Probably the relief, but we all just seemed to carry ourselves differently, and I felt different, but I didn't know how to articulate it 'cause it sounded a bit weird in my head. And I remember saying it to a friend of mine and she was like "Oh yeah, I'm the same, I feel lighter" so yeah, just like freer or lighter or something. So yeah, I think just having a place where we were all together to party and dance was so important … I'm proud of what we did, repealing the 8th was a good thing. It wasn't done perfectly … but it was fundamentally a good thing to get rid of that from the constitution … to not have future generations of women growing up with that feeling, that their body is written into the Constitution.'

Recounting her memories of the referendum, Muireann explains how her activist experience "completely changed how (she) felt about (her) body". She juxtaposes the experience of openly celebrating the referendum results through activities like dancing, with the way in which she previously would have felt "ashamed" of her body and would have felt compelled to "hide" her body away. Britt and Heise (2000) explain how the experience of shame compels the subject to participate in 'hiding behaviours', while pride, on the other hand, facilitates greater engagement with 'expansive' bodily conduct in public space (253–254). Moreover, they explain how the *collective* engagement of social movement actors in 'expansive' bodily behaviour in public space contributes to the creation of an affective atmosphere of pride (Britt and Heise 2000, 253). In this vein, it becomes clear why activists like Muireann felt it was important for Repeal campaigners to "have a place" where they could "be together to party and dance". Not only did the physicality of the celebrations provide a mode of catharsis for activists; it constituted a final act of 'coming out' for Repeal activists, allowing them to define their bodies in *their own terms*, not as objects of shame, but as sources of power, pride, and even pleasure.

I wanted to know more about the ways in which Muireann's everyday life and bodily experiences had changed since the referendum. After pausing to reflect on my question, Muireann recounted meeting with fellow campaigners in the days following the vote and noting how they all "looked different" and seemed to "carry (themselves) differently". Muireann makes sense of this transformation by describing it as the embodied manifestation of the "relief" they all felt after the campaign victory. Reminiscent of Mairead's description of the repeal of the 8th amendment as the removal of a "weight", Muireann reflects on how both she and her colleagues felt "lighter" after the referendum. Muireann contrasts this "lighter", "freer" feeling with a previous state of being wherein she felt that her body was "written into the Constitution". The phrasal verb 'to write into' indicates a process of 'adding' something (usually a rule or condition) to an agreement, contract, or law.[4] Describing her understanding of the fact that her body had been "written into the Constitution" through the 8th amendment, Muireann (re)invokes the intimate connection between the feminized, reproductive body and the Irish nation-building project – wherein the targeted reproductive coercion of specific gendered and racialized bodies becomes a condition for the construction of the nation-state (Yuval-Davis 1997).

Listening to Muireann's testimony, I reflected again upon about how the referendum victory appeared to translate into the removal of a set of *embodied restrictions* or the elimination of a *blockage* which affected the literal movement of Muireann's body-in-space. Referring to the celebrations which took place on the night of 26 May, Muireann goes so far as to describe the experience of dancing with her comrades as a physical "casting off" of a set of constraints she had experienced not only in "the months beforehand" (presumably, referring to the limitations that had been placed upon campaigners by the 'Yes' campaign in terms of how they should comport themselves with members of the public) but throughout her "whole lifetime". After our interview, I thought further about Muireann's analogy of "growing up with that feeling" of having your body "written into the Constitution". I envisioned my own body being physically held down onto a page; wrestling against a string of words which wrangle their way around my neck and limbs, prohibiting my movement, holding me firmly in place.

Speaking to Aoibhinn, I asked her as well to describe the ways in which her everyday experience had been transformed since the referendum. She spoke in similar terms to Muireann, explaining how she felt that was able to literally *move through the world differently* now that the 8th amendment had been repealed. As I discussed in Chapter 1, Aoibhinn described how, prior to the referendum, she "always had the abortion fund in the bank" or "the ability to get that loan out of the Credit Union". She described how she always felt "a bit scared" and would siphon money aside as an emergency fund which she could draw on if she needed to travel to England to access an abortion there. Further comparing her everyday life and her feelings about her body before and after the 2018 referendum, she described how she used to feel a sense of "constriction and capture". I wanted to know more about whether and in what ways these feelings and experiences had been transformed now that the 8th amendment had been banished to the annals. She explained:

> 'Yes, like before the campaign, before I was even aware of it, I always felt these hands on my body, and I was always a bit scared … Like, that feeling of constriction and capture and hands on me. That knowledge that people were protected by law to do whatever they wanted to my

body. They could section me. Like, I have a mental health history, it's not an exaggeration, it's not unreal to say that I could be raped and then sectioned to be forced to continue a pregnancy. Like, if I was incarcerated, the reality of those things were with me all the time. I texted somebody on the 26th to say "I'm walking around town like fucking Kanye" 'cause it was like, "Come at me!" do you know? I'm protected.'

Recalling life under the 8th amendment, Aoibhinn described being constantly burdened with "the reality" of the fact that she could be "sectioned" or "incarcerated" and that "people were protected by law to do whatever they wanted to my body". Indeed, as explained in Chapter 1, the 8th amendment was directly transposed into the Health Service Executive's National Consent Policy (de Londras and Enright 2018). This meant that upon becoming pregnant, medical practitioners were entitled to make interventions 'on behalf' of the foetus, without the consent of or in contravention of the wishes of the pregnant person (de Londras and Enright 2018, 2). Doctors were permitted to force-feed or perform unwanted medical procedures on pregnant people, wherever these interventions were considered necessary to protect the life of the 'unborn'.

Recounting how this reality was "with (her) all the time", Aoibhinn reinvokes the relentlessness of the felt burden of reproductive oppression under the constitutional abortion ban. Her testimony is important because it forces us to (re)consider the subtle, nefarious but far-reaching effects of anti-abortion laws which have consequences not only in the moment wherein access to abortion is sought and denied, but which can create conditions which directly shape the everyday physical and emotional experience of the gestational subject. In the same way as the concept of 'abortion work' pushes us to expand the *temporal framework* within which we conceptualize reproductive violence, Aoibhinn's comparison of her embodied and affective life pre- and post-Repeal again highlights the diffuse temporality of reproductive inequality as it operates via anti-abortion laws, but also points to the broader meaning of abortion activism in terms of the potential *embodied consequences* of reproductive justice movements.

Referring specifically to her bodily experience under the 8th amendment, then, Aoibhinn's testimony illustrates how, in an environment wherein abortion is systematically inaccessible, such as Ireland, the reproductive body (or, the potentially pregnant/pre-pregnant body) comes to be experienced as a 'fragile encumberance' or a 'burden, which must be dragged along, and at the same time *protected*' (Young 1980, 147, my emphasis). Aoibhinn describes how this experience was transformed, however, in the aftermath of the referendum. Sitting up in her chair and puffing her chest outwards, Aoibhinn explained how, the day after the vote, she was "walking around town like Kanye". As she spoke, she demonstrated this walk, feigning steps and raising her arms before swinging them, exaggeratedly, from side to side.

Listening to Aoibhinn, I was reminded of feminist phenomenologist Iris Marion Young's (1980) description of 'feminine existence' as characterized by the 'failure to make use of lateral space' (137). Feminine embodiment, Young argues, is defined by 'inhibited intentionality', with women failing to 'put their whole bodies into engagement' (Young 1980, 145). Aoibhinn's account illustrates how the repeal of the 8th amendment transformed the literal, physical experience of how she, as a gendered, subject-body, moves through the world. Henceforth, her quotidian embodied experience was characterized, not by the sense of "capture and constriction" (as she described to me when recounting her experience of growing up under the 8th amendment) but by an openness, an expansiveness and intentionality that she had not previously felt.

What Aoibhinn and her colleagues are describing here then is how, through their activism, Repeal campaigners successfully transformed their *embodied experience of the world* and, specifically, the literal *movement of their bodies-in-space*. Moreover, they transformed how they *felt about their bodies*, thereby reconstructing themselves as *embodied subjects*. In the following excerpt, Muireann describes how her involvement in the Repeal the 8th campaign caused her to reflect upon and to thematize other aspects of her quotidian embodied experience in a more explicit fashion. She describes how she began to reconceptualize reproductive rights as a "very physical thing" which signified what people or society "think is OK" to "do to your body". Muireann explains how her involvement in the abortion rights movement helped her to "connect the dots" and to make sense of the other forms of bodily objectification and gendered or reproductive violence that women and feminized people in Ireland face:

> 'I think … growing up, when you become aware of reproductive rights, it's a very physical thing 'cause it's about your body and what people think is OK, so I think it made me aware of wider issues of how women's bodies are treated in society and the low-level kind of casual sexual assault, cat-calling, the commodification of women's bodies that we experience our entire lives. So, it kind of made me join up those dots in a lot of ways, and the shame that surrounded my body and women's bodies my entire life, and then realizing that there could be another way, realizing that that didn't have to be the way. So, I think it was a feeling that my body had been under attack, for the duration of the campaign, but also my entire life as a woman, so realizing that, but also realizing that my body had also gotten me through this incredibly tense, difficult period … and you can see it in photos we took on the 26th of May, we just look so gaunt. Just these

caverns under our eyes, everyone had lost so much weight. We just looked like physical wrecks. So, the feeling that my body had been under attack but also the feeling that my body had gotten me through, and we had gotten through it together. We had walked past those posters together, and we had come out the other side, and I wasn't going to be ashamed of it anymore.'

Explaining how herself and her colleagues "had lost so much weight" and were "physical wrecks" in the weeks following the referendum, Muireann demonstrates how the process of social transformation is a 'collective, embodied' project which requires 'hard work' and an intensive 'investment of bodily resources' (Sutton 2007, 144). Importantly, Muireann's testimony exemplifies the important role of the gendered body in the movement for abortion rights in Ireland, but also signifies how political activity around abortion rights allowed campaigners an opportunity to challenge or reconceptualize their own perceptions of their embodied capabilities. Recounting her experience of regularly being forced to walk past or encounter violent anti-abortion imagery, Muireann explains how while she felt that one on hand, her body had "been under attack" through the campaign, she suddenly recognized that it was her body which had also "gotten (her) through this incredibly, tense, difficult period".

In this way, Muireann describes how her activism helped her to develop a greater sense of confidence or trust within her body. Interestingly, Muireann's testimony illustrates how, while she continued to understand her body as an *object* of surveillance and violence (which was consistently "under attack"), as a result of her activist experience, she came to appreciate and understand her body in relation to its capacity to engage in acts of resistance or social change (Young 1980). In other words, Muireann no longer understood her body purely as an object, but instead recognized her agency and political subjectivity in its embodied state. This idea of 'split subjectivity', that is, experiencing the body as subject and object at the same time, is typical of the experience of feminine embodiment according to Young (49).

Blathnaid also spoke at length about how her involvement in the Repeal the 8th campaign changed the way that she related to her body. Specifically, Blathnaid explained how her activism endowed her with a greater degree of *confidence* in her bodily capacities, specifically increasing her awareness of the fact that she could harness her labour to change society and the cultural landscape. Like Muireann, Blathnaid emphasizes how the material labour performed by the activist body is so imperative to processes of social change. She situates the work of the Repeal the 8th movement in the context of a longer history of abortion activism and women's rights organizing in Ireland and makes a point to indicate the transnational connections and consequences of the Irish abortion rights campaign, which she says has had a "ripple effect" across the world.

> 'It felt like I was on fire. It felt like I was unstoppable. I was fierce and I was probably the most confident I've ever been ... it was that confidence and I still feel it, I still feel it here [points to chest] it's not left. It's still there, it's still resounding and it's in my chest. And it fuelled me and it's still fuelling me ... I looked around and I genuinely felt like the world had changed. And I had contributed to that change, and I had harnessed my labour – organizing and trying to get more and more people involved – I felt like I had the power to harness the labour of others, to achieve that change. Not just to work super hard, but I felt like I mattered. I felt like we changed the political landscape of Ireland, we changed the cultural landscape of Ireland. We were part of a historical movement that people are going to be talking about that for decades and decades and decades. We made that mark. And that was what started out as a couple of hundred people who had been around from the 80s who were super active. And it's just amazing to look at, to be part of, such an amazing movement that has really shaken the structures of Irish society and the wider international impact of that and seeing that ripple effect across the world. ... I'm fuelled now with a fire that was lit, that doesn't seem like it's ever going to go out.'

In a similar fashion to Aoibhinn, Blathnaid sat up in her chair as she spoke. She rolled her hand into a ball and banged her fist against her chest, as she described to me how being a part of the abortion rights movement had helped to feel "fierce", "unstoppable" and "fuelled her with a fire" that "doesn't seem like it's ever going to go out". Listening to Blathnaid explain how she felt "fuelled with fire", I remembered my discussion with Saoirse who spoke despairingly about the anger which circulated among the pro-choice community in the aftermath of the Together for Yes campaign, lamenting that she didn't know "what was going to happen to all that" anger. Perhaps, then, Blathnaid's testimony was evidence of the potentially positive effects of that anger: which she safeguarded, honed, and reinvested directly into her social justice activism, post-Repeal.

Explaining how their quotidian embodied experiences *and* their self-understanding as embodied subjects were transformed through the campaign to repeal the 8th amendment, Blathnaid and her activist colleagues shed light on what I term the 'embodied consequences' of the movement for abortion rights in Ireland. With the concept 'embodied consequences', I am building upon Marco Giugni's (2008) work on the 'political biographical and cultural consequences' of social movements (1582). Giugni argues that, within conventional social movement scholarship, it is the political or policy outcomes of a movement which are given the most sustained, analytical attention. Giugni argues that for social movement actors, however, their involvement in activism often produced more subtle, yet equally significant cultural effects *and* has biographical consequences for those who dedicate portions of their lives to political organizing (2008).

With the framework of the 'embodied consequences', I want to highlight then how activism in relation to abortion or reproductive rights operates not only to secure specific legal, political, or policy outcomes, but in fact, serves to bring about new conceptions of embodied reproductive life and new understandings and relations to gendered, reproductive embodiment, in a broader sense. In this vein, when analysing the 'embodied consequences' of the movement to repeal the 8th amendment, it is important to examine not only how activists' quotidian embodied experience, or their own self-understanding as embodied subjects has been transformed, but also, how the movement for abortion rights challenged or overhauled existing norms in relation to gendered and reproductive embodiment in Ireland, more generally.

Describing her involvement in the abortion rights movement as an "earthquake ... a good earthquake" in her life, Eabha explained how her ideas about motherhood and relationship to her own (maternal) body were completely altered on account of her involvement in the Repeal campaign. She disclosed how six months after the referendum, her marriage "broke up". After her involvement in the campaign, she explains, she had to "start asking some really tough questions" about "bodily autonomy", "personal autonomy", and "shame". She elaborated upon how the campaign prompted her to question new ways of "being a woman", since, for the previous "two decades", she had "bought into a way of being a woman that didn't fit". Part of this progression, she shared with me, included a process of "unpicking motherhood". I asked her to explain in more detail what exactly this entailed:

'I had these ideas that you'd have to breastfeed until your boobs fell off, until your nipples were bleeding, didn't matter. It didn't matter if you never slept, you had to do this because that's what good mothers did. And you had to keep going and keep going until it broke you. And that's what I did. And it did. Literally broke me, to the point where I very nearly had to be hospitalized. Because I was told, that's what you had to do. That you could no longer have any needs of your own, that having needs of your own is a selfish thing. Because mothers, particularly in Ireland and I know it's elsewhere, but I had internalized the idea that mums, mothers, didn't have their own stories, they were all about somebody else. And otherwise, you were a shit mom, a bad mum.'

Eabha explained to me how after the referendum, she felt "stronger" and like she had "found worth" in things "outside of what society told (her) to do". Her testimony confirms research by feminist social movement scholars, specifically that of Barbara Sutton (2010) who explains that, in the context of 'sexist political cultures', women's activism can serve to 'create alternative notions of embodied womanhood' (174–175). In Eabha's testimony, she indicates how this discourse around maternal sacrifice operates as constraint or burden which is *felt* directly in, or which has material consequences for the gendered, reproductive body. Sociologist Pam Lowe (2016) describes how 'normative ideas about women's role as mothers' constrain the choices women make (2). Specifically, Lowe explains, the idea of maternal sacrifice is central to the ways in which norms about gender and motherhood are constructed and function (2016).

Under the rubric of maternal sacrifice, women are compelled to 'put the welfare of children, whether born, in utero, or not yet conceived, over and above any choices and/or desires of their own' (Lowe 2016, 3). As Eabha explains, she had previously understood that "being a woman" meant "breastfeeding until your boobs fell off ... until your nipples were bleeding", confirming the popular (gendered) assumption that maternity requires constant 'corporeal generosity' (Diproses 2002 in Hird 2007, 2). In relation to the idea of the 'embodied consequences' of the abortion rights movement then, Eabha's testimony indicates how the campaign helped her to unpack and challenge these social norms around maternity and maternal embodiment. In the aftermath of the campaign Eabha explains, she began to reject idea of motherhood as a type of sacrificial embodiment and was instead finding "new ways" of being a 'Mom'.

To conclude, the repeal of the 8th amendment produced not only a series of political, legal, and policy consequences, but signaled a range of *embodied consequences*, for women and gestating people in Ireland. The victory of the repeal movement signified not only the introduction of legal abortion services in the state, but the ushering in of new modes of gendered and reproductive embodiment. This analysis demonstrates how, through their activist practices, abortion campaigners in Ireland have successfully transformed the conditions of their quotidian, embodied, gendered experience; reconstructed their relationships to their bodies and reconceptualized their own self-understanding as embodied subjects; and finally, challenged and overhauled accepted social norms and values in relation to gendered, reproductive embodiment. This research illustrates then how, in the Irish context, abortion activism itself can be conceptualized as a *reparative act* by which campaigners reconfigure the conditions which construct their everyday embodied and affective experience in the world.

7

Conclusion

A 'new' story about women's bodies and Irish abortion politics

The intellectual 'seed' which would eventually become this book was planted during the summer of 2015. I had just finished my undergraduate degree in Trinity College Dublin and was working for a language school in the city, trying to save money before moving to the Netherlands where I was planning to pursue postgraduate study. As I have described in the Introduction to this book, public support for the Repeal the 8th campaign grew exponentially in the period between 2012 and 2018, as was evidenced in the increasingly large crowds which gathered every September for the annual 'March for Choice' in Dublin city centre. Having moved to the Netherlands in late August 2015, I would miss the fourth annual March for Choice themed 'Breaking the Silence' which was scheduled to take place on 26 September. From a little under 700 miles away, I followed coverage of the protest which brought an estimated 10,000 activists to the Dublin streets: the largest annual March for Choice to date, at this point (AWID 2015).

As the abortion rights movement gained momentum during the early 2010s, so too did the movement to 'save' the 8th amendment. Two months prior to the 2015 March for Choice, an All-Ireland 'Rally for Life' took place in Dublin on Saturday 15 July (Rally for Life 2015). Walking to and from work in the days preceding and following the 'Rally for Life', I was confronted with various anti-abortion posters strewn around the city centre. I remember one image in particular; a black-and-white line-drawing purporting to describe the anatomy of a pregnant woman's body. On the left-hand side of the image was a line which went from the top of the woman's head, all down her left side, to her feet. Pointing to this line was an arrow, connected to a speech bubble. Inside the speech bubble was text which read 'Your body'. On the right-hand side of the image was another line which ran from the top to the bottom of her stomach area. A separate arrow pointed to this portion of her body, connecting to a second speech bubble, the text in which read 'Not your body'.

Examining this image, I was confronted with a profound sense of what feminist theorist Clare Hemmings (2012) might call 'affective dissonance'. Hemmings describes the experience of 'affective dissonance' as the gap which ensues between one's 'sense of self and the possibilities for its expression and validation' in the world (154). In other words, affective dissonance arises, Hemmings describes, when one is confronted with a stark differential in terms of how one views and understands one's own self/body and the ways in which one's self/body is conceptualized and treated by society at large. Hemmings explains that while experiences of affective dissonance cannot 'guarantee feminist mobilisation', it can often produce a 'sense of injustice and then a desire to rectify' that injustice (2012, 157). As such, the experience of affective dissonance, Hemmings argues, is critical for the creation of feminist solidarity; it 'has to arise', she says, 'if a feminist politics is to emerge'.

Being regularly confronted with various types of anti-abortion imagery, like the one just described, I started to reflect upon how these representations conflicted with my own experience and understanding of my reproductive body. Moreover, I began to think about how these posters *reproduce* and *normalize* a particular way of seeing women and pregnant people, one which hinges primarily upon their bodily objectification. I started to wonder, then, what difference would it make to the abortion debate, if we were to focalize alternative representation of the intimate, bodily worlds of women and gestating people? One which aligned more meaningfully with their actual lived experience? What if people understood the feelings, the emotions, the flesh-and-blood vulnerability of living under the weight of the 8th amendment? What difference would it make to abortion debate if we centralized the quotidian bodily experience of having to constantly negotiate and resist the effects of Ireland's reproductive laws?

Employing a qualitative research methodology based on in-depth interviews with abortion activists, this book exposes the subtle yet pervasive power of anti-abortion laws and policies to shape the embodied subjectivities of women and gestating people. It reveals how, in the case of Ireland, the constitutional abortion ban historically moulded the relationship of women (and people who may become pregnant) to their reproductive bodies. Illustrating how anti-abortion regulations mobilize the disciplinary power of anticipatory logics, this book explains how, under the shadow of the 8th amendment, women and gestating people in Ireland came to live their bodies out-of-space-and-time as 'future aborting bodies'. Highlighting how reproductive oppression is felt at the level of the affected body, this book unveils how the quotidian thought-patterns, bodily labours, and emotional experiences of women and gestating people were shaped by and through the need to 'prepare' for crisis pregnancies and to circumvent the powerful effects of the 8th amendment, in their everyday lives.

Pre-existing scholarship on Irish abortion politics has focused largely on how Irish laws have exiled abortion-seekers, forcing them to travel abroad to access abortion services (Rossiter 2009). Postcolonial scholarship exemplifies how this system of banishing 'sexual transgressors', either through institutionalization or forced emigration, worked to fabricate an ideal of Irish identity predicated on the supposed sexual purity of Irish women (Fischer 2017, 754). Other research has investigated the impact of the 8th amendment in the delivery of healthcare, and on the legal decision-making capacities of medical practitioners and pregnant people in Ireland (de Londras and Enright 2018). *Embodying Irish Abortion Reform*, by comparison, is the first to highlight and examine how the embodied subjectivities of women and gestating people in Ireland were shaped and moulded by the constitutional abortion ban and by the culture and infrastructure of reproductive coercion which surrounded it. In this vein, *Embodying Irish Abortion Reform* tells a different story about abortion and women's bodies in Ireland.

One of the key findings of this book is that women and people who may become pregnant in Ireland have historically been forced to perform a unique and thus far untheorized form of reproductive labour which I term 'abortion work'. From the moment they became aware of their potential to become pregnant and of the inaccessibility of abortion in Ireland, the activists interviewed in this research described how they began to devise strategies and plans for how they might access a clandestine abortion at home or for how they might travel abroad to access abortion care. Activists described to me in detail their 'abortion contingency plans', which include funnelling money away monthly into a special account or 'abortion fund', researching clinics and hospitals abroad where they might be able to access abortion services, or figuring out potential travel arrangements including deciding whether they would fly or travel by ferry to Great Britain.

This book also explores the role of the gendered reproductive body in the movement for reproductive rights in Ireland. In particular, it highlights the integral role of women's emotions, specifically the emotions of anger, shame, and indignation, which propelled many activist bodies into the protest space. In her pathbreaking research on the ACT UP organization, Deborah Gould discusses the 'emotional habitus' of AIDS activists in the United States in the late 1980s, illustrating the contingent relationship between their 'emotional habitus' – understood as the 'socially constituted, prevailing ways of feeling and emoting' – and political mobilization (Gould 2009, 10). Gould explains how intensive affective experiences of grief and despair surrounding the AIDS crisis reconfigured the emotional habitus of LGBTQIA+ activists, exploding their political horizons and paving the way for more aggressive, antagonistic forms of political organizing and direct action.

This book describes how the 'emotional habitus' of women and gestating people in Ireland was transformed by the death of Savita Halappanavar in 2012. Ms Halappanavar, a migrant woman who had moved to Ireland from India, died after being denied a life-saving abortion, at the hands of the Irish state. More than half of the activists I spoke to described Ms Halappanavar's death as an event which spurred them to become involved in the Repeal the 8th campaign. As I have described, the overwhelming experience of anger, shame, and indignation at Ms Halappanavar's death catalysed a process of intensive meaning-making for Irish women, who were forced suddenly to reconsider their subjective relationship to the state and who were forced, ultimately, to put their bodies on the line to safeguard their own and each other's physical autonomy and wellbeing.

Analysing the explicitly 'embodied' aspects of political campaigning, this book reveals the essential role played by the gendered body in transforming Ireland's political and cultural landscape with respect to the 2018 abortion referendum. It explores how specific activist practices – including collective marches, mass 'sit ins', and public speaking events – played an important role in allowing Irish feminist activists to challenge the geopolitical separation between private and public sphere on which Ireland's anti-abortion regime has historically been predicated. By forcefully inserting their feminized bodies into the political sphere, Irish abortion activists challenge 'the discursive fields within which the female body is constructed in society' and in doing so, contest existing ideas about who is 'entitled' to act as a political agent (Sasson-Levy and Rapoport 2003, 397). Moreover, these explicitly 'physical' aspects of campaigning provided activists an opportunity for emotional catharsis and a method to challenge and reconceptualize their own understandings of their bodily capabilities.

For Irish abortion activists, the protest body became the vehicle, agent, and outcome of their political resistance. Activists use their bodies to 'do' politics, by the waving of flags and banners in the streets, through the carrying of signs or the displaying of activist symbols on their bodies, and through the wearing of political garments or dress including the black-and-white 'Repeal' jumper which was launched by the 'Repeal project' campaign in early 2016. Through this act of 'gestural dress', activists use their bodies to transmit goodwill, solidarity, and care to abortion-seekers and to create and sustain new forms of intimacy and sociality among the community of abortion activists. Exploring activists' relationship with/to the black-and-white sweatshirt, this book argues that the wearing of the Repeal jumper functioned as an embodied consciousness-raising activity, as well as an act of situated bodily resistance.

This book also proposes the idea that movements for reproductive rights and justice have 'embodied consequences', as well as legal and cultural effects. In the case of the Repeal the 8th campaign, Irish activists sought to secure specific legal objectives but also to transform and reconstruct hegemonic modes and norms of gendered and reproductive embodiment. In the pre-Repeal the 8th context, Irish women describe how their everyday, bodily, and reproductive lives were dominated by feelings of fear, vulnerability, and precarity. In an effort to pre-empt the possible effects of the 8th amendment, they explain how their everyday bodily practices – including their reproductive and productive labours – were shaped by the need to 'prepare' for crisis pregnancies in some way, shape, or form. In the aftermath of the referendum, by contrast, they describe how their feelings and relationships to their bodies changed and were now characterized instead by a sense of openness, expansiveness, and intentionality which they had not formerly experienced.

Through their activism, abortion campaigners in Ireland successfully transformed their everyday, embodied experience and, specifically, the literal movement of their bodies-in-space. Moreover, they transformed how they felt about their bodies and how they understand themselves as embodied subjects. With the framework of the 'embodied consequences', this book highlights how activism in relation to abortion or reproductive rights operates not only to secure specific legal, political, or policy outcomes, but in fact serves to bring about new conceptions of embodied reproductive life and new understandings and relations to gendered, reproductive embodiment, in a broader sense. This book illustrates then how, in the Irish context, abortion activism itself can be conceptualized as a reparative act by which campaigners reconfigure the conditions of their everyday embodied and affective experience in the world.

Conceptual contributions to the study of reproductive (in)justice

This book offers several contributions to the study of abortion politics, feminist protest movements, and reproductive (in)justice. For decades, reproductive justice scholars have asked us to go beyond the liberal focus on repressive laws and policies which restrain our reproductive rights and to pay attention instead to the ways in which reproductive injustice is embedded in the fabric of our world through social norms and societal structures which stratify the reproduction of various social groups and which create certain groups of bodies as more vulnerable to reproductive violence (Price 2010; Roberts 2015; Ross 2017). In this sense, the reproductive justice framework pushes us to analyse both the structural nature of reproductive injustice and to consider the more obtuse methods by which reproductive oppression is creatively operationalized in our society. This book makes an innovative contribution to contemporary reproductive justice scholarship then by exploring how reproductive oppression is experienced at the level of the affected body. Specifically, it examines the thus far under-researched issue of the effects of anti-abortion laws and regulations at the level of embodied subject formation.

In this vein, this book builds upon histories of feminist scholarship on the social construction of sex/gender by exploring how the gendered, reproductive body is produced through power relations, in this case, via the norms and structures which govern abortion. As political philosopher Clare Chambers writes, 'power is not a repressive force coming from outside the individual, constraining her actions, but a creative force manifested in the individual's everyday life' (2008, 23). The reinforcement of particular norms and processes at the level of the body is produced through 'two processes', Chambers explains, 'the threat of surveillance and thus sanctions for nonconformity ... and sheer force of habit' (2009, 24). Chambers confirms that the exercise of power is 'not confined to those moments when an identifiable senior figure imposes a formal requirement' but manifests in our everyday lives (2008, 26). Power, she concludes, operates when it 'suggests forms of human subjectivity' (Chambers 2008, 32).

Embodying Irish Abortion Reform argues then that while power is wielded in the form of reproductive oppression, reproductive oppression itself can take several forms. Feminist theorist Iris Marion Young divides oppression into five categories: 'exploitation, marginalization, powerlessness, cultural imperialism, and violence'. Young describes oppression as a 'condition of groups' but explains that while 'structural oppression involves relations among groups, these relations do not always fit the paradigm of conscious and intentional oppression of one group by another' (Young 1990, 41). Oppression is 'structural', Young clarifies; it emanates 'not from a few people's choices and policies' but 'is embedded in unquestioned norms, habits, and symbols' (Young 1990, 41). This book affirms Young's theories, illustrating how reproductive oppression is exercised not only through anti-abortion policies which withhold access to care at a specific moment in time. Instead, as this book exemplifies, abortion laws wield reproductive oppression by shaping the *everyday* bodily practices, feelings, and experiences of the gestating subject in a variety of subtle yet coercive ways.

To paraphrase Chambers (2008), Ireland's anti-abortion regime has historically suggested particular forms of embodied subjectivity for women and gestating people living in this context. In fact, this book argues that the regulation of reproductive politics in Ireland can be understood as a system of spatial, affective, and temporal regulation which cumulatively acts as an assemblage of disciplinary forces upon the body of the gendered, reproductive subject. Returning to Young's conceptualization of the 'five faces of oppression', Young describes how oppression can manifest through violence which can be understood either as 'direct victimization' or as 'the daily knowledge shared by all members of oppressed groups that they are liable to violation' (Young 1990, 62). Returning to my analysis of the embodied effects of the 8th amendment, Young's framework allows us to conceptualize how the knowledge that one might need and be denied a (potentially life-saving) abortion, itself operates as a form of reproductive oppression, in the Irish case.

In this vein, the concept of 'abortion work' – which I propose and define here as the cognitive, affective, and physical, bodily labour which is unequally imposed on women and those who may become pregnant, as they plan for, prepare for, and negotiate clandestine abortions – can be conceptualized both as a material manifestation of this experience of reproductive oppression, and as emblematic of the efforts of Irish women to resist and circumvent reproductive violence. With the concept of 'abortion work', I am building upon the work of feminist scholars like Andrea Bertotti who coined the term 'fertility work' to describe the 'labor and responsibility associated with navigating a couple's fertility', including the work of adopting, managing, and planning contraceptive methods (Bertotti 2013, 13).

The concept of 'fertility work' was further elaborated by Kimport who describes 'fertility work' as entailing not only the 'physical burdens of contraception' but also the 'associated time, attention, and stress' (Littlejohn 2013 and Bertotti 2013 in Kimport 2018, 2). Kimport argues that gender inequality is reproduced when the responsibility of preventing pregnancy (and the responsibility of 'fertility work', more broadly) is unquestioningly and disproportionately assigned to women. With this book, I argue that the assignation of 'abortion work' to women and gestating people in Ireland is emblematic of the state's attempt to discipline women's fertility and to burden women with an additional, unacknowledged from of reproductive work.

'Abortion work' can be compared both to 'fertility work' and to the 'mental load' of navigating and organizing reproductive and domestic labour, in so far as much 'abortion work' comprises cognitive or 'thinking work' and thus it constitutes an invisible form of reproductive labour (Bertotti 2013; Reich-Stiebert et al). Moreover, like 'fertility work', 'abortion work' is unequally distributed across the lines of gender, 'race', class, and disability. Predominantly, it is women who are burdened with 'abortion work', and 'abortion work' is more complicated for migrant women, for example, who must think about navigating visa applications and language barriers as part of making their 'abortion contingency plans', and for working-class women, who may have to contend with additional potential economic burdens, in comparison to their middle-class counterparts. Finally, as Reich-Stiebert et al (2023) explain, just as the 'mental load' brings with it 'negative implications for women's well-being and mental health', 'abortion work' brings with it a longitudinal experience of anxiety, vulnerability, and fear (466).

What makes 'abortion work' different then, at least in the Irish context, is its distinctive affective quality. Women like Eithne and Sadbh are faced with a chronic sense of anxiety, panic, or fear, the product of living with the 'life-threatening risk' of the 8th amendment hanging over them (Connolly 2020). Moreover, while many women do 'abortion work' in an attempt to offset or circumvent their vulnerability to reproductive violence, in some cases, doing 'abortion work' can increase one's vulnerability to structural harms, for example, criminalization. Thus, while not all aspects of 'abortion work' are invisible, in contexts where abortion is illegal, even the more explicitly 'physical' aspects of 'abortion work' – for example, purchasing and keeping stock of illegal abortion pills – must remain necessarily *invisibilized* in order to protect women and abortion-seekers, and their allies.

Embodying Irish Abortion Reform argues that 'abortion work' can be conceptualized as a form of reproductive labour with a distinctly subversive quality. Through the doing of 'abortion work', women and people who may become pregnant engage their cognitive abilities, their emotional labour, and their physical bodies to resist state-mandated regimes of compulsory pregnancy. It is important to note that while much 'abortion work' is done in the shadows, solidarity networks and activist groups like Speaking of Imelda and the Abortion Support Network in Ireland have historically played an important role in assisting abortion-seekers to bring their 'abortion contingency plans' to fruition.

Finally, through doing 'abortion work', these women and pregnant people in Ireland transform their relationships to their bodies. While on the one hand we can see the burden of 'abortion work' as emblematic of the state's efforts to punish women and people who may become pregnant, we can also see through the doing of 'abortion work', a method by which these individuals reappropriate their embodied labour to preserve and defend their bodily autonomy. In a post-*Roe* v *Wade* world, where abortion rights and access to safe, legal abortion care is being rolled back across a myriad of countries worldwide, this conceptual framework could be transposed to explore and explain the lived experiences of women in other geopolitical contexts, and will be increasingly useful (for scholarship, policy, and political advocacy) to exemplify and emphasize the immediate and long-term effects of anti-abortion laws.

This book also proposes an innovative 'embodied approach' to the study of reproductive politics. Following the 'organizational' or 'cultural' perspectives, existing social movement scholarship traditionally focuses on either the policy or political outcomes of social movements (Giugni 2008). Through developing the concept of the 'embodied consequences' of reproductive rights and justice movements, this book allows us to analyse how activists' quotidian embodied experiences or bodily-ways-of-being are transformed through (their involvement in) reproductive activism. The concept of 'embodied consequences' is particularly useful for the study of reproductive rights activism, explaining how political activity in this realm can be motivated not only by the need to change laws but by the desire to challenge hegemonic representations of gendered embodiment and to contribute alternative visions of the reproductive process which are grounded in the complex, lived, affective experiences of the gestating person.

In the same way as the concept of 'abortion work' pushes us to expand the temporal framework within which we conceptualize reproductive violence, the framework for analysing the 'embodied consequences' of the Irish abortion rights campaign highlights the diffuse temporality of reproductive inequality as it operates via anti-abortion laws. This framework also points to the broader meaning of abortion activism in terms of the capacity for reproductive rights campaigners to not only challenge and transform existing sex and gender norms in a given context through their work but indicates how through political campaigning feminist protestors may find the opportunity to revolutionize their quotidian embodied and emotional experiences in a wider sense.

Finally, this book contributes to contemporary research on feminist protest movements, and specifically to scholarship on the 'material culture' or protest objects produced by feminist activists. In its focus on feminist material culture, *Embodying Irish Abortion Reform* highlights several important transnational connections in contemporary feminist scholarship on gender and politics. Specifically, it identifies similar methods of visual, artistic, and cultural production in the campaign for abortion rights in Ireland and across several countries in Latin America. Focusing specifically on the role of transnational symbols, such as the green scarf for abortion rights in Argentina, the orange voting hand in Uruguay, and the black-and-white Repeal jumper in Ireland, this book exemplifies how such protest objects work in a similar vein in these contexts to convey political meaning, fortify collective identity, and stir public emotions. Devising the concept of 'gestural dress' to describe the unique intimacy and sociality generated through the wearing of the Repeal jumper in Ireland, this book follows in the footsteps of Latin American social movement scholarship, in reaffirming the importance of putting the body 'on the line' or *poner el cuerpo* in contemporary feminist protest movements.

Limitations to the book and avenues for future research

The primary limitations of this research are methodological in nature. Forty-three activists were interviewed, ranging in age from early 20s to late 60s. Thirty-seven or 86 per cent of the 43 participants were both White and born in Ireland. This signifies an over-representation of 'White-Irish' people who make up only 82 per cent of the national population (CSO 2016). This book also did not include any participants from an Irish Traveller background. The over-representation of participants from a White, settled, middle-class background is likely correlated with my own identity and subjectivity and with my decision to engage a 'snowball' sampling technique. As critics of the snowball sampling method rightly identify, this method is dependent on a 'referral process' which often entails a strong 'selection bias' and risks producing a homogeneous participant group (Parker et al 2019, 4).

According to the initial research design, I planned to travel across Ireland to conduct face-to-face, in-depth qualitative interviews with activists working in diverse urban and rural communities. Although the first half of the data collection was carried out in-person, the restrictions imposed in March 2020 because of the COVID-19 pandemic – halfway through my fieldwork trip – which included a moratorium on face-to-face empirical research, meant that data collection had to be paused and the research design re-evaluated and rearranged at this point. When I recommenced data collection in January 2021 interviews were carried out entirely via online methods to protect and safeguard the health and safety of myself and the research participants. Having to collect data via online methods necessitates engaging with participants who had access to personal computers or smartphones and comprehensive network connections. This meant that activists without these resources were potentially excluded from the data collection process. To mitigate this, I conducted telephone interviews in some cases.

This book identifies several important topics for future research into reproductive politics, which have relevance both within and outside of the Irish context. First, with the concept of 'abortion work', which I have explored extensively in Chapter 3, this research transforms and expands our understanding of the *embodied experience* and *temporality* of reproductive oppression. Through the concept of 'abortion work', I have illustrated how 'anticipation' – which has become the organizing principle of (reproductive) biomedicine and reproductive politics, more widely – has reached back *even before conception*, to shape and transform the affective experiences and intimate, everyday bodily *practices* of the potentially pregnant body-subject (Franklin and Ragone 1998; Adams et al 2009). 'Abortion work', I argue, can be conceptualized as a previously unacknowledged form of *gendered, reproductive labour* which is unequally distributed across class and racial categories, and which is imposed as a financial, emotional, physical, psychological, and *embodied burden* on women and others who may become pregnant.

Further research is needed, then, into the concept of 'abortion work', specifically in geopolitical contexts where abortion remains illegal or is practically inaccessible. At the time of writing, abortion rights face renewed contestation in a slew of countries worldwide. In June 2022, the US Supreme Court overturned Roe V Wade, ending the federal right to an abortion (Donegan 2023). A year later, the Maltese government chose to backtrack from a previous proposal to decriminalize abortion on health grounds, passing a law which would require doctors providing abortion to people whose health is in grave jeopardy to refer them first to a three-doctor medical panel before an abortion can be granted (Amnesty International 2023). In April 2024, the Italian parliament passed a measure allowing anti-abortion activists to enter abortion clinics (Giuffrida 2024). In Argentina, the hard-won victories of the abortion rights campaign are in jeopardy under the new administration of Javier Milei, whose anti-abortion rhetoric has been linked with the uptake in doctors refusing to provide abortion care across the state (Barber 2024). With access to abortion being rolled back in a number of countries, increased analytical attention is required to understand how abortion-seekers differentially experience and negotiate these restrictions in their everyday lives, within their national and local contexts.

In relation to the Irish context, under the legislation implemented following the repeal of the 8th amendment in 2018, abortion remains criminalized and is accessible only in a very limited array of circumstances (ARC and Grimes 2021). The Health (Regulation of the Termination of Pregnancy) Act 2018 provides for abortion only up to 12 weeks 'on request', and beyond 12 weeks only where there is a risk to the life or health of the pregnant person or where the pregnancy in question entails a fatal foetal anomaly (ARC and Grimes 2021). Data published by the Abortion Rights Campaign in September 2021 illustrates that while substantial numbers of abortion-seekers are now able to access terminations within the state, large numbers who do not meet the narrow eligibility criteria to access legal abortions continue to have to travel outside of the jurisdiction (ARC and Grimes 2021). Additional research is needed then to investigate how structures of reproductive injustice are sustained and perhaps reformulated within Ireland's new legislative regime, and specifically to explore how the burden of 'abortion work' continues to be unequally distributed among marginalized groups.

As I explored in Chapter 6, the decision to disband the grassroots abortion rights campaign and to reconvene various 'pro-choice' activist groups under the banner of Together for Yes – the civil society organization which campaigned for a 'Yes' vote in the 2018 referendum – proved to be a somewhat contentious move. To this day, debate is ongoing within Irish abortion activist circles with regards to the tactics of the official referendum campaign, and more specifically, in terms of the medical, legal, political, and policy repercussions of Together for Yes's conciliatory strategy. In particular, the decision made by the 'Yes' campaign to concede to government's proposition to 'water down' the recommendations of the Citizens Assembly and to put forward legislation which omitted the proposal for 'socio-economic' abortion up to 22 weeks, in place of a proposal which would allow abortion 'on request' only until 12 weeks, has been strongly scrutinized by activist groups and medical and legal experts alike (Enright 2018; de Londras 2020; ARC and Grimes 2021).

In the run-up to the abortion referendum in May 2018, Taoiseach (Prime Minister) Leo Varadkar reiterated that, if the 8th amendment was successfully repealed and were abortion legislation eventually passed, terminations beyond 12 weeks would remain 'illegal except in very specific circumstances', while 'late term abortions' would be completely forbidden (Ryan 2018). The decision by the Irish government to invoke a 12-week gestational limit as part of the proposed abortion legislation (which is substantially more restrictive than abortion legislation in other European contexts, including Great Britain, France, the Netherlands, and Spain) was motivated primarily by the fact that large volumes of abortion pills (which allow for termination in 'early pregnancy' – up to 12 weeks) were already being imported into the country at the time of the referendum in 2018 (Ryan 2018). The Health Act 2018 would thus allow for 'medical abortions' (induced by mifepristone and misopristol) to be carried out 'safely' in the community under the 'regulation' of the person's GP (Ryan 2018). According to the Chief Medical Officer, the 12-week limit is to be 'strictly interpreted' (NWCI 2021, 19).

As ARC's data demonstrates, the 12-week gestational time limit combined with Ireland's mandatory three-day waiting period between initial consultation and accessing abortion services cumulatively constitute significant barriers to reproductive autonomy for those seeking abortion services inside the Irish state. Data published in 2019 indicates that upwards of 375 Irish residents travelled to access abortions in England and Wales, with most of these seeking care during the second trimester of pregnancy (NWCI 2021, 3). Further research is needed then to examine the effects of the 12-week gestational limit on abortion access, as instigated under the Health (Regulation of Termination of Pregnancy) Act 2018, and to understand how *temporality* continues to act as a disciplinary force in the regulation of the reproductive lives of women and gestating people in the Irish context. As I have argued elsewhere, 'time works as a coercive force in *two directions*' for abortion-seekers who are compelled to secure terminations as early as possible but to refrain from making 'quick decisions' (O'Shaughnessy 2019b, para 14, my emphasis).

Applying a queer feminist phenomenological method to analyse the testimony of women and people growing up in the shadow of the 8th amendment, this book provides an alternative, embodied, affective history of the movement for abortion rights in Ireland. This research reveals that the struggle to repeal the constitutional abortion ban in Ireland was not only a struggle to secure reproductive rights. It was a struggle to alleviate an ongoing and violent condition of gendered, racialized, embodied *vulnerability* and *labour* forcibly imposed on women and gestating people; to reconfigure and transform the relation of the feminized reproductive subject to their bodies; and ultimately, to allow the potentially pregnant embodied subject to *move through the world* free of the burden of reproductive coercion which has historically constituted an integral part of the Irish nation-building project.

By restoring women, pregnant people, abortion-seekers, and feminist activists to the centre of knowledge production and political debate in relation to reproductive politics, this book attempts to contribute to feminist scholarship on reproduction and embodiment, by generating a 'non-patriarchal account of the reproductive process' (Franklin 1991, 203). Reaffirming and advocating for the epistemological, political, and ethical utility of participant testimony to make 'visible those forms of power that had previously been concealed', this research deploys a collaborative, feminist methodology which locates activists within and prioritizes their embodied and affective experiences, to create alternative, phenomenological models of reproductive and gendered bodily life (Ahmed and Stacey 2001, 4).

For the Irish abortion rights movement, a foundational element of activist work has been attempting to break the silence which has historically characterized the Irish abortion debate, to 'learn to talk' about abortion and about the affective, bodily experience of living under the 8th amendment (Griffin et al 2019, 48). In a country where, for centuries, pregnant women and their children were compulsorily removed from the social landscape through incarceration in Magdalene Laundries, Mother and Baby Homes, or through forced emigration; where Catholic Church teachings prevented and actively stigmatized any level of openness and transparency around sex and reproduction; in a country where women's accounts of their lived experiences continued to be treated with scepticism and contempt, giving testimony in relation to one's intimate, bodily life arguably constitutes a type of radical feminist activism in itself.

To conclude, as abortion rights continue to be contested, both in Ireland and across the globe, feminist scholars must continue to try to find new ways to challenge the hegemony of the foetal image which functions to marginalize and disenfranchise women and pregnant people within both the medical and political spheres (Duden 1993). By refocusing the feelings, thoughts, emotions, vulnerabilities and everyday bodily experiences of women and people in Ireland living under and mobilizing against systems and structures of reproductive oppression, this research delineates one method whereby we might shift the terms of scholarly and legislative debate. In providing an alternative account of the *embodiment of abortion politics*, this research paves the way for a more politically grounded, theoretically engaged, and affectively attuned study of reproductive injustice which has further application both in Ireland and beyond.

Acknowledgements

Parts of this chapter are adapted from O'Shaughnessy (2024).

Notes

Series Editors' Preface
[1] We are using the term 'women' here because the struggle for abortion rights in the 20th century was characterized as a struggle for women's reproductive rights. However, we acknowledge that not all those who can become pregnant and who may require an abortion define themselves as women.

Chapter 1
[1] The Employment Equality Act (1977) made 'unlawful in relation to employment certain kinds of discrimination on ground of sex or marital status' and established 'a body to be known as the Employment Equality Agency to amend the Anti-Discrimination (Pay) Act 1974' (*Employment Equality Act* 1977).

[2] Women who had just given birth were considered, according to guidelines from the Catholic Church, to be 'unclean' and thus had to be 'churched' for a period of four to six weeks upon their return to the community (Smyth 2019).

[3] Prior to the Abortion Act 1967, the 'door' to abortion access for Irish women in England had already been opened under the *Rex* ruling wherein gynaecologist Alex Bourne was acquitted for providing a life-saving termination to a 15-year-old pregnant girl (Luibheid 2006). After this point, abortion was technically legally permissible in England, although under a highly restrictive set of circumstances.

[4] The 'Billings' Method refers to a method of family planning whereby changing patterns of cervical mucus are monitored through self-evaluation to determine periods of fertility (see Betts 1984).

[5] All names cited in this book are pseudonyms.

[6] In the aftermath of the *Roe* v *Wade* ruling, the pro-life movement in the United States began to reorganize itself throughout the early 1970s to push for a constitutional convention to secure a 'human life amendment'. The Human Life Amendment would 'declare that all life begins at conception', thereby making abortion illegal (Ginsburg 1989, 72).

[7] In 2010, Michelle Harte, who was receiving cancer treatment, became pregnant and was forced to travel to the UK to receive an abortion. During the time she had to wait while applying for a passport and making the subsequent journey to the UK, she was forced to stop her cancer treatment. Ms Harte subsequently died from her illness in 2011 (Roche 2018).

[8] The Supreme Court ruling in *McGee* v *Attorney General* in 1973 ruled that the right to privacy in marriage included the right to import contraceptives for personal use (Mahon 1987, 64).

[9] While the Irish government was negotiating the terms of the Maastricht Treaty, it lobbied for an appendage which would prohibit Irish women from appealing to European laws

NOTES

in an effort to override Irish abortion regulations (Luibhéid 2006). Reification of the Maastricht Treaty, as Luibheid explains, allowed the Irish state to protect its 'pro-natalist' policy towards White, Irish women, while discouraging immigration from non-EU states.

[10] For more information see Irish Family Planning Authority (nd). As Theresa Reidy (2019) explains, it is important to note that after 1983, 'no subsequent referendum proposal which sought to make abortion provision more restrictive was passed' (27).

[11] In July 2019, members of parliament (MPs) at Westminster passed legislation changing abortion laws and extending same-sex marriage rights to Northern Ireland. These changes would come into effect if devolution was not restored in Stormont by 21 October. Since devolution was not restored until early 2020, the new legal framework for abortion came into effect on 31 March 2020, technically allowing for terminations in the first 12 weeks of pregnancy and in cases of fatal foetal anomaly. To this day, the Department of Health in Northern Ireland has yet to commission full services across the state (McCormack 2021).

[12] As Calkin (2020) notes, numbers of 'abortion travellers' from Ireland began to decline after 2006/2007 following the establishment of 'pill networks' (76). Between 'twenty-five and sixty shipments of pills have been intercepted every year since 2009' (2020).

[13] As Sutton and Vacarezza remind us, 'the Fifth Feminist Encuentro [Meeting] of Latin America and the Caribbean, held in Argentina in 1990, established 28 September as the Day of Abortion Rights for Women of Latin America and the Caribbean. On that day in the year 1871, Brazil passed the Lei do Ventre Livre (Free Womb Law) that declared the freedom of enslaved women's children who were born after the promulgation of the law (No. 2.040). By choosing that day, feminists were denouncing that almost two centuries after the start of slavery abolition in Brazil, motherhood was still not always free ("Declaración de San Bernardo" 1991 [1990]). Thus, on 28 September the feminist calendar mobilizes – more or less explicitly – abolitionist legacies, to proclaim that "womb freedom" is still an unfulfilled emancipatory project in the region' (Sutton and Vacarezza 2021, 13).

[14] Only 26 abortions were carried out in Irish hospitals under this law in 2014 (Bardon 2015). By comparison, in the year previous to this, an estimated 3,679 Irish abortion-seekers travelled to access abortions in clinics and hospitals in England and Wales (Murray 2016, 668).

[15] The 'Black Monday' protest was the culmination of months of activism by a network called the Polish Women's Strike. It took place on 3 October 2016. Over 14,000 women and men marched on the streets of 140 cities in Poland to protest the country's abortion laws (Cullen and Korolczuk 2019).

[16] Sonja Mackenzie's (2013) concept of 'structural intimacies' has also been useful in helping me to think about the power of testimony or 'stories' to illustrate the 'meeting of interpersonal lives and social structural patterns' (7). The framework of 'structural intimacies', Mackenzie explains, develops a 'rhetorical space at the nexus of large-scale social forces, local cultural worlds, and their embodiment in the sexual' (Mackenzie 2013, 8).

[17] In the interest of protecting the anonymity of respondents, I have explicitly chosen to utilize broad identification categories to reflect respondent's cultural and ethnic backgrounds. In terms of sociodemographic information, respondents are generally identified as coming from 'national' or 'migrant' backgrounds. This is to reflect the fact that, since 2005, even for second-generation migrants who are born in Ireland, they may not be entitled to national citizenship (unless at least one of their parents was also an Irish citizen) (see https://www.citizensinformation.ie/en/moving-country/irish-citizenship/your-right-to-irish-citizenship/ [Accessed 25 February 2024]).

Chapter 2

[1] Generally, asylum-seekers waiting processing of their applications are instructed not to travel outside the state during this time as they may forfeit their asylum application.

Furthermore, the cost of travelling to Great Britain to access an abortion was estimated at this time to be approximately €1,000; a heavy financial burden for many women including pregnant asylum-seekers (Lentin 2015).

Chapter 3

[1] I use the word 'perception' here as it is important to make clear that while women like Eabha or Emer may have come to experience a degree of 'shared' vulnerability under the 8th amendment after Ms Halappanavar's death, the specific threat of reproductive violence that these women experience under the 8th amendment will always have been shaped and mediated through the intersecting forces of misogyny, racism, classism, ableism, and so on. That is to say that while the 8th amendment did act as a 'life-threatening force' to all women and gestating people, the weight and effects of this force are always already different for racialized, classed, and otherwise marginalized body-subjects.

Chapter 4

[1] Using Pralat's (2021) framework, we can conceptualize the act of 'coming out' as an abortion activist as making explicit what is, in this context, considered to be a queer 'orientation' towards abortion; or perhaps as a process of making one's (non-normative) *feelings* towards abortion explicit.

[2] *Nouvel Observateur* (2007).

[3] *Merriam-Webster Dictionary*, 'Catharsis'. Available at: https://www.merriam-webster.com/dictionary/catharsis (Accessed 23 February 2024).

[4] *Online Etymology Dictionary*, 'Gesture'. Available at: https://www.etymonline.com/word/gesture#etymonline_v_6053 (Accessed 19 February 2024).

[5] *Britannica Dictionary*, 'Gesture'. Available at: https://www.britannica.com/dictionary/gesture (Accessed 19 February 2024).

[6] Goss.ie, 'Oliver Callan Hits Out at the Repeal the 8th Campaign', https://goss.ie/showbiz/oliver-callan-hits-repeal-8th-campaign-83319 (Accessed 19 Februrary 2024).

Chapter 5

[1] *Collins Dictionary*, 'Agreement', https://www.collinsdictionary.com/dictionary/english-french/agreement (Accessed: 23 February 2024).

[2] A similar argument is made by Sara Ahmed (2021) in her book *Complaint!* when she says that women who call attention to a problem often 'become' the problem.

Chapter 6

[1] *Cambridge Dictionary*, 'Valve'. Available at: https://dictionary.cambridge.org/dictionary/english/valve (Accessed 23 February 2024).

[2] *Online Etymology Dictionary*, 'Valve'. Available at: https://www.etymonline.com/word/valve (Accessed 24 February 2024).

[3] *Online Etymology Dictionary*, 'Relieve'. Available at: https://www.etymonline.com/word/relieve (Accessed 24 February 2024).

[4] *Merriam Webster*, 'Write into'. Available at: https://www.merriam-webster.com/dictionary/write%20into#:~:text=phrasal%20verb,was%20written%20into%20the%20contract (Accessed 24 February 2024).

References

Accapadi, M.M. (2007) 'When White Women Cry: How White Women's Tears Oppress Women of Color', *College Student Affairs Journal*, 26(2), pp 208–215.

Adams, V., Murphy, M. and Clarke, A.E. (2009) 'Anticipation: Technoscience, Life, Affect, Temporality', *Subjectivity*, 28(1), pp 246–265.

Åhäll, L. (2018) 'Affect as Methodology: Feminism and the Politics of Emotion', *International Political Sociology*, 12(1), pp 36–52.

Ahmed, S. (2006) *Queer Phenomenology: Orientations, Objects, Others*. Durham, NC: Duke University Press.

Ahmed, S. (2010) 'Happy Objects', in M. Gregg and G. Seigworth (eds) *The Affect Theory Reader*. Durham, NC: Duke University Press, pp 29–51.

Ahmed, S. (2014a) *The Cultural Politics of Emotion*. Edinburgh: Edinburgh University Press.

Ahmed, S. (2014b) 'Selfcare as Warfare', *feministkilljoys*, 25 August. Available at: https://feministkilljoys.com/2014/08/25/selfcare-as-warfare/ (Accessed 18 August 2021).

Ahmed, S. (2017) 'Smile!', *feministkilljoys*, 2 February. Available at: https://feministkilljoys.com/2017/02/02/smile/ (Accessed 9 August 2021).

Ahmed, S. (2021) *Complaint!* Durham: Duke University Press.

Ahmed, S. and Stacey, J. (2001) 'Testimonial Cultures: An Introduction', *Cultural Values*, 5(1), pp 1–6.

AIMS Ireland (2017) 'How Does the 8th Amendment Affect Continuing Pregnancy in Ireland?', 23 November. Available at: http://aimsireland.ie/how-does-the-8th-amendment-affect-continuing-pregnancy-in-ireland-aims-ireland/ (Accessed 28 October 2021).

Amnesty International (2023) 'Malta: Lives Put at Risk as Parliament Waters Down Bill Seeking to Partially Decriminalize Abortion' 28 June. Available at: amnesty/org.en/latestnews/2023/06/malta-lives-put-at-risk-as-parliament-waters-down-bill-seeking-to-partially-decriminalize-abortion/ (Accessed 19 April 2024).

Apata, G.O. (2020) '"I Can't Breathe": The Suffocating Nature of Racism', *Theory, Culture, & Society*, 37(7–8), pp 241–254.

ARC (2020) 'What happened during Ireland's First Year of Legal Abortion?', 23 September 2020. Available at: abortionrightscampaign.ie/what-happened-during-irelands-first-year-of-legal-abortion/ (Accessed 14 March 2022).

ARC and Grimes, L. (2021) 'Too Many Barriers: Experiences of Abortion in Ireland after Repeal', September. Available at: abortionrightscampaign. ie/facts/research/ (Accessed 29 November 2021).

Ashley, W. (2014) 'The Angry Black Woman: The Impact of Pejorative Stereotypes on Psychotherapy with Black Women', *Social Work in Public Health*, 29(1), pp 27–34.

AWID (2015) 'The Abortion Rights Campaign "Breaking the Silence" in Ireland', 27 September. Available at: awid.org/member-profiles/abortion-rights-campaign-breaking-silence-ireland (Accessed 19 April 2024).

Ballif, E. (2023) 'Anticipatory Regimes in Pregnancy: Cross-Fertilising Reproduction and Parenting Culture Studies', *Sociology*, 57(3), pp 476–492.

Barber, H. (2024) '"The Stigma Has Returned": Abortion Access in Turmoil in Javier Miley's Argentina', *The Guardian*, 18 March. Available at: https://www.theguardian.com/global-development/2024/mar/18/argentina-abortion-javier-milei#:~:text=1%20month%20old-,'The%20stigma%20has%20returned'%3A%20abortion%20access%20in,turmoil%20in%20Javier%20Milei's%20Argentina&text=Javier%20Milei's%20anti%2Dabortion%20rhetoric,medical%20professionals%20across%20the%20country (Accessed 19 April 2024).

Bardon, S. (2015) '26 terminations under Protection of Life during Pregnancy Bill', *The Irish Times*, 29 June. Available at: https://www.irishtimes.com/news/health/26-terminations-under-protection-of-life-during-pregnancy-bill-1.2266839 (Accessed 19 April 2024).

Bardon, S. (2018) 'Simon Harris Tells Opposition of Difficulty over Referendum Date', *Irish Times*, 31 January. Available at: https://www.irishtimes.com/news/politics/simon-harris-tells-opposition-of-difficulty-over-referendum-date-1.3374289 (Accessed 23 February 2024).

Barry, U. (1988) 'Abortion in the Republic of Ireland', *Feminist Review*, 29, pp 57–63.

Bartlett, A. and Henderson, M. (2016) 'What is a Feminist Object? Feminist Material Culture and the Making of the Activist Object', *Journal of Australian Studies*, 40(2), pp 156–171.

Bergen, S. (2022) '"The kind of doctor who doesn't believe doctor knows best": Doctors for Choice and the Medical Voice in Irish Abortion Politics, 2002–2018', *Social Science & Medicine*, 297, Article 114817.

Berry, D. (2018) 'PIC: LGBTQ Member Viciously Attacked in Dublin for Wearing a "Repeal" Jumper', *Lovin Dublin*, 28 April. Available at: https://lovindublin.com/dublin/repeal-jumper-attack-dublin (Accessed 29 November 2021).

REFERENCES

Bertotti, A.M. (2013) 'Gendered Divisions of Fertility Work: Socioeconomic Predictors of Female Versus Male Sterilization', *Journal of Marriage and Family*, 75(1), pp 13–25.

Betts, K. (1984) 'The Billings Method of Family Planning: An Assessment', *Studies in Family Planning*, 15(6), pp 253–266.

Bloomer, F. and Fegan, E. (2014) 'Critiquing Recent Abortion Law and Policy in Northern Ireland', *Critical Social Policy*, 34(1), pp 109–120.

Bock von Wülfingen, B., Brandt, C., Lettow, S., and Vienne, F. (2015) 'Temporalities of Reproduction: Practices and Concepts from the Eighteenth to the Early Twenty-first Century', *History and Philosophy of the Life Sciences*, 37(1), pp 1–16.

Britt, L. and Heise, D. (2000) 'From Shame to Pride in Identity Politics', in S. Stryker, T.J. Owens and R.W. White (eds) *Self, Identity, and Social Movements*. Minneapolis: University of Minnesota Press, pp 252–268.

Burns, E. (2018) '#10thdss: Intersectionality and the Irish Abortion Rights Campaign of 2018', 19 September. Available at: https://emmaqburns. com/2018/09/19/10thdss-intersectionality-and-the-irish-abortion-rig hts-campaign-of-2018/ (Accessed 5 August 2021).

Butler, J. (1988) 'Performative Acts and Gender Constitution: An Essay in Phenomenology and Feminist Theory', *Theatre Journal*, 40(4), pp 519–531.

Butler, J. (2015) 'Bodies in Alliance and the Politics of the Street', in *Notes Toward a Performative Theory of Assembly*. Cambridge, MA: Harvard University Press, pp 66–98.

Butler, J. (2016) 'Rethinking Vulnerability in Resistance', in *Vulnerability in Resistance*. Durham: Duke University Press, pp 12–28.

Cahillane, L. (2018) 'Delaying Tactics or Useful Deliberative Exercises? The Irish Citizens' Assembly and the Convention on the Constitution', *IACL-AIDC Blog*, 4 December. Available at: https://blog-iacl-aidc.org/ debate-the-citizens-assembly-in-ireland/2018/12/3/delaying-tactics-or-useful-deliberative-exercises-the-irish-citizens-assembly-and-the-convent ion-on-the-constitution (Accessed 14 September 2021).

Calkin, S. (2019) 'Healthcare not Airfare! Art, Abortion and Political Agency in Ireland', *Gender, Place & Culture*, 26(3), pp 338–361.

Calkin, S. (2020) 'Abortion Pills in Ireland and Beyond: What Can the 8th Amendment Referendum Tell Us about the Future of Self-Managed Abortion?', in K. Browne and S. Calkin (eds) *After Repeal: Rethinking Abortion Politics*, London: Zed, pp 73–89.

Calkin, S., de Londras, F. and Heathcote, G. (2020) 'Abortion in Ireland: Introduction to the Themed Issue', *Feminist Review*, 124(1), pp 1–14.

Campbell, E. (2018) 'My Experience of the Together for Yes (TFY) Campaign', *Sexual and Reproductive Health Matters*, 10 October. Available at: http://www.srhm.org/news/my-experience-of-the-together-for-yes-tfy-campaign/ (Accessed 8 November 2021).

Carnegie, A. and Roth, R. (2019) 'From the Grassroots to the Oireachtas', *Health and Human Rights*, 21(2), pp 109–120.

Cavanagh, N. (2016) 'Repeal Jumpers: When Fashion Becomes Political', *The Irish Times*, 21 September. Available at: https://www.irishtimes.com/student-hub/repeal-jumpers-when-fashion-becomes-political-1.2800024?mode=sample&auth-failed=1&pw-origin=https%3A%2F%2Fwww.irishtimes.com%2Fstudent-hub%2Frepeal-jumpers-when-fashion-becomes-political-1.2800024 (Accessed 14 September 2021).

Chakravarty, D., Feldman, A., and Penney, A. (2020) 'Analysing Contemporary Women's Movements for Bodily Autonomy, Pluriversalizing the Feminist Scholarship on the Politics of Respectability', *Journal of International Women's Studies*, 21(7). Available at: https://vc.bridgew.edu/cgi/viewcontent.cgi?article=2349&context=jiws (Accessed 12 June 2021)

Chambers, C. (2008) *Sex, Culture, and Justice: The Limits of Choice*, Philadelphia: Pennsylvania State University Press.

Chemaly, S. (2018) *Rage Becomes Her*. New York: Simon & Schuster.

Chen, C.W. and Gorski, P.C. (2015) 'Burnout in Social Justice and Human Rights Activists: Symptoms, Causes, and Implications', *Journal of Human Rights Practice*, 7(3), pp 366–390.

Clifford, A.M. (2002) 'Abortion in International Waters off the Coast of Ireland: Avoiding a Collision between Irish Moral Sovereignty and the European Community', *Pace International Law Review*, 14(2), pp 385–433.

Cohen, E.F. (2018) *The Political Value of Time: Citizenship, Duration, and Democratic Justice*. Cambridge: Cambridge University Press.

Commission of Investigation into Mother and Baby Homes (2021) *Final Report of the Commission of Investigation into Mother and Baby Homes*. Commission of Investigation into Mother and Baby Homes. Available at: https://www.gov.ie/en/publication/d4b3d-final-report-of-the-commission-of-investigation-into-mother-and-baby-homes/ (Accessed 15 February 2022).

Connolly, L. (2002) *The Irish Women's Movement: From Revolution to Devolution*. Dublin: The Lilliput Press.

Connolly, L. (2020) 'Explaining Repeal: A Long-term View', in K. Browne and S. Calkin (eds) *After Repeal Rethinking Abortion Politics*. London: Bloomsbury Academic, pp 36–52.

Conroy, D. (2016) 'Passing the Buck on the Eighth to the Citizens' Assembly is so Unfair', *independent.ie*, 17 October. Available at: https://www.independent.ie/opinion/comment/passing-the-buck-on-the-eighth-to-the-citizens-assembly-is-so-unfair-35135545.html (Accessed 4 September 2021).

REFERENCES

Cosgrave, A. (2016) 'Repeal Project is My Micro Contribution to a Movement Spanning Decades', *Her.ie*. Available at: https://her.ie/repeal/repeal-project-founder-anna-cosgrave-repeal-project-is-my-micro-contribution-to-a-movement-spanning-decades-308025 (Accessed 19 February 2024).

Central Statistics Office (CSO) (2016) 'Census of Population 2016 - Profile 8 Irish Traveller's, Ethnicity, and Religion', Available at: cso.ie/en/releasesandpublications/ep/p-cp8iter/p8e/#:~:text=The%20largest%20group%20in%202016,mixed%20background"%20(1.5%25) (Accessed 19 April 2024).

Cullen, P. and Korolczuk, E. (2019) 'Challenging Abortion Stigma: Framing Abortion in Ireland and Poland', *Sex Reproduction Health Matters*, 27(3), 1686197.

Darling, O. (2020) 'Storytelling and the Repeal of the 8th Amendment: Narrative and Reproductive Rights in Ireland', *Rejoinder*. Available at: https://irw.rutgers.edu/rejoinder-webjournal/issue-5-storytelling-for-social-change/483-storytelling-and-the-repeal-of-the-8th-amendment-narrative-and-reproductive-rights-in-ireland (Accessed 22 June 2021).

De Londras, F. (2020) '"A Hope Raised and Then Defeated"? The Continuing Harms of Irish Abortion Law', *Feminist Review*, 124(1), pp 33–50.

De Londras, F. and Enright, M. (2018) 'The Case for Repealing the 8th', in F. de Londras and M. Enright, *Repealing the 8th: Reforming Irish Abortion Law*. Bristol: Bristol University Press, pp 1–14.

Dolezal, L. (2015) *The Body and Shame: Phenomenology, Feminism and the Socially Shaped Body*. London: Lexington.

Donegan, M. (2023) 'A Year Ago Roe v Wade Was Overturned: Grieve for the New America', *The Guardian*, 23 June. Available at: https://www.theguardian.com/commentisfree/2023/jun/23/roe-v-wade-overturned-abortion#:~:text=We%20do%20not%20like%20to,them%20%E2%80%93%20and%20grieve%20for%20them (Accessed 19 April 2024).

Dorsey, K. and Chen, E. (2020) 'Understanding Respectability Politics and How it Informs Sociopolitical Change', *Studio ATAO*, 30 June. Available at: https://www.studioatao.org/post/understanding-respectability-politics (Accessed 12 August 2021).

Duden, B. (1993) *Disembodying Women: Perspectives on Pregnancy and the Unborn*. Cambridge, MA: Harvard University Press.

Duffy, D.N. (2020) 'From Feminist Anarchy to Decolonisation: Understanding Abortion Health Activism Before and After the Repeal of the 8th Amendment', *Feminist Review*, 124(1), pp 69–85.

Duffy, D.N., Freeman, C. and Rodríguez Castañeda, S. (2023) 'Beyond the State: Abortion Care Activism in Peru', *Signs: Journal of Women in Culture and Society*, 48(3), pp 609–634.

Duffy, M. (2007) 'Doing the Dirty Work: Gender, Race, and Reproductive Labor in Historical Perspective', *Gender and Society*, 21(3), pp 313–336.

Earner-Byrne, L. (2003) 'The Boat to England: An Analysis of the Official Reactions to the Emigration of Single Expectant Irishwomen to Britain, 1922–1972', *Irish Economic and Social History*, 30, pp 52–70.

Edelman, L. (2004) *No Future: Queer Theory and the Death Drive*. Durham, NC: Duke University Press.

Enright, M. (2018) '"The Enemy of the Good": Reflections on Ireland's New Abortion Legislation', *feminists@law*, 8(2).

Fenton, J. (2017) 'A "Repeal" Jumper was Placed on the Altar of this Dublin Church', *Lovin Dublin*, 7 August. Available at: https://lovindublin.com/pics/pic-a-repeal-jumper-was-placed-on-the-altar-of-this-dublin-church (Accessed 26 May 2021).

Ferriter, D. (2009) *Occasions of Sin: Sex and Society in Modern Ireland*. London: Profile.

Field, L. (2018) 'The Abortion Referendum of 2018 and a Timeline of Abortion Politics in Ireland to Date', *Irish Political Studies*, 33(4), pp 608–628.

Finn, C. (2018) 'There Was Talk that Dublin Castle Would Be Muted. That Is Not What Happened', thejournal.ie. Available at: https://www.thejournal.ie/dublin-castle-repeal-the-eighth-4037521-May2018/ (Accessed 14 September 2021).

Fischer, C. (2017) 'Revealing Ireland's "Proper" Heart: Apology, Shame, Nation', *Hypatia*, 32(4), pp 751–767.

Fischer, C. (2019) 'Abortion and Reproduction in Ireland: Shame, Nation-Building and the Affective Politics of Place', *Feminist Review*, 122(1), pp 32–48.

Fitzsimons, C. (2021) *Repealed: Ireland's Unfinished Fight for Reproductive Justice*. London: Pluto Press.

Fletcher, R. (2005) 'Reproducing Irishness: Race, Gender, and Abortion Law', *Canadian Journal of Women and the Law*, 17, pp 365–404.

Fletcher, R. (2018) '#RepealedThe8th: Translating Travesty, Global Conversation, and the Irish Abortion Referendum', *Feminist Legal Studies*, 26(3), pp 233–259.

Flynn , E. (2018) 'The Case of Travellers and Traveller Voices', in C. Florescu et al (eds) *We've Come a Long Way: Reproductive Rights of Migrants and Ethnic Minorities in Ireland*. Sao Paolo: editora Urutau, pp 89–93.

Ford, T. (2013) 'SNCC Women, Denim, and the Politics of Dress', *The Journal of Southern History*, 39(3), pp 625–658.

Foucault, M. (1978) *The History of Sexuality*, 1st American edn. New York: Pantheon Books.

REFERENCES

Franklin, S. (1991) 'Fetal Fascinations: New Dimensions to the Medical-Scientific Construction of Fetal Personhood', in S. Franklin, C. Lury J. and Stacey (eds) *Off-Centre: Feminism and Cultural Studies*. New York: HarperCollins Academic, pp 190–205.

Franklin, S. and Ragone, H. (1998) *Reproducing Reproduction: Kinship, Power, and Technological Innovation*, Philadelphia: University of Pennsylvania Press.

Freeman, C. (2020) 'Viapolitcs and the Emancipatory Possibilities of Abortion Mobilities', *Mobilities*, 15(6), pp 896–910.

Friedan, B. (2010 [1963]) *The Feminine Mystique*. London: Penguin.

Gilmartin, M. and Kennedy, S. (2019) 'A Double Movement: The Politics of Reproductive Mobility in Ireland', in C. Sethna and G. Davis (eds) *Abortion Across Borders: Transnational Travel and Access to Abortion Services*. Baltimore: Johns Hopkins University Press, pp 123–143.

Ginsburg, F. (1989) *Contested Lives: The Abortion Debate in the American Community*. Berkeley: University of California Press.

Giuffrida, A. (2024) 'Italy Passes Measures to Allow Anti-Abortion Activists to Enter Abortion Clinics', *The Guardian*, 16 April. Available at: https://www.theguardian.com/world/2024/apr/16/italy-passes-measures-to-allow-anti-abortion-activists-to-enter-abortion-clinics (Accessed 19 April 2024).

Giugni, M. (2008) 'Political, Biographical and Cultural Consequences of Social Movements', *Sociology Compass*, 2(5), pp 1582–1600.

Goffman, E. (1963) *Stigma: Notes on the Management of Spoiled Identity*. London: Penguin Books.

Goodwin, J. and Pfaff, S. (2001) 'Emotion Work in High-Risk Social Movements: Managing Fear in the US and East German Civil Rights Movement', in J. Goodwin, J.M. Jasper, and F. Poletta (eds) *Passionate Politics: Emotions and Social Movements*. Chicago: University of Chicago Press, pp 282–302.

Goold, I. (2014) 'ABC v Ireland', in J. Herring and J. Wall (eds), *Landmark Cases in Medical Law*. Oxford: Hart Publishing, pp 307–340.

Gordon, A. (2008) *Ghostly Matters: Haunting and the Sociological Imagination*. Minneapolis: University of Minnesota Press.

Gorska, M. (2021) 'Why Breathing Is Political', *Lambda Nordica*, 26(1), pp 109–117.

Gould, D.B. (2009) *Moving Politics: Emotion and Act Up's Fight Against AIDS*. Chicago: University of Chicago Press.

Griffin, G., O'Connor, O. and Smyth, A. (2019) *It's a Yes! How Together for Yes Repealed the Eighth and Transformed Irish Society*. Dublin: Orpen Press.

Griffin, N. (2024) 'Twelve of Ireland's Maternity Hospitals Still Do Not Offer Surgical Abortions', *Irish Examiner*, 2 March. Available at: irishexaminer.com/news/arid-41343551.html (Accessed 19 April 2024).

Grimes, L. (2016) 'They Go to England to Preserve Their Secret: The Emigration and Assistance of the Irish Unmarried Mother in Britain 1926–1952', *Restrospectives*, 5(1), pp 51–65.

Guittar, N.A. (2011) 'Out: A Sociological Analysis of Coming Out'. Electronic Theses and Dissertations. https://stars.library.ucf.edu/etd/1934

Guittar, N.A. (2013) 'The Meaning of Coming Out: From Self-Affirmation to Full Disclosure', *Qualitative Social Review*, 9(3), pp 169–187.

Haraway, D. (1988) 'Situated Knowledges: The Science Question in Feminism and the Privilege of Partial Perspective', *Feminist Studies*, 14(3), pp 575–599.

Haughton, M., Hoover, S., and Murphy, C.L. (2022) 'Think Outside My Box: Staging Respectability and Responsibility in Ireland's Repeal the 8th Referendum', *Feminist Encounters: A Journal of Critical Studies in Culture and Politics*, 6(1), p 11.

Hemmings, C. (2012) 'Affective Solidarity: Feminist Reflexivity and Political Transformation', *Feminist Theory*, 13(2), p 15.

Henley, J. (2018) 'Irish Abortion Referendum: Yes Wins with 66.4% – as it Happened', *The Guardian*, 29 May. Available at: https://www.theguardian. com/world/live/2018/may/26/irish-abortion-referendum-result-count-begins-live (Accessed 14 March 2022).

Higginbotham, E.B. (1993) *Righteous Discontent: The Women's Movement in the Black Baptist Church, 1880–1920*. Cambridge, MA: Harvard University Press.

Hill Collins, P. (1996) 'The Social Construction of Black Feminist Thought', in A. Garry and M. Pearsall (eds) *Women, Knowledge, Reality: Explorations in Feminist Philosophy*. New York: Routledge, pp 222–248.

Hill Collins, P. (2009 [1990]) *Black Feminist Thought: Knowledge, Consciousness, and the Politics of Empowerment*, 2nd edn. New York: Routledge.

Himmelweit, S. and Plomien, A. (2014) 'Feminist Perspectives on Care: Theory, Practice and Policy', in M. Evans, C. Hemmings, M. Henry, H. Johnstone, S. Madhok, A. Plomein and S. Wearing et al (eds) *The SAGE Handbook of Feminist Theory*. London: SAGE, pp 446–464.

Hird, M.J. (2007) 'The Corporeal Generosity of Maternity', *Body & Society*, 13(1), pp 1–20.

Hochschild, A.R. (1979) 'Emotion Work, Feeling Rules, and Social Structure', *The American Journal of Sociology*, 85(3), pp 551–575.

Hochschild, A.R. (2012 [1983]) *The Managed Heart: Commercialization of Human Feeling*. Berkeley: University of California Press.

Holland, K. (2014) '"March for Choice" Attracts Thousands in Dublin', *The Irish Times*, 27 September. Available at: https://www.irishtimes.com/ news/social-affairs/march-for-choice-attracts-thousands-in-dublin-1.1944 267?mode=sample&auth-failed=1&pw-origin=https%3A%2F%2Fwww. irishtimes.com%2Fnews%2Fsocial-affairs%2Fmarch-for-choice-attracts-thousands-in-dublin-1.1944267 (Accessed 3 November 2021).

REFERENCES

Holmes, M. (2004) 'Feeling Beyond Rules: Politicizing the Sociology of Emotion and Anger in Feminist Politics', *European Journal of Social Theory*, 7(2), pp 209–227.

hooks, b. (1995) 'Performance Practice as a Site of Opposition', in C. Ugwu (ed) *Let's Get It On: The Politics of Black Performance*. Seattle: Bay View Press, pp 210–219.

Hourihane, A.M. (2018) 'Let Women Celebrate Repeal of the Eighth', *The Times*, 17 August. Available at: https://www.thetimes.co.uk/article/let-women-celebrate-repeal-of-the-eighth-mrwpcrpr6 (Accessed 14 September 2021).

Inglis, T. (1997) 'Foucault, Bourdieu and the Field of Irish Sexuality', *Irish Journal of Sociology*, 7(1), pp 5–28.

Inglis, T. (1998) *Lessons in Irish Sexuality*. Dublin: University College Dublin Press.

Irish Family Planning Authority (nd) *History of Abortion in Ireland*. Available at: https://www.ifpa.ie/advocacy/abortion-in-ireland-legal-timeline/ (Accessed 7 December 2021).

Irish Statute Book (1861) *Offences Against the Person Act 1861*. Available at: https://www.irishstatutebook.ie/eli/1861/act/100/enacted/en/print.html (Accessed 24 November 2021).

Irish Statute Book (nd) *Eighth Amendment of the Constitution Act, 1983*. Available at: https://www.irishstatutebook.ie/eli/1983/ca/8/enacted/en/html (Accessed 20 February 2024).

Jasper, J.M. (1997) *The Art of Moral Protest: Culture, Biography, and Creativity in Social Movements*. Chicago: University of Chicago Press.

Jasper, J.M. (1998) 'The Emotions of Protest: Affective and Reactive Emotions in and around Social Movements', *Sociological Forum*, 13(3), pp 397–424.

Jones, T. and Norwood, K.J. (2017) 'Aggressive Encounters and White Fragility: Deconstructing the Trope of the Angry Black Woman', *Iowa Law Review*, 102(5), pp 2017–2069.

Justice for Magdalenes Research (2021) 'About the Magdalene Laundries'. Available at: http://jfmresearch.com/home/preserving-magdalene-history/about-the-magdalene-laundries/ (Accessed 24 November 2021).

Kennedy, L., O'Boyle, M., and Kane, A. (2021) *The 8th*. Black Tabby Films. Available at: https://the8thfilm.com/ (Accessed 29 October 2021).

Kimport, K. (2018) 'More Than a Physical Burden: Women's Mental and Emotional Work in Preventing Pregnancy', *The Journal of Sex Research*, 55(9), pp 1096–1105.

Kimport, K. and Littlejohn, K.E. (2021) 'What are We Forgetting? Sexuality, Sex, and Embodiment in Abortion Research', *The Journal of Sex Research*, 58(7), pp 863–873.

Koivunen, A., Kyrola, K., and Ryberg, I. (2018) 'Vulnerability as a Political Language', in A. Koivunen, K. Kyrola and I. Ryberg (eds) *The Power of Vulnerability: Mobilising Affect in Feminist, Queer and Anti-racist Media Cultures*. Manchester: Manchester University Press.

Leahy, P. (2018) 'Irish Times Exit Poll Projects Ireland has Voted by Landslide to Repeal Eighth', *The Irish Times*, 25 May. Available at: https://www.irishtimes.com/news/politics/irish-times-exit-poll-projects-ireland-has-voted-by-landslide-to-repeal-eighth-1.3508861?mode=sample&auth-failed=1&pw-origin=https%3A%2F%2Fwww.irishtimes.com%2Fnews%2Fpolitics%2Firish-times-exit-poll-projects-ireland-has-voted-by-landslide-to-repeal-eighth-1.3508861 (Accessed 14 September 2021).

Lentin, R. (2003) 'Pregnant Silence: (En)gendering Ireland's Asylum Space', *Patterns of Prejudice*, 37(3), pp 301–322.

Lentin, R. (2004) 'Strangers and Strollers: Feminist Notes on Researching Migrant M/others', *Women's Studies International Forum*, 27(4), pp 301–314.

Lentin, R. (2015) 'After Savita: Migrant M/others and the Politics of Birth in Ireland', in A. Quilty, S. Kennedy and C. Conlon (eds) *The Abortion Papers Ireland: Volume 2*. Cork: Cork University Press, pp 179–188.

Lentjes, R., Alterman, A., and Arey, W. (2020) '"The Ripping Apart of Silence": Sonic Patriarchy and Anti-Abortion Harassment', *Resonance: The Journal of Sound and Culture*, 1(4), pp 422–442.

Locke, J. (2007) 'Shame and the Future of Feminism', *Hypatia*, 22(4), pp 142–162.

Lorde, A. (1981) 'Keynote Address: The NWSA Convention "The Uses of Anger"', *Women's Studies Quarterly*, 9(3), pp 7–10.

Loughlin, E. (2021) 'Half of the Country's Maternity Hospitals Do Not Offer Full Abortion Services', *Irish Examiner*, 25 March. Available at: https://www.irishexaminer.com/news/arid-40250726.html (Accessed 3 December 2021).

Lowe, P. (2016) *Reproductive Health and Maternal Sacrifice: Women, Choice and Responsibility*. London: Palgrave Macmillan.

Lowe, P. and Hayes, G. (2019) 'Anti-Abortion Clinic Activism, Civil Inattention and the Problem of Gendered Harassment', *Sociology*, 53(2), pp 330–346.

Luddy, M. (2007) 'Sex and the Single Girl in 1920s and 1930s Ireland', *The Irish Review*, 35, pp 79–91.

Luddy, M. (2011) 'Unmarried Mothers in Ireland 1880–1973', *Women's History Review*, 20(1), pp 109–126.

Luibhéid, E. (2006) 'Sexual Regimes and Migration Controls: Reproducing the Irish Nation-state in Transnational Contexts', *Feminist Review*, 83(1), pp 60–78.

Mackenzie, S. (2013) *Structural Intimacies: Sexual Stories in the Black AIDS Epidemic*. New Brunswick: Rutgers University Press.

Macra Na Feirme (2022) *About Us*. Available at: https://macra.ie/pages/about (Accessed 21 February 2022).

Mahon, E. (1987) 'Women's Rights and Catholicism in Ireland', *New Left Review*, 166, pp 53–78.

Martin, A. (2002) 'Death of a Nation: Transnationalism, Bodies and Abortion in Late Twentieth-century Ireland', in T. Mayer (ed) *Gender Ironies of Nationalism*. London: Routledge, pp 65–88.

Martin, E. (2001 [1989]) *The Woman in the Body: A Cultural Analysis of Reproduction*. Boston: Beacon Press.

Masheti, N. (2021) 'Race and Ethnicity Shouldn't Matter in Maternity Care. But They Do', *Irish Examiner*, 3 October. Available at: irishexaminer.com/opinion/commentanalysis/arid-40723003.html (Accessed 19 April 2024).

McAvoy, S. (2013) 'Vindicating Women's Rights in a Fetocentric State: The Longest Irish Journey', in N. Giffney and M. Shildrick (eds) *Theory on the Edge: Irish Studies and the Politics of Sexual Difference*. New York: Palgrave Macmillan.

McCarthy, J. (2016) 'Reproductive Justice in Ireland: A Feminist Analysis of the Neary and Halappanavar Cases', in M. Donnelly and C. Murray (eds) *Ethical and Legal Debates in Irish Healthcare: Confronting Complexities*. Manchester: Manchester University Press, pp 9–23.

McCormack, J. (2022) 'Abortion in NI: Timeline of Key Events', *BBC News* 8 June. Available at: https://www.bbc.co.uk/news/uk-northern-ireland-politics-56041849#:~:text=March%202020,take%20effect%20from%2031%20March (Accessed 19 April 2024).

McCrave, C. (2019) 'Doctors Warn that Our Hospitals are Still Not Ready to Offer Abortions', *theindependent.ie*, 10 January. Available at: https://www.independent.ie/irish-news/health/doctors-warn-that-our-hospitals-are-still-not-ready-to-offer-abortions-37698005.html (Accessed 14 September 2021).

McGill, M. (2019) '"Enough judgement": Reflections on Campaigning for Repeal in Rural Ireland', in K. Browne and S. Calkin (eds) *After Repeal Rethinking Abortion Politics*. London: Bloomsbury Academic, pp 109–123.

McGreevy, R. (2017) 'Citizens' Assembly Backs Abortion Rights in Wide Range of Circumstances', *The Irish Times*, 23 April. Available at: https://www.irishtimes.com/news/ireland/irish-news/citizens-assembly-backs-abortion-rights-in-wide-range-of-circumstances-1.3058170?mode=sample&auth-failed=1&pw-origin=https%3A%2F%2Fwww.irishtimes.com%2Fnews%2Fireland%2Firish-news%2Fcitizens-assembly-backs-abortion-rights-in-wide-range-of-circumstances-1.3058170 (Accessed 21 February 2022).

McKimmons, E. and Caffrey, L. (2021) 'Discourse and Power in Ireland's Repeal the 8th Movement', *Interface: A Journal for and about Social Movements*, 13(1), pp 193–224.

MERJ (2019) 'Migrants and Ethnic Minorities Being Left Behind by Ireland's Abortion Legislation', *Migrants and Ethnic Minorities for Reproductive Justice*. Available at: https://merjireland.org/index.php/2019/09/09/migrants-and-ethnic-minorities-being-left-behind-by-irelands-abortion-legislation/ (Accessed 29 November 2021).

Millar, E. (2017) *Happy Abortions: Our Bodies in the Era of Choice*. London: Zed.

Mishtal, J., Reeves, K., Chakravarty, D., Grimes, L., Stefani, B., Chavkin, W., Duffy, D., Favier, M., Horgan, P., Murphy, M., Lavelanet, A.F. and Scott, J. (2022) 'Abortion Policy Implementation in Ireland: Lessons from the Community Model of Care', *PLOS ONE*, 17(5).

Moraga, C. (1983) 'Preface', in C. Moraga and G. Anzaldua (eds) *This Bridge Called My Back: Writings by Radical Women of Colour*. New York: Kitchen Table Press, pp xiii–xix.

Moraga, C. and Anzaldua, G. (eds) (1983) *This Bridge Called My Back: Writings by Radical Women of Colour*. New York: Kitchen Table Press.

Morgan, L.M. and Roberts, E.F.S. (2012) 'Reproductive Governance in Latin America', *Anthropology & Medicine*, 19(2), pp 241–254.

Morse, F. (2012) '"Abortion Tears Life Apart" Advert Sparks Anger in Dublin', *Huffington Post*, 18 June. Available at: https://www.huffingtonpost.co.uk/2012/06/18/anti-abortion-adverts-posters-billboards-ireland_n_1605316.html (Accessed 21 February 2022).

Murray, C. (2016) 'The Protection of Life During Pregnancy Act 2013: Suicide, Dignity and the Irish Discourse on Abortion', *Social & Legal Studies*, 25(6), pp 667–698.

Nayak, A. (2007) 'Critical Whiteness Studies: Critical Whiteness Studies', *Sociology Compass*, 1(2), pp 737–755.

Needham, M. (2019) *Compostela*. Directed by Donal O'Kelly, New Theatre, 11 September.

Nouvel Observateur (2007) 'Text: Le "Manifeste des 343 salopes" paru dans le Nouvel Obs en 1971', 27 November. Available at: https://www.nouvelobs.com/societe/20071127.OBS7018/le-manifeste-des-343-salopes-paru-dans-le-nouvel-obs-en-1971.html (Accessed 19 February 2024).

NWCI (National Women's Council of Ireland) (2018) 'Launch of Together for Yes!', 13 April. Available at: https://www.nwci.ie/news/article/launch_of_together_for_yes (Accessed 23 February 2024).

NWCI (National Women's Council of Ireland) (2021) 'Accessing Abortion in Ireland: Meeting the Needs of Every Woman'. Available at: https://www.nwci.ie/images/uploads/15572_NWC_Abortion_Paper_WEB.pdf (Accessed 11 March 2022).

O'Cionnaith, F. (2016) 'Dail Returns: TDs Face Discipline for Repeal Jumpers', *Irish Examiner*, 28 September. Available at: https://www.irishexaminer.com/news/arid 20423123.html (Accessed 23 February 2024).

REFERENCES

O'Connell, H. (2012) 'Senator's Criticism of Abortion Ads as "Odious Abuse of Taxpayer-funded Privilege"', *thejournal.ie*, 28 June. Available at: https://www.thejournal.ie/senators-criticism-of-abortion-ads-an-odious-abuse-of-taxpayer-funded-privilege-503197-Jun2012/ (Accessed 1 June 2021).

O'Connor, A. (2016) 'Here's How These Repeal Jumpers Sold Out in One Day and Became an Irish Phenomenon', *The Daily Edge*, 5 July. Available at: https://www.dailyedge.ie/repeal-jumpers-2862018-Jul2016/ (Accessed 26 May 2021).

O'Halloran-Bermingham, A.R. (forthcoming) 'Shame, Abortion, and Nation: Affective Experiences of People Who Have Left Ireland for Abortion Care', PhD thesis. University of Cambridge.

O'Hare, M.F., Manning, E., Corcoran, P. and Greene, R.A. (2023) *Confidential Maternal Death Enquiry in Ireland, Report for 2019–2021.* Cork: MDE Ireland. Available at: https://www.ucc.ie/en/media/research/nationalperinatalepidemiologycentre/documents/MaternalDeathEnquiryReport2019-2021.pdf (Accessed 19 April 2024).

O'Keefe, T. (2006) 'Menstrual Blood as a Weapon of Resistance', *International Feminist Journal of Politics*, 8(4), pp 535–556.

O'Shaughnessy, A. (2019a) 'Why I'm Marching: Maximum Energy and Effort Deserves more than the Minimal Level of Provision', *Abortion Rights Campaign: Why I'm Marching*, 10 September. Available at: https://www.abortionrightscampaign.ie/2019/09/10/why-im-marching-maximum-energy-and-effort-deserves-more-than-the-minimal-level-of-provision/ (Accessed 16 October 2021).

O'Shaughnessy, A. (2019b) 'A Race Against the "Body Clock": Abortion and the Temporal Politics of the "Waiting Period"'. Available at: hhttps://www.researchgate.net/publication/376523187_A_Race_against_the_Body_Clock_Abortion_and_the_Temporal_Politics_of_the_Waiting_Period (Accessed 19 April 2024).

O'Shaughnessy, A. (2021) 'Triumph and Concession? The Moral and Emotional Construction of Ireland's Campaign for Abortion Rights', *European Journal of Women's Studies*, pp 233–249.

O'Shaughnessy, A. (2024) 'On the Embodied Experience of Anti-Abortion Laws and Regulations: The Gendered Burden of "Abortion Work"', *Body and Society*. https://doi.org/10.1177/1357034X24125420

O'Shaughnessy, A., Roth, R., Carnegie, A., and Grimes, L. (2023) 'Unruly Bodies (of Knowledge): Influencing Irish Abortion Policy through Evidence-Based Abortion Activism', *Community Development Journal*, 2 December. https://doi.org/10.1093/cdj/bsad032

O'Sullivan, E. and O'Donnell, I. (eds) (2012) *Coercive Confinement in Ireland: Patients, Prisoners and Penitents.* Manchester: Manchester University Press.

Orozco, E. (2017) 'Feminicide and the Funeralization of the City: On Thinking Agency and Protest Politics in Ciudad Juarez', *Theory & Event*, 20(2), pp 351–380.

Parker, C., Scott, S. and Geddes, A. (2019) 'Snowball Sampling', in P. Atkinson, S. Delamont, A. Cernat, J. Sakshaug and R. Williams (eds) *SAGE Research Methods Foundations*. London: SAGE.

Parkins, W. (2000) 'Protesting Like a Girl: Embodiment, Dissent and Feminist Agency', *Feminist Theory*, 1(1), pp 59–78.

Pedwell, C. and Whitehead, A. (2012) 'Affecting Feminism: Questions of Feeling in Feminist Theory', *Feminist Theory*, 13(2), pp 115–129.

Phelan, P. (1993) *Unmarked: The Politics of Performance*. London: Routledge.

Pitts-Taylor, V. (2014) 'A Feminist Carnal Sociology: Embodiment in Sociology, Feminism, and Naturalized Philosophy', *Qualitative Sociology*, 38, pp 19–25.

Pollack Petchesky, R. (1987) 'Fetal Images: The Power of Visual Culture in the Politics of Reproduction', *Feminist Studies*, 13(2), pp 263–292.

Pollack Petchesky, R. (1990) *Abortion and Woman's Choice: The State, Sexuality and Reproductive Freedom*. Boston: Northeastern University Press.

Polletta, F. and Jasper, J. (2001) 'Collective Identity and Social Movements', *Annual Review of Sociology*, 27, pp 283–305.

Porter, E. (1996) 'Culture, Community and Responsibilities: Abortion in Ireland', *Sociology*, 30(2), pp 279–298.

Power, J. (2017) 'Number of Abortion Pills Seized by Irish Customs Declines', *The Irish Times*, 24 April. Available at: https://www.irishtimes.com/news/health/number-of-abortion-pills-seized-by-irish-customs-declines-1.3059156 (Accessed 3 November 2021).

Pralat, R. (2021) 'Sexual Identities and Reproductive Orientations: Coming Out as Wanting (or Not Wanting) to Have Children', *Sexualities*, 24(1/2), pp 276–294.

Price, K. (2010) 'What Is Reproductive Justice? How Women of Color Activists Are Redefining the Pro-Choice Paradigm', *Meridians*, 10(2), pp 42–65.

Quinn, H. (2018) 'My Protest Body: Encounters with Affect, Embodiment, and Neoliberal Political Economy', *New Proposals: Journal of Marxism and Interdisciplinary Inquiry*, 9(2), pp 51–65.

Rally for Life (2015) 'Dublin 2015: Dublin City Centre: 4 July 2015: 2pm'. Available at: rallyforlife.net/dublin-2015/ (Accessed 19 April 2024).

Reed, J.-P. (2015) 'Social Movement Subjectivity: Culture, Emotions, and Stories', *Critical Sociology*, 41(6), pp 935–950.

Reich-Stiebert, N., Froehlich, L., and Voltmer, J.-B. (2023) 'Gendered Mental Labor: A Systematic Literature Review on the Cognitive Dimension of Unpaid Work Within the Household and Childcare', *Sex Roles*, 88(11–12), pp 475–494.

Reidy, T. (2019) 'The 2018 Abortion Referendum: Over Before it Began!', in K. Browne and S. Calkin (eds) *After Repeal: Rethinking Abortion Politics*. London: Zed Books, pp 21–35.

Rivetti, P. (2019) 'Race, Identity and the State After the Irish Abortion Referendum', *Feminist Review*, 122(1), pp 181–188.

Roberts, D.E. (2015) 'Reproductive Justice, Not Just Rights', *Dissent*, 62(4), pp 79–82.

Roche, B. (2018) 'Mother Might Still Be Alive but for Eighth Amendment – Gynaecologist' *Irish Times*, 13 May. Available at: https://www.irishtimes.com/news/ireland/irish-news/mother-might-still-be-alive-but-for-eighth-amendment-gynaecologist-1.3493958 (Accessed 26 November 2021).

Rosen, C. (2016) 'Women on Waves, Ireland, and the Abortion Ship Pilot Mission', *Women Leading Change*, 1(2), pp 28–37.

Ross, L.J. (2017) 'Reproductive Justice as Intersectional Feminist Activism', *Souls*, 19(3), pp 286–314.

Rossiter, A. (2009) *Ireland's Hidden Diaspora: The Abortion Trail and the Making of the London-Irish Underground 1980–2000*. London: IASC Publishing.

RTÉ (2017) 'Tens of Thousands Take Part in March for Choice Rally', *RTÉ News*, 30 September. Available at: https://www.rte.ie/news/ireland/2017/0930/908737-march-for-choice/ (Accessed 3 November 2021).

Ryan, O. (2018) 'Q&A: Why Has the Government Chosen 12 Weeks as the General Time Limit for Abortion?', thejournal.ie, 3 May. Available at: https://www.thejournal.ie/12-weeks-abortion-ireland-3988241-May2018/ (Accessed 28 September 2021).

Safronova, V. (2018) 'Lawyer in Rape Trial Links Thong with Consent, and Ireland Erupts', *The New York Times*, 15 November. Available at: https://www.nytimes.com/2018/11/15/world/europe/ireland-underwear-rape-case-protest.html (Accessed 23 June 2023).

Saguy, A.C. (2020) *Come Out, Come Out, Whoever You Are*. Oxford: Oxford University Press.

Sánchez-Rivera, R. (2022) 'Coloniality and Reproductive Coercion in Puerto Rico in Light of the End of Roe v. Wade', *Society for Cultural Anthropology: Fieldsights*, 3 October. Available at: https://culanth.org/fieldsights/coloniality-and-reproductive-coercion-in-puerto-rico-in-light-of-the-end-of-roe-v-wade (Accessed 19 April 2024).

Sasson-Levy, O. and Rapoport, T. (2003) 'Body, Gender, and Knowledge in Protest Movements: The Israeli Case', *Gender & Society*, 17(3), pp 379–403.

Scally, G. (2018) *Scoping Inquiry into the CervicalCheck Screening Programme*. Final Report. Available at: http://scallyreview.ie/wp-content/uploads/2018/09/Scoping-Inquiry-into-CervicalCheck-Final-Report.pdf. (Accessed 19 April 2024).

Scannell, Y. (2007 [2001]) 'The Constitution and the Role of Women', in A. Hayes and D. Urquhart (eds) *The Irish Women's History Reader.* London: Routledge.

Sedgwick, E.K. (2008) *Epistemology of the Closet.* Berkeley: University of California Press.

Sethna, C. and Davis, G. (eds) (2019) *Abortion across Borders: Transnational Travel and Access to Abortion Services.* Baltimore: Johns Hopkins University Press.

Sewell, W.H. (1996) 'Historical Events as Transformations of Structures: Inventing Revolution at the Bastille', *Theory and Society*, 25(6), pp 841–881.

Shildrick, M. (1997) *Leaky Bodies and Boundaries: Feminism, Postmodernism and (Bio)ethics.* London: Routledge.

Skeggs, B. (2002) *Formations of Class and Gender: Becoming Respectable.* London: SAGE.

Smith-Oka, V. (2012) 'Bodies of Risk: Constructing Motherhood in a Mexican Public Hospital', *Social Science & Medicine*, 75(12), pp 2275–2282.

Smyth, L. (2016 [2005]) *Abortion and Nation: The Politics of Reproduction in Contemporary Ireland.* London: Routledge.

Smyth, M. (2019) 'My Mother was Weak and Unwell as She Struggled up St Michael's Hill to be "Churched"', *The Irish Times*, 21 June. Available at: https://www.irishtimes.com/life-and-style/people/my-mother-was-weak-and-unwell-as-she-struggled-up-st-michael-s-hill-to-be-churched-1.3922537 (Accessed 24 November 2021).

Stambolis-Ruhstorfer, M. and Saguy, A.C. (2014) 'How to Describe It? Why the Term *Coming Out* Means Different Things in the United States and France', *Sociological Forum*, 29(4), pp 808–829.

Strike 4 Repeal (2017) 'Strike 4 Repeal 8th March'. Available at: http://strike4repeal.org/ (Accessed 29 November 2021)

Sutton, B. (2007) 'Poner el Cuerpo: Women's Embodiment and Political Resistance in Argentina', *Latin American Politics and Society*, 49(3), pp 129–162.

Sutton, B. (2010) *Bodies in Crisis: Culture, Violence, and Women's Resistance in Neoliberal Argentina.* New Brunswick: Rutgers University Press.

Sutton, B. and Vacarezza, N.L. (2021) *Abortion Rights and Democracy.* London: Routledge.

Taylor, V. (2000) 'Mobilizing for Change in a Social Movement Society', *Contemporary Sociology*, 29(1), p 219.

Tithe an Oireachtais – Houses of the Oireachtas (2020) 'History of Parliament in Ireland'. Available at: https://www.oireachtas.ie/en/visit-and-learn/history-and-buildings/history-of-parliament-in-ireland/ (Accessed 20 February 2024).

Tremblay, J.T. (2019) 'Feminist Breathing', *differences*, 30(3), pp 92–117.

Ui Bhriain, N. (2012) 'These Billboards Simply Bring the Reality of Abortion into Focus', *thejournal.ie*, 22 June. Available at: https://www.the journal.ie/readme/abortion-billboards-youth-defence-pro-life/ (Accessed 21 February 2022).

Vacarezza, N.L. (2021b) 'Orange Hands and Green Kerchiefs Affect and Democratic Politics in two Transnational Symbols for Abortion Rights', in B. Sutton and N.L. Vacarezza (eds) *Abortion and Democracy: Contentious Body Politics in Argentina, Chile, and Uruguay*. London: Routledge, pp 70–91.

Vacarezza, N.L. (2021a) 'The Green Scarf for Abortion Rights: Affective Contagion and Artistic Reinventions of Movement Symbols', in C. Macón, M. Solana, and N.L. Vacarezza (eds) *Affect, Gender and Sexuality in Latin America*. Cham: Springer International, pp 63–86.

Wade, P. (2017) *Degrees of Mixture, Degrees of Freedom: Genomics, Multiculturalism, and Race in Latin America*. Durham: Duke University Press.

Wagonner, M. (2017) *The Zero Trimester: Pre-Pregnancy Care and the Politics of Reproductive Risk*. Berkeley: University of California Press.

Walsh, A. (2020) 'Feminist Networks Facilitating Access to Misoprostol in Mesoamerica', *Feminist Review*, 124(1), pp 175–182.

Weerawardhana, C. (2018) 'White Women's Mascot: Dr Savita Halappanavar and the Racial Politics of Abortion Rights', *Dr Chamindra Weerawardhana*, 30 October. Available at: https://fremancourt.medium.com/white-wom ens-mascot-savita-halappanavar-and-the-racial-politics-of-abortion-rig hts-c33daf65d544 (Accessed 6 August 2021).

Weiss, G. (2021) 'Feminist Phenomenology', in K.Q. Hall and Ásta (eds) *The Oxford Handbook of Feminist Philosophy*. Oxford: Oxford University Press, pp 63–71.

Weissman, A.L. (2017) 'Repronormativity and the Reproduction of the Nation-State: The State and Sexuality Collide', *Journal of GLBT Family Studies*, 13(3), pp 277–305.

Whittier, N. (2012) 'The Politics of Visibility: Coming Out and Individual and Collective Identity', in G.M. Many, R.V. Kutz-Flamenbaum, D.A. Rohlinger and J. Goodwin (eds) *Strategies for Social Change*. Minneapolis: University of Minnesota Press, pp 145–169.

Yangzom, D. (2016) 'Clothing and Social Movements: Tibet and the Politics of Dress', *Social Movement Studies*, 15(6), pp 622–633.

Young, I.M. (1980) 'Throwing Like a Girl: A Phenomenology of Feminine Body Comportment Motility and Spatiality', *Human Studies*, 3(1), pp 137–156.

Young, I.M. (1990) *Justice and the Politics of Difference*. Princeton: Princeton University Press.

Young, I.M. (2005) *On Female Body Experience: Throwing Like a Girl and Other Essays*. Oxford: Oxford University Press.

Yuval-Davis, N. (1997) *Gender and Nation*. London: Sage.

Index

References to endnotes show both the page number and the note number (147n16).

12 weeks limit 15, 121, 143, 144
22 week (proposed) limit 143

A

'ABC judgement' 12–13
Abortion Act 1967 (Britain) 5, 10, 26
abortion mobilities 28
abortion pills 11, 28, 67, 89, 124, 140, 144
Abortion Rights Campaign (ARC) 12, 13,
    19, 43, 44, 77, 87, 90, 110, 122, 143
'abortion stories' 68–70
Abortion Support Network (ASN) 11, 140
'Abortion Tears Her Life Apart' 43–52
'abortion work' 37–42, 76, 112, 135, 139–143
'abortion-free Ireland' narrative 48
Accapadi, M.M. 106
access to abortions post-Repeal 121–122
'accompaniment' organizations 10–11
acompañamiento 81
acoustical agency 51
activist burnout 117–124
Adams, V. 39, 40, 41
adoption 5, 14, 27
advertisements 43–44, 45
Advertising Standards Agency of Ireland
    (ASAI) 44
aesthetic regimes 47–48
affect theory 16, 17, 36
affective alienation 104
affective dissonance ix, 134
affective labour 37–38, 39, 40
    see also emotions
Ahmed, S. 17, 18, 20, 32, 33, 36, 41, 56, 93,
    95, 96, 100, 103, 104, 145
AIDS activism 19, 46, 135
Ailbhe 54, 55, 78, 79
AIMS Ireland 13, 53, 124
air, different kinds of 114
AkiDwA 13
Alliance for Choice Belfast 87
All-Ireland 'Rally for Life' 133

Amnesty International 90, 143
anger 56, 59, 100–108, 136
Anti-Amendment Campaign 6, 9
Anti-Austerity Alliance/People Before Profit 78
anticipation, disciplinary force of 38–42
    see also fear
Aoibhinn 40–41, 76, 77, 126, 127–128
Aoife 103–104
Apata, G. 114
Argentina 17, 64, 84, 143
Article 8 of European Convention on Human
    Rights 13
Ashley, W. 106
asylum seekers 33, 120, 122
aural rhetoric 50
Aurora 11
auto-ethnography 19, 21, 117
autonomy 92, 98–99, 112, 121–122, 131

B

Bacik, I. 44, 50
'backstreet' abortions 5
badges 96, 109
Ballif, E. 40
Barry, U. 6–7
Bartlett, A. 78, 79
Bergen, S. 98–99
Bertotti, A. 37, 139
billboard campaigns 43–44, 45, 46, 56
biomedical models 16, 40
Black and ethnic minority women 60, 61,
    88, 105–106, 114, 124
    see also Halappanavar, Savita; migrant
    women; racism
Black feminism 16, 18, 20, 114
Black Monday/CzarnyProtest 13
Black Women's Baptist Church movement 88
Blathnaid 83–84, 129–130
Bloomer, F. 10
bodily containment 20, 77
bodily knowledge 47

INDEX

body language 19, 94
body politics 93
Bon Secours Mother and Baby Home, Tuam 14
'bottom-up' knowledge production 8–9, 16
Bowers v Hardwick 46
Boylan, P. 110
breath/breathing 114–115, 116–117
Britt, L. 125
burnout 117–124
Burns, E. 87
Butler, J. 17, 36, 71

C

Caffrey, L. 9–10, 12
Calkin, S. 27–28, 47–48, 67, 89
Callan, O. 82
calls to action 70
Campbell, E. 87
cancer screening 14–15
canvassing 91–100, 101
care, compassion, change ('three C's') 89, 93
Carlow 91
Carnegie, A. 10, 12, 13, 43, 57
catharsis 75, 109–117
Catholic Church
  author's grandmother 3
  'churching' 3
  investigations into Mother and Baby
    Homes 14
  and Irishness 3
  patriarchal church 20
  Pope Francis 84
  'pro-amendment' campaigning 6
  shame 59, 145
  superiority of Catholic Celts 26
  teachings of sexuality 35, 145
  as white saviours 61
Cavanagh, N. 78
CervicalCheck 14–15
Chakravarty, D. 54, 90
Chambers, C. 138
Chemaly, S. 101, 102, 105, 107
Chen, C.W. 118–119, 121
Chen, E. 102, 104
church-state apparatus 20, 83
Ciara 82, 96, 97–98, 99
Citizens Assembly 72, 86, 143
Clarke, A. 39
classism 17, 62, 99
Clodagh 110, 112, 114
clothing 64, 77–85, 96–100, 136
Coalition to Repeal the Eighth
  Amendment 13, 30, 87, 89
Cohen, E. 41–42
collective identity 48, 56, 67–68, 80
colonialism 1, 5, 26, 61
'coming out' 64–72, 87–88, 92, 101, 125
Commission of Investigation into Mother and
  Baby Homes 14

compassion 59, 61, 89, 93, 94, 102
Confidential Maternal Death Inquiry Report
  2019–2021 60–61
Connolly, L. 6, 9, 28, 29, 35, 39, 43, 53, 140
conservativism 2–3, 27, 87, 97
Constitution of Ireland (1937) 1, 2, 6–7, 10,
  125–126
  see also Eighth amendment
contingency plans 34, 35, 126, 135, 137, 139, 140
contraception 2, 6, 34, 139
Corless, C. 14
Cosgrave, A. 77
Cosmopolitan 29
costs of abortion 37, 39, 41, 67, 126, 135
'county homes' 4–5, 27
cover stories 33–38
COVID-19 19, 142
Criminal Law Amendment Act 1935 2
criminalization of abortion 7, 10, 42, 59,
  124, 143
critical feminist scholarship 16, 17

D

Daly, C. 31
Darling, O. 69–70
Davis, G. 5, 26, 28
de Londras, F. 7, 10, 15, 122, 127, 135
De Valera, Eamon 1
deaf community 66–67
decolonization 74
Deirdre 70, 71, 123
demonstrations 55, 70, 74–76
  see also marches
depoliticization of abortion 99
direct action 46, 47, 49
Direct Provision centres 91, 120, 123
disability 67, 112, 120, 122, 123
doctors, trust in 98–99
Doctors 4 Choice 98–99
Dolezal, L. 8, 16, 111
domestic labour 95–96, 103, 139
Dorsey, K. 102, 104
Dublin 30, 45, 55–56, 73, 82–83, 90,
  109–110, 123, 124, 133
Duden, B. 49
Duffy, D.N. 38, 81, 82

E

Eabha 25–26, 28, 37, 39, 56, 131–132
Earner-Byrne, L. 28
Easter Rising 30
Eighth amendment
  avoidance in medical circles 58
  Citizens Assembly 72
  effect on immobile/incarcerated women 35, 53
  history of 6–7, 8, 13–14, 15, 29
  see also referendum 2018; Repeal the
    8th campaign
Eimear 29–30, 119–120

Eithne 33, 36, 39, 53, 139–140
embodied consequences 124–132, 136–137, 141
embodied infrastructure 52, 55, 56, 62
embodied solidarity 52, 57, 62, 70
embodied vulnerability 24, 70, 92, 144
Emer 57, 79–80, 81
emotions
  abortion travel 28–29
  anger 56, 100–108, 135, 136
  bodily intensities 18
  emotion management 91–100
  emotional habitus 46–47, 48–49, 52, 135–136
  emotional labour 34, 81, 87, 94–95, 101–108, 120–121
  emotional scripts 94
  emotionality of politics 51
  emotive dissonance 104
  fear 33–34, 35–36, 40, 104–108, 137
  and political life 19
  and power 18
  shame 58–62, 135, 136
  as social and cultural practices 18–19
Employment Equality Act 1977 2
England *see* travel
Enright, M. 7, 10, 13–14, 32, 112, 122, 127, 135, 143
erasure of the pregnant person 51
Eurocentrism 90
European Convention on Human Rights 13
European Court of Human Rights 12, 13
European Union (EU) 10
events 46

F

Facebook 45, 48
facial expressions 19, 94–96
family planning clinics 29
farming class 35
fear 33–34, 35–36, 40, 104–108, 137
Fegan, E. 10
feminist breathing 116
feminist ethic of care 81
Feminist Legal Studies 9
feminist material culture 141
feminist objects 78
feminist phenomenology 16–17
feminist politics 80
feminist scholarship 8, 18, 38, 49–50, 63, 107, 111, 116, 128, 132, 138
feminist sociology 17
feminist technoscience 40
feminist 'testimonial politics' 20
ferries/boats 28, 37
Ferriter, D. 2, 35, 111
fertility work 37, 38, 139
Fionnula 73–74
Fischer, C. 4, 26, 27, 59, 135

Fitzsimons, C. 13, 119, 120
'Five Faces of Oppression' 38
Fletcher, R. 26, 115–116
floating abortion clinics 11
floating signifiers 112
Flynn, E. 33
Flynn, T. 69, 110
focus groups as campaigning tool 90, 98
foetal anomalies 15, 31, 86, 99, 121, 143
foetal heartbeats 53
foetal personhood 50
foetocentrism 16, 122, 145
forced emigration of pregnant women 5, 27, 145
Ford, T. 96, 97
Foucault, M. 17
France 69
Franklin, S. 16, 145
Free, Safe, Legal 83
Freeman, C. 28
Friedan, B. 95
friends/family experiences of abortion 49, 55, 57
'future aborting bodies' 134

G

gay liberation movement 67, 70
gender inequality 32
gender roles 2, 3, 4–5, 32, 94–98, 107, 111, 120–121
gendered body 7–8, 36, 63, 76–77, 129, 136
gendered displacement 27
geopolitics 27–28, 48, 80, 142
gestural dress 64, 81–85, 141
ghosts 113
Gilmartin, M. 5, 26, 27
Giugni, M. 130–131, 141
Goffman, E. 51
Gomperts, R. 11
'good' versus 'bad' abortions 60
Goodwin, J. 74
Gordon, A. 113
Gorski, P.C. 118–119, 121
Gould, D. 18, 19, 46, 47, 55, 56, 135
GPO (General Post Office), Dublin 30
grandmother, author's 1, 2–3
grassroots campaigning 12, 34, 43, 78, 87, 102, 117, 120, 143
Great Famine (1845–1852) 1–2
green scarves 13, 78, 79, 141
'Green Wave' 13
Griffin, G. 87, 89–90, 145
Grimes, L. 5
Guittar, N.A. 65

H

Halappanavar, Savita 11–12, 43, 52–60, 77, 79, 90–91, 105, 113, 115, 136
Hamilton ruling 29

INDEX

Haraway, D. 9, 16
Harris, S. 86, 124
Harte, M. 146n6
Haughton, M. 91
Hayes, G. 51
healing 117–124
Health (Regulation of Termination of
  Pregnancy) Act 2018 15, 121, 122, 123,
  124, 143, 144
Health Service Executive National Consent
  Policy 7, 127
healthcare during pregnancy 7
Heise, D. 125
Hemmings, C. ix, 134
Henderson, M. 78, 79
hidden diaspora 47
Higginbotham, E.B. 88, 99–100, 107
Higgins, M.D. 121
High Court 29
higher education 25–26
Hill Collins, P. 8, 16, 20, 106
Himmelweit, S. 81
Hird, M.J. 121, 132
Hochschild, A. 19, 94–95, 101, 104
home, intention to keep women in the 2
Homes Commission of Investigation 14
hooks, b. 74
Human Life Amendment Campaign (US) 6
human rights 13, 15, 98
hyper-visibilization of the pregnant
  body 68–69

I

'I Believe Her' 14
identity politics 67
imagery 44, 49, 50, 51, 116, 129, 133–134
incarcerated women 35, 53
incendiary objects 83
induced miscarriages 35–36
information about abortion 10, 11, 26, 29, 30
Ingle, R. 69, 110
Inglis, T. 111
in-group policing 102
institutionalization of pregnant women 4–6,
  27, 48, 111, 145
intentional experience 77
intergenerational activism 112
International Safe Abortion Day 12
internet blocks 26
intersectionality 58, 88, 90–91, 105, 107,
  109–117, 120
interview methods 19–20
intimidation 50
invisible work 34, 36, 48, 140
Irish Choice Network 43, 44, 55, 56
Irish Council for Civil Liberties 90
Irish Family Planning Association 90
Irish Free State 1, 3, 4, 5, 27, 30, 59, 111
Irish Pregnancy Counselling Centre 6, 9, 29

Irish Women United 9
Irish Women's Abortion Support Group
  (IWASG) 10–11, 29
Italy 143
It's a Yes! 89–90

J

Jasper, J.M. 48, 54, 55, 56
Joint Oireachtas Committee (JOC) 86
Jones, T. 106
Justice for Magdalenes Research 5

K

Kennedy, S. 5, 26, 27, 56
Kimport, K. 37, 139
Kivlehan, D. 12
Knights of Columbanus 6
Koivunen, A. 36

L

language choices 91–93, 103
Laoise 83, 98, 99
Latin America 11, 13, 17, 64, 78, 79, 80, 81,
  93–94, 141, 143
Lentin, R. 33, 61, 116
Lentjes, R. 50, 51
liberalization 10, 31, 87
Life Institute 44
lived experience 16, 20
Locke, J. 58, 61–62
Lorde, A. 18, 102, 105, 107
Lowe, P. 51, 60, 132
Luddy, M. 4
Luibhéid, E. 27

M

Mackenzie, S. 147n16
MACRA 97
Magdalene Laundries 4–5, 27, 48, 59, 84,
  109, 112, 145
Mairead 45, 46, 47, 112, 113–114, 115
Malta 142
mandatory waiting periods 42
March for Choice 12, 45, 70, 71, 73, 133
marches 70, 73, 75, 76, 124, 133
Marianism 3
'marriage bar' 2
married women and abortion 60
Martin, A. 1, 3, 10, 27
Martin, E. 9
massed bodies 18, 71, 74, 75
material culture 78, 141
  see also protest objects
maternal deaths 11–12, 60, 124
maternal sacrifice 132
McCarthy, J. 11, 12, 43, 53
McCullagh, P. 109
McGee ruling 9
McGill, M. 96–97

169

McKimmons, E. 9–10, 12
McQuaid, John 1
media attention 78–79, 82–83, 105, 110
medical expertise, prioritization of 99
memorials 115
men 1, 34
mental load 34, 36, 38
#MeToo 66
middle classes 34, 53, 54, 57, 58, 60, 62, 91, 97, 99, 107
middle ground 90, 91
migrant women
  abortion migration 27
  'abortion work' 38–39, 139
  access to abortions post-Repeal 122
  anger 105
  embodied solidarity 57
  ignored by Together for Yes campaign 91
  Irish Free State 4
  logistics of travel for abortions 33–34
  research participants 20
  Savita Halappanavar as 11–12, 53–54, 60
  'subverting the nation' 33
  Together for Yes 87
Migrants and Ethnic Minorities for Reproductive Justice 116, 120
Milei, J. 143
Milk, H. 70
Millar, E. 94, 98
miscarriage 11, 35–36, 43, 53
misogyny 14, 55, 60, 62, 84, 97, 98, 99, 116
'Miss X' 10, 12, 26
Moraga, C. 116
morality 4, 54, 55, 56, 94, 97, 99
  see also shame; stigma
Morgan, L.M. 7
Mother and Baby Homes 4–5, 14, 48, 145
motherhood, idealization of 4, 26–27, 131
Muireann 49, 50, 51, 52, 56, 59, 75, 77, 95, 114–115, 124–126, 128–129
Mullingar 90
multiculturalism 60
Murphy, M. 39
Murray, C. 13

N

National Women's Council of Ireland 13, 87, 90
nationalism 1, 2, 3, 89
nation-building 4–5, 26, 27, 59, 126, 145
Need Abortion Ireland 11
Needham, M. 117
negligence cases 58
neoliberalism 17, 53
Nilsson, L. 49
noise/sound 50, 75
non-consensual listening 50
non-verbal language 19, 94–96
nonviolent resistance 80

Northern Ireland 10, 20, 87
Norwood, K.J. 106
Nuala 118
nurturing sites 51

O

objectification of the feminine body 49, 51, 52, 62, 128, 134
O'Connell bridge closure 73
O'Connor, O. 87
O'Connor, S. 69
O'Donnell, I. 27
Offences Against the Persons Act 1861 5, 6, 10
Office of Censorship of Publications 29
O'Gorman, C. 84
O'Halloran-Bermingham, A.R. 41
Onanuga, Bimbo 12, 61
Oonagh 92, 93
Open Line Counselling 29
orange 'voting hand' 80, 141
Orlaith 60, 61, 66–67
O'Shaughnessy, A. 23, 59, 60, 61, 89, 94, 99, 110, 121, 144
O'Sullivan, E. 27
'other' groups 91, 117

P

pañuelazo 79
Parkins, W. 74
patriarchy 1, 20, 69, 74, 106
Pedwell, C. 18
People Before Profit 55
performing politics 72–77, 104
personal experience of abortion 66, 68–70
Pfaff, S. 74
Phelan, V. 15
Phelen, P. 68
Plomien, A. 81
Poland 13, 72, 147n15
politics and the gendered body 8–9
politics of concealment 86–108
politics of revelation 72, 87–88, 92
politics of visibility 9, 16, 68, 69–70, 72
Pollack Petchesky, R. 50, 68, 94
Polletta, F. 48
poner el cuerpo 64, 84, 103, 141
Pope Francis 84
Positive Options 26
postcode lottery 122
postcolonialism 3, 4, 33, 58–62, 89, 94, 135
poster campaigns 25–26, 43–52, 56
poststructuralism 16, 17
power
  and breath/breathing 114
  emotional labour 95
  and emotions 18
  'five fields of power' 17
  gendered body as site of 7, 17

INDEX

geopolitics 27–28
massed bodies 74
reproductive oppression 138
structural power relations 32
trust in doctors 98
Pralat, R. 66
pre-abortion space 40–41
pregnancy advisory and referral
organizations 29
Pregnancy Counselling Centres 6, 9, 29
pre-pregnancy 'abortion work' 40,
127–128, 134
primary care services 122, 144
pro-choice movement 6, 13, 15, 29, 43–52,
69, 72, 73, 84, 86–87
see also Repeal the 8th campaign; Together
for Yes
pro-life movement 6, 9–10, 43–52, 133–134
pro-natalism 33, 36
Protection of Human Life in Pregnancy Bill
2002 10
Protection of Life During Pregnancy Act
(PLDPA) 13
protest activism 25–26, 55, 63–85, 124, 136
protest objects 13, 18, 50, 78, 136, 141
public harassment 51
public space accessibility 71

Q

queer theory 16, 17, 144
Quinn, H. 117

R

race 61, 90, 106, 116
racism 17, 32, 55, 57, 62, 88, 91, 105–106,
114, 116
'Rally for Life' 133
Rancière, J. 47–48
rape 10, 14, 27
Rapoport, T. 15, 64, 136
Reed, J.-P. 51, 52
referendum 1983 6, 29, 54, 83–84
referendum 1992 10
referendum 2002 10, 49
referendum 2018 13–14, 15, 59, 72–73, 84,
86–108, 109, 124
Referendum Bill (2018) 86
Reich-Stiebert, N. 34, 39, 139
Reidy, T. 147n10
Repeal jumpers 64, 77–85, 96, 97, 136, 141
Repeal the 8th campaign 8–9, 13–15, 43–62,
69, 97–98, 110, 112, 115, 120
representational power 68
reproductive governance 7–8, 16, 38, 76, 77
reproductive habitus 32
reproductive justice 137–141
reproductive labour 38, 103
reproductive mobility 5–6
reproductive rights 128

reproductive violence 38, 127, 128, 137,
139, 140, 141
repronormativity 32
research methods 19–21, 141–142
resistance 8, 18, 80, 83, 85, 92, 136
respectability 86–108, 124
revelation, politics of 72, 87–88, 92
Rex v Bourne 27, 146n3
Reynolds, A. 69
right to access information on abortion
services 10, 29
right to choose 87
right to life of the unborn 6, 9, 29
right to respect for private life 13
right to travel abroad for abortion
services 10, 26, 29
risk to woman's life 12, 13, 121, 143
Rivetti, P. 53, 62, 91
Roberts, E.F.S. 7
Roe v Wade viii, 28, 140, 142
Roisin 31, 33
Roscommon 90, 97
Rossiter, A. 47, 135
Roth, R. 10, 12, 13, 43, 57
'Rugby Rape Trial' 14
rural areas 30, 96–97, 122, 123

S

sacrifice 121, 132
Sadbh 34–35, 36, 39, 72–73, 139–140
Saguy, A. 65, 66, 70, 92
same-sex marriage referendum 90, 118
Saoirse 44, 46, 48, 52, 68, 93, 94, 101, 102,
103, 130
Sasson-Levy, O. 15, 64, 136
Scannell, Y. 2
second-trimester abortions 120
secrecy 67
Sedgwick, E. 65
self-managed abortions at home 11
sepsis 11, 43, 53
Sethna, C. 5, 26, 28
Sewell, W. 46, 48, 55
sexual purity 1–2, 59
sexuality scholarship 65–66, 70, 111
shame 58–62, 67, 68, 94, 109–117, 125, 131,
135, 136
Shauna 104–105, 106, 120–121
Shildrick, M. 28
ship, abortion 11
silencing of women's voices 20, 47
sin 111, 112
Sinead 109
Skeggs, B. 88, 107
smiling 95–96
Smith, D. 17
Smith-Oka, V. 32
Smyth, A. 87, 89, 98
snowball sampling 19, 142

social class 34–35, 37, 39, 88, 91
social justice 19, 83–84, 95, 100, 102, 121, 130
social media campaigning 12, 82–83, 119
social movement scholarship 8–9, 18, 48, 53, 54, 63, 141
Society for the Protection of the Unborn (SPUC) 6, 29, 84
socioeconomic abortion 143
Spanish Women's Abortion Support Group 11
spatial orientations 25–33, 70, 71
Speaking of Imelda 10–11, 140
spectres/ghosts 112–113, 123–124
speech acts 51, 66, 71
speech politics 91–100
split subjectivity 129
Stacey, J. 20, 145
Stambolis-Ruhstorfer, M. 65, 92
Steinem, G. 77
stigma 12, 27, 67, 68, 70, 71, 78, 91, 145
stillborn babies 61
stories, preparing 31, 33–38
storytelling 66, 68–70
streets, coming out onto the 70–71, 73
Strike 4 Repeal 72, 73–74, 75
structural intimacies 147n16
structural violence 74
student activism 31
suffering 94, 99, 103, 107
suffragettes 74
suicide 10, 49
surveillance 40, 50, 69, 129, 138
Sutton, B. 9, 16, 17–18, 64, 74, 84, 103, 118, 129, 132
symbolic interactionism 19
symbolic violence 16

T

Taylor, V. 48
telephone hotlines 30
temporality 38–42, 113–114, 127, 142, 144
Termination for Medical Reasons 13
terminology used in campaigning 91–93, 103
testimony 20–21
'three C's strategy' 89, 93–94
three-day waiting limit 144
Together for Yes 15, 19, 59, 86–110, 116, 119, 122, 143
tone policing 101
trans men 87
transnational feminist solidarity 11
travel
 cost of 37, 39, 40–41, 67, 126, 135
 importance of the actual journeys 28–29
 invisible work 36
 logistics 33, 36–37, 38–39
 post-Repeal 15, 143, 144
 right to travel abroad for abortion services 10, 26, 29
 Together for Yes 89

travel abroad for abortion services 10–11, 26–27, 31–33, 144
 wearing Repeal jumper 80–81
Traveller women 33, 62, 87, 91
Tremblay, J.-T. 116
Tuam Mother and Baby Home 14
'two-tier' approach to abortion provision 13

U

Ui Bhriain, N. 44
uncare, state of 82
Union of Students in Ireland 90
United Left Alliance 55
unmarried mothers 4, 27
unpaid work 38
US 6, 28, 67, 142

V

valves 115, 117
Varadkar, L. 124, 144
viapolitics 28
vigils 55, 59
violence 16, 17, 50, 57, 74, 84, 129, 137–141
Virgin Mary 3, 27, 33, 94
virginity, prizing of 34–35
visual media 49, 51
 see also imagery
voice, democratic nature of 74
vulnerability 36, 56, 58, 70, 77, 83–84, 118
 see also embodied vulnerability

W

Wade, P. 60
Wagonner, M. 40
Wallace, M. 31
wanted pregnancies 60
Waszack, E. 116
websites, blocking access to 26
Weerawardhana, C. 60
Well Woman Centre 29
whiteness 58–62, 74, 90, 106, 107, 141–142
Whittier, N. 67–68
Wicklow 97
Women on Waves 11
Women's Liberation Movement 9
Women's Right to Choose 6, 29
women's rights language 92, 93, 99
working classes 39, 41, 88, 89, 120, 139

X

'X case' 10, 12, 26

Y

'Yes' campaign 86–108, 109, 120, 124, 126, 143
 see also Together for Yes
Young, I.M. 38, 127, 128, 129, 138–139
Youth Defence 43–52, 56, 76

Z

zero trimester 40